BEST BODY BEST BONES

Your Doctor's Exercise R_x Prescription

Your Step-by-Step Guide to Feeling Great, Looking Terrific, Living Longer and Fit Body & Bones

Introduction

National award-winning author and health expert, Dr. Raymond Cole, follows up his step-by-step guide to prevent and treat osteoporosis: ***Osteoporosis: Unmasking a Silent Thief*** with this equally empowering guide to "feeling great, looking terrific and living longer."

Best Body Best Bones is a comprehensive, yet easy to use handbook encompassing all aspects of physical fitness and wellness. Packed with practical information, ***Best Body Best Bones*** serves as an authoritative tool to motivate and to encourage. Dr. Cole directs us on how to establish and pursue our own personalized fitness and nutritional program to enhance our life. Blessed with tremendous insight and the gift of caring, Dr. Cole provides us with just the right blend of information and guidance to promote us towards a lifetime of happiness and physical fitness. You will benefit immediately from the first person stories and the well-established principles which supply ongoing direction and support.

Dr. Cole draws from his years of clinical experience and ongoing study, as well as from his own transformation to a healthy lifestyle, to provide a foundation of fitness to build from. Whether or not you have ever engaged in a fitness program before, ***Best Body Best Bones*** is a powerful guide for transforming your life.

Gary W. Gray, PT

Published by

Wellpower Publications
107 Chicago St.
Brooklyn, MI 49230

Phone (517) 592-WELL(9355)
Or
Phone 1-877-DOC-COLE (toll free)

E-Mail recfcc@aol.com

Library of Congress Catalog Number
2001 132970
Library of Congress Cataloging – In – Publication Data

ISBN 0-917073-04-5

Printed in the United States of America

First Edition

Great care has been taken to provide accurate and authoritative information in regard to the subject matter covered. The manual is intended for healthy adults, age 18 and over. This manual is solely educational and informational and not intended as medical advice. It is used and/or sold with the understanding that neither the author nor publisher is engaged in rendering medical or other professional services to you and that without personal examination and consultation the author and publisher do not render judgment or advice to you for a medical condition. Please consult your medical or health professional for medical advice. Discuss the information in this manual with your physician before using any of it to determine if it is right for you. The material in this book is not intended as a substitute for consulting with your physician and obtaining medical supervision for any activity, procedure, or suggestion in regards to your health. The author and publisher assume no medical or legal responsibility for having the contents herein considered as a prescription or for any consequences arising from the use of the information contained herein. You, or the medical or health professional who treats you, assume full responsibility for the use of the information in this book. Please pay particular attention to the precautions and warnings. While every attempt has been made to provide accurate and up-to-date information, the author/publisher makes no representation, express or implied, with regard to the accuracy of the information contained in this book, and legal responsibility or liability cannot be accepted by the author or the publisher for any errors or omissions that may be made or for any loss, damage, injury or problems suffered or in any way arising from the use of information in this book.

Acknowledgements

Special thanks to my wife, Francine Cole, D.O., and son, Chris Cole, and daughter, Kim Cole, for their love, patience and support over the time it took to write this book. Thanks also to BT for his invaluable help, wit and unique sense of humor.

Thanks also to Scott Fisher, Registered Physical Therapist, from Gary Gray's Irish Hills Physical Therapy, and Kris Beyer, Certified Personal Trainer and owner of Kris' Physical Evidence Health Club in Brooklyn, MI, for their suggestions. Special thanks to Michael Friday from The Exponent in Brooklyn, MI, for his great layout, design and suggestions.

I also deeply appreciate the assistance of Marci Tolford, Aleta Johns, Denise Phelps, Julie Mattis, Pat Kwiatkowski, Debbie Smith, Sheena Johns, Jennifer Enbody, Cindy Colvin, Kathy Sada, Raymond Mooney, P.A.-C. and Gary Gray, P.T.

I want to acknowledge the unselfish work worldwide of the **KIWANIS** International Members. 292,000 Kiwanis members in over 8,400 communities in 79 countries are devoted to the principle of service, to the advancement of individual, community and national welfare and to the strengthening of international goodwill. KIWANIS Is Where-ever A Need Is Served! Kiwanians serve… meet a need… make a difference!

A portion of the sale of each book is donated to **KIWANIS** to help the local community clubs, national and international service programs and to assist in **KIWANIANS FOR A FIT AMERICA!**

Dedication

To Kim and Chris

ABCs of Healthy Living

Always *Carry Happiness With You* or you can search the world and you'll never find it!

Bring *Out The Finest Every Moment* in yourself and others each day!

Choose *Carefully and Control Wisely Your Thoughts, Feelings, Words and Actions!*

Do *The Right Thing* because it's the right thing to do**!**

Effect *Others For Positive Change* rather than being at the effect of others!

Focus *Each Day* on becoming better and better in every way!

Love Always,
Dad

Table of Contents

Best Body Best Bones
Your Doctor's Exercise R$_x$ Prescription

Introduction To Fitness

Table of Contents

Key Components of a Fitness Program

The Actual Exercise Program

Table of Contents

Tailoring Fitness To You

Other Fitness Considerations

Table of Contents

Weight Loss & Fitness

Table of Contents

Lifelong Fitness

Fitness Wisdom

Other

FITNESS Rx

Introduction to Fitness

Chapter I

WHAT IS FITNESS?

What if you lost 50 percent of your sight? Wouldn't you fight with everything you have to get it back? Now for the clincher! What if you lost 50 percent of your sight, could have easily prevented it but didn't act to prevent your vision loss. Wouldn't you be really angry with yourself then? But that's exactly what's happening with most individuals, only it's something more important than their eyesight. It's their actual life energy, physical, emotional, and mental well being and life expectancy. Are you one of those who are just getting by on 50 percent octane or:

Do you want to feel good, look good and live longer?

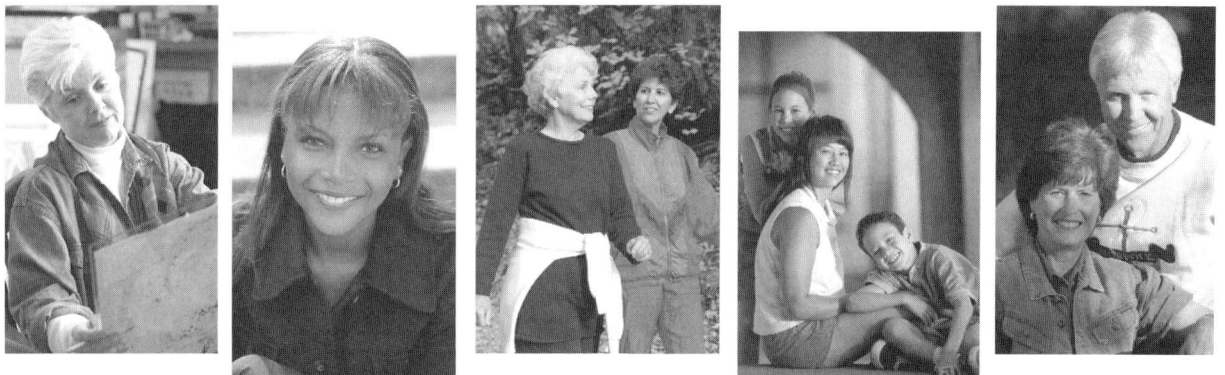

Great news! You can with just a little time and effort getting Physically Fit! Fitness is that state of well being in which performance is optimal. You function at 100 percent efficiency rather than just 50 percent. Think of getting fit as giving your car a tune-up so that it performs better. Can you use a tune-up today?

Fitness is optimal (oxygen) aerobic capacity, muscle strength, endurance, flexibility, balance, posture, and body composition so that we do, look and feel our best. Simply stated, it's the superb functioning of our bodies. Some of the results of fitness are a stronger heart, being less "winded" when performing work, a slimmer physique, more definition of our musculature, increased mental alertness and more physical energy. Regular exercise is the way to get physically fit.

Degrees of fitness vary depending upon such things as one's age, gender, heredity, individual physical characteristics, health, current fitness level and goals. What is considered good physical fitness for one individual's life may not be for another. We all come in different shapes and sizes with particular characteristics that make each of us unique. And don't forget, our goals are different also. For example, a 21-year-old young man may direct his program to be more physically fit in the area of muscular strength and body composition, whereas, a 41-year-old middle-age woman may direct her program to be more physically fit in the area of aerobic capacity. On the other hand, a 74 year old elderly woman may direct her program to be more physically fit in the area of flexibility.

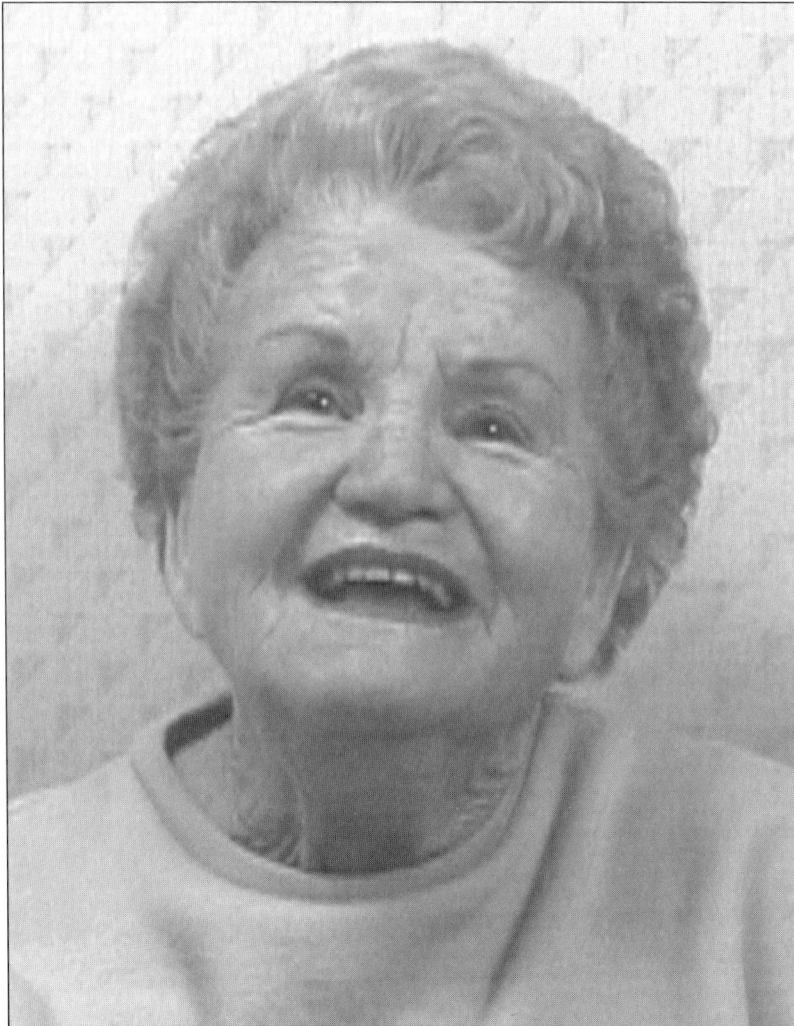

"I've got the perfect place to walk because I live out in the boondocks in Addison on a small lake on a dead end street. I walked two miles before I came here today and I typically walk two miles most days. I also do some exercises on the floor and some stretching. Not too long ago I bought myself a treadmill 'cause I like to exercise all year 'round and I was afraid I'd fall on the ice. It's really good for exercising in the winter.

If I go even two days without exercising, this ole body tells me about it. The older you get the more you need to exercise. I'm 83 years young, not 83 years old!"

Christine Collins—Age 83

When your body is conditioned, you experience more energy, are stronger, have more vigor and experience a dramatic boost in your vitality. Fitness improves the efficiency of your heart and lungs, reduces total cholesterol and is one of the best means of raising "good" cholesterol. It lowers blood pressure so your heart and blood vessels don't have to strain as much and reduces the risks of diabetes, heart disease and some cancers. It provides improved sleep, better mental alertness and acuity and increased ability to live an active independent lifestyle and to deal with the stressors of everyday life. It creates an improved appearance by creating better posture, more defined musculature, causes weight loss, and helps our body's immunity to illnesses. But that's not all. There are a wealth of other benefits including feeling more confident, competent, improved self-image and in total control of your life. And these are just some of the benefits! The list goes on and on.

When you can experience the best, why settle for anything less? So go for it! Experience for yourself the Number One reason people exercise – to feel good! *Commit to and act now to begin a Fitness Program For Life, Your Life! You'll be glad you did!*

Chapter 2

HOW DECONDITIONING SNUCK UP ON US

Until recently, physical labor was the lot of the vast majority of humanity. Over the past half-century, however, the balance has shifted toward occupations and lifestyle that involve more mental than physical activity. Elevators replaced stairs and automobiles replaced walking. People migrated to the cities as America became a mechanized society.

In today's computerized, technological society, much labor is now accomplished by the push of a button. While the dishwasher or gas-burning furnace does the work, we sit in front of the television or our computer. The sitting that we do, however, is in part responsible for the tiredness that we complain of, the obesity many exhibit, even the low back problems many have. It is also the prime cause of deconditioning.

The seductive trap of deconditioning caught most Americans unaware. The first shock came during the Korean War when a surprising number of young men couldn't pass the most elementary fitness test. Ten years later, President John F. Kennedy's Council on Physical Fitness was formed to develop and maintain basic standards of fitness among America's youth. Today there is an even greater awareness of the importance of regular exercise and physical fitness. But the problem is far from solved. The truth is the majority of Americans do not do any type of exercise activity at all. While health spas are thriving and the sales of walking shoes, jogging suits, walkmans and portable radios are booming, many Americans are still less fit than ever.

Now for the clincher!

Only one in every ten (10 percent) individuals is physically fit.

- Six of every ten individuals (60 percent) are totally or regularly inactive.

- Sedentary lifestyle contributes to one in three deaths from heart disease.

- More people die yearly from deconditioning (250,000) than from motor Vehicle accidents (50,000), breast cancer (46,000), and uterine cancer (13,000) combined.

Individuals who exercise regularly experience 36 percent lower healthcare cost and 54 percent shorter hospital stays. For the 10 percent who exercise the benefits are beyond the imagination of an individual who has always been sedentary.

But there's even more space age data to consider. When the first astronauts went into space a remarkable phenomena was observed. Not only did the astronauts' muscle tissue atrophy because of their weightless condition, but their bone mass decreased rapidly as well. In other words, when we work against gravity we stretch, condition, and strengthen our bone cells. And if that's not a convincing argument for regular conditioning then consider this history lesson. From skeletons discovered in the mid 1700s and early 1800s, researchers have found that modern day pre- as well as post-menopausal women have lower bone densities at the hip than women of these earlier eras.

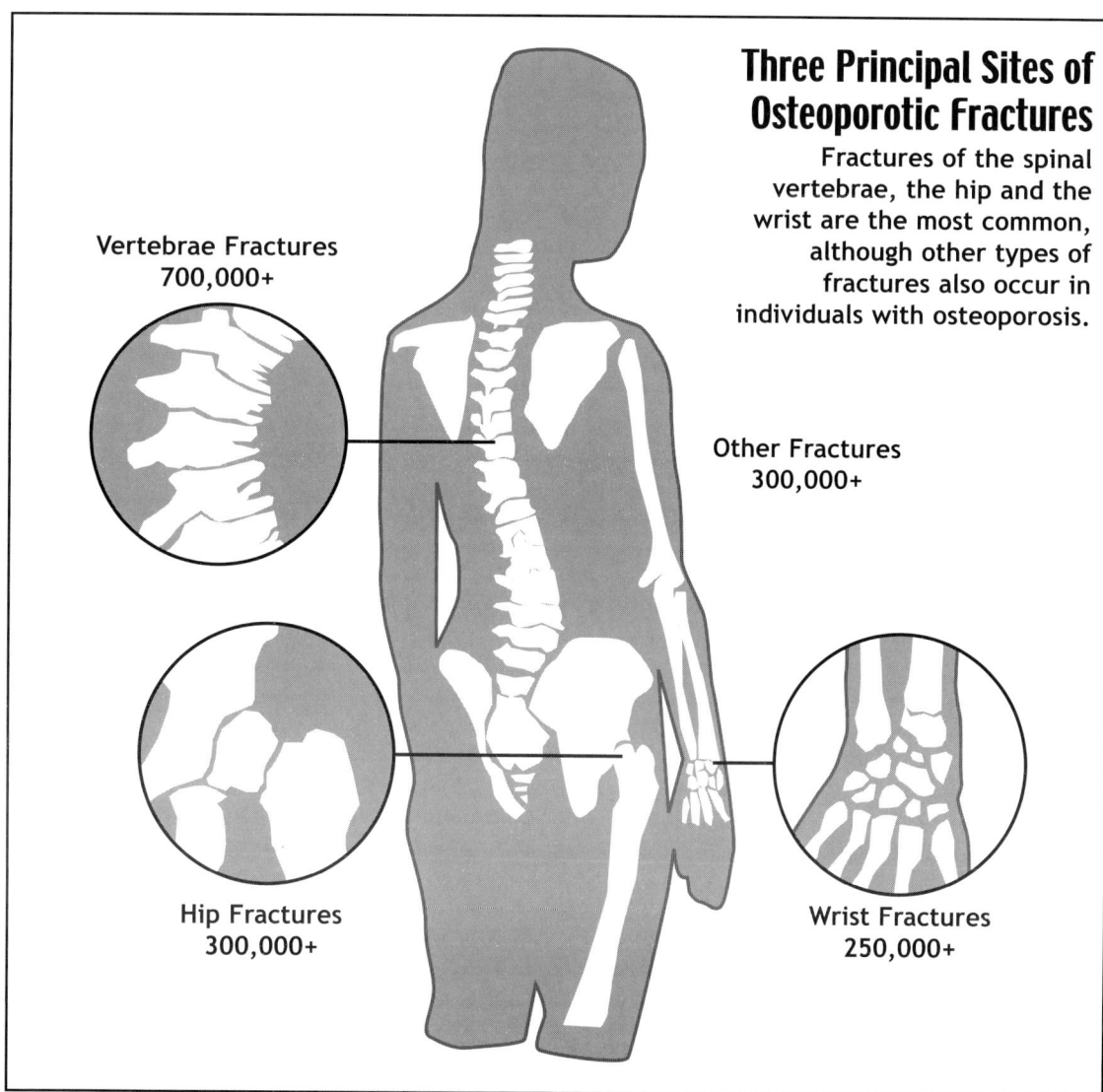

Three Principal Sites of Osteoporotic Fractures

Fractures of the spinal vertebrae, the hip and the wrist are the most common, although other types of fractures also occur in individuals with osteoporosis.

Vertebrae Fractures
700,000+

Other Fractures
300,000+

Hip Fractures
300,000+

Wrist Fractures
250,000+

Low Bone Density Contributes to more than 1.5 Million Fractures Each Year

This supports the theory that osteoporosis tends to be a disease of our modern civilization and of deconditioning.

Why Regular Exercise
Is More Important Today Than Ever

How important is exercise? Important enough for some nutritionists to say that they would rather see a person eat junk food and exercise regularly than eat health food and not exercise! They are not recommending that people eat junk food but saying, however, that without exercise even the best diet can not be metabolized properly.

Chapter 3

But... I CAN'T EXERCISE BECAUSE

Most Common Excuses Given Not To Exercise

• *"I'm too old to begin to exercise"*

The good news is that exercise refreshes everyone. It has no contraindications due to age and is an all-natural tonic from the fountain of youth that anyone can take.

Exercise is not limited to any age. In fact, in many ways exercise is of more benefit with increasing age. *Elderly individuals often have the most to gain by beginning to exercise.*

Our metabolism slows down as we get older (notice even though individuals eat the same amount as they get older they put on weight). One good way to rev it up is to exercise. Regular exercise can give you as much as a 15 percent increase in metabolism. Even more good news though! You'll be glad to know recent studies have demonstrated dramatic physiologic benefits if exercise is begun at any age. Sounds incredible but often the most astonishing "turn your life around" results are obtained in the sedentary elderly. An inactive 75-year-old woman with multiple-chronic medical conditions once said to me, **"If I'd known I was going to live so long, I'd have taken better care of myself when I was younger!"** Listen up, retirees! We are never too old to begin a daily brisk walk around the neighborhood.

We either "use it or lose it" after the age of 30. After this physiologic prime we begin to lose muscle mass at about one-half pound a year, and bone mass density at about 1/2-1 percent a year.

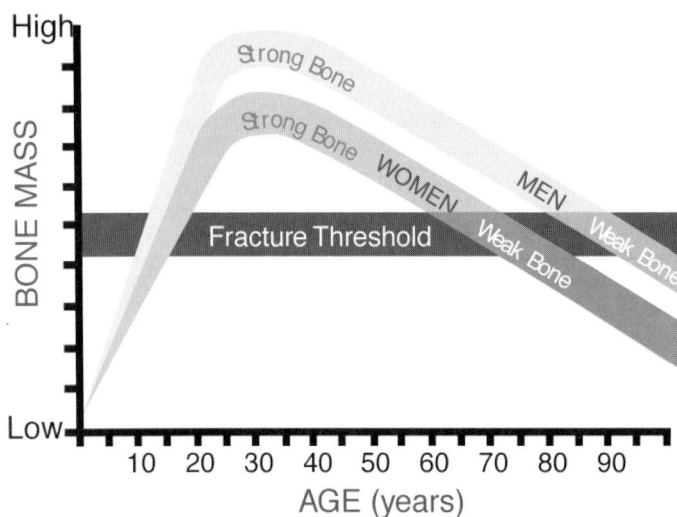

Bone Mass Over Time

Bone mass changes with age in men and women. This chart is characteristic for most people. In general, men usually have greater bone mass than women.

But that's not all. We progressively experience decreasing balance and coordination and slower reflexes. And if this were not enough there's decreasing flexibility, the hardening of our arteries and blood vessels and of course, the dreadful, obvious sign of aging...decreasing skin tone and its resultant wrinkles.

But there is good news and I've saved it for last. As we become older we can take steps to slow and reverse the deteriorating processes of aging. Exercising for fitness reverses the muscle wasting that begins at age 30 and exercising with light weights can add defined stronger lean muscle tissue to your physique so that you can look and feel good at any age. It improves circulation as well as balance, flexibility and the other degenerative changes of aging. Ask and any geriatric specialist will tell you that the best anti-aging pill is the exercise pill.

"I exercise for 2-3 hours several times a week...I start out on a treadmill, then a bike with arm movements, then I do stretches, then I do dumbbells...I feel good! Cut down on my eating and lost 10 pounds...I snack on pretzels and figured out each small pretzel is about 6 calories and can be worked off by about one minute on the treadmill."

George Denton – Age 69

You're never too old to begin building a healthier life. Even 100 year old persons benefit from cardiovascular and musculoskeletal fitness. If an elderly individual is too weak and frail to safely begin an exercise program, then he or she should be evaluated by and a program begin under a well-trained certified physical therapist. Sometimes a home health care agency can arrange for a physical therapist to come into the home of an elderly individual who cannot make it to a physical therapist's office. Medicare covers this therapy with the diagnosis of muscle wasting, muscle weakness, osteoporosis and poor balance.

Another important benefit of maintaining flexibility, mobility, and muscle strength is that it improves balance and thereby helps to prevent falls.

Falls are the major traumatic etiology of osteoporotic fractures in the elderly which account for 65,000 deaths each year.

As we increase in age flexibility exercises become increasingly important. I'm sure you can think of someone now who has lost mobility and in a sense "rusted up." If we aren't mobile, then our muscles and bones weaken. All too often there is rapid progressive deterioration in geriatric individuals once mobility is lost. Maintaining flexibility and maximum mobility is a prime consideration in the elderly and for treatment of osteoporosis.

Fracture Fear

Fear of ending their days in a nursing home due to a catastrophic event such as a hip fracture is a greater fear for most of the elderly than dying. Many view going into a nursing home as the "kiss of death" and fear they will never come out again.

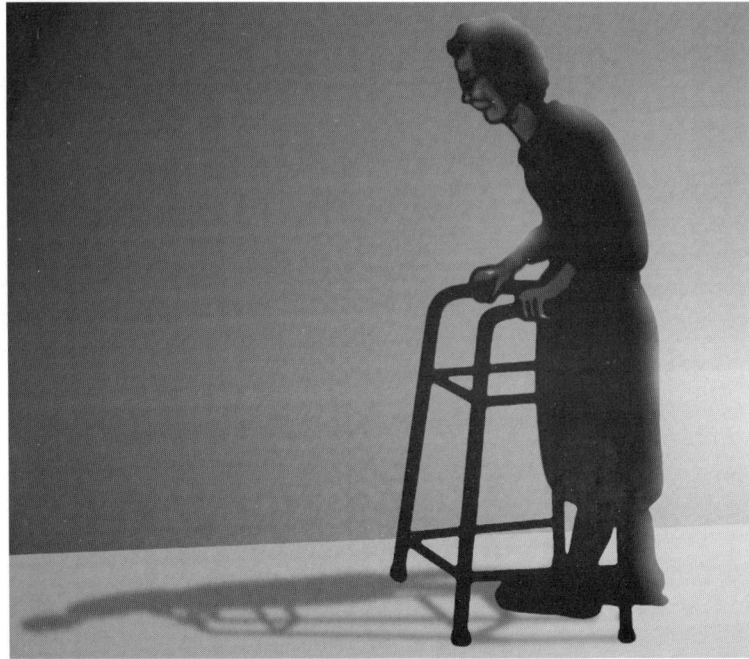

Exercise is the best anti-aging pill and probably the best means available today of enabling one's Golden Years to be lived to their fullest potential. Not only does it increase the length of one's life by decreasing the risk of heart attacks, stroke, diabetes, high cholesterol, hypertension, etc., but it increases the quality of one's life. Notice the vibrant personality, energy and optimism of someone you know who exercises regularly. Notice the control of their life and the halo effect onto other areas of their life. Notice how they radiate this confidence, competence and optimism to others around them. When it comes to your health, don't settle for less than the best!

• *"I'm old, and I could get hurt with weights"*

Some elderly have a fear of weights and a fear of getting injured with them. Start low and *go slow*. If elderly, buy a pair of two-pound dumbbells and begin to exercise with them. Do the arm dumbbell exercises while sitting on a chair without arms. If you have difficulty even getting up from a chair then begin to exercise by getting up and down from your chair 10 times. This is a modified squat exercise. If you need a walker for support, that's fine, it'll strengthen your arms and your sitting and standing limb girdle muscles in one exercise. For some, getting up from an armchair is the best way to begin using the armrests of the chair for help with the initial inertia of getting up. Going through your fear of starting is the best way to conquer it. If you've been waiting for the right time to begin, then wait no longer. Just do it!

• "I'm too out of shape and weak to start"

A graduated program is just what the doctor ordered. Think about it, muscles require resistance to become stronger. Elderly individuals with muscle weakness, severe muscle wasting, osteoporosis and poor balance often benefit the most in terms of quality of life, particularly the very elderly who have difficulty even getting up out of a chair due to weak limb girdle musculature.

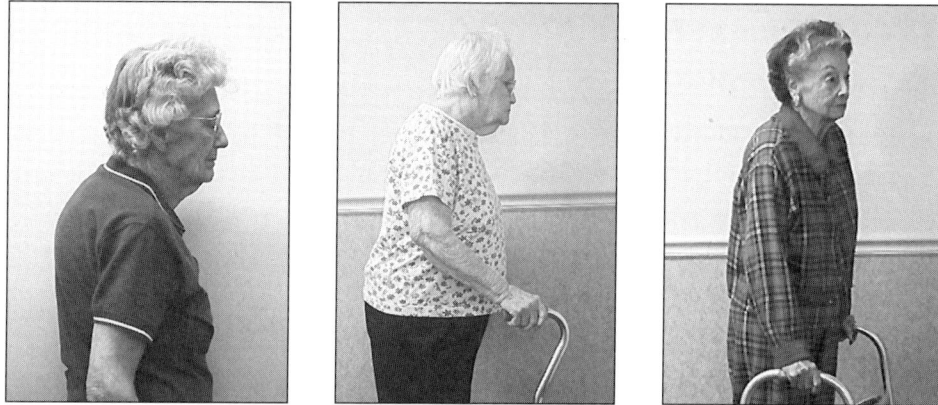

Once a frail individual becomes bedridden due to muscle weakness, they usually continue on a downhill spiral and die within a short time thereafter. Any well-trained geriatric physician knows the utmost importance of keeping elderly individuals' strength up and keeping them mobile and active. If you'd like to become stronger and healthier, thinking about it won't get you there. There's no better way to get there than by doing it!

• "I have osteoarthritis" or "I have osteoporosis" or I have...

Having a chronic disease such as osteoarthritis, osteoporosis, rheumatoid arthritis, chronic obstructive pulmonary disease or the like does not mean a person should not exercise. In fact, *individuals debilitated with chronic disease often stand to benefit the most from a moderate exercise program.* One's bones and joints are more apt to "rust up" from disuse than wear out from use. Osteoarthritic joints hurt more in the morning but feel better during the day if used. The obvious recipe for feeling better then is moderate exercise. The key is moderation, not overdoing it.

• "My low back hurts"

Interestingly, individuals who exercise have less incidence of low back pain than others. Of course these individuals shouldn't run, jump rope, walk on a steep incline, or perform impact aerobics, but a program such as stretching, walking, recumbent bike-riding, muscle-strengthening with light dumbbells, and low back exercises is extremely beneficial. About 95 percent of the population will experience low back pain at one time or another in their lives. Weak abdominal muscles, the middle-age spread and increased weight contribute significantly in most of these. No doubt about it, a good exercise program is a valuable tool for correcting this condition. *A low back and abdominal strengthening program will tremendously help individuals with back pain.*

• *"I get plenty of exercise at work"*

Upon more intense questioning, I usually find that individuals using this excuse are not getting adequate cardiovascular aerobic fitness exercise and good muscle strengthening/toning exercise.

• *"I get plenty of exercise running after the kids"*

Mere movement may not be enough for aerobic and muscular fitness or do anything for your muscular-skeletal strength and flexibility. As your kids get older you may want to exercise with them or participate with them in various athletic or sporting activities.

• *"I don't have the time to exercise – I work all the time"*

Create time. You might shut off the TV or consider moderate physical activity for 20-30 minutes six times a week in the form of a treadmill or a recumbent exercise bike with free weights conveniently located in front of the television. When you plan your day in the morning see if you can eliminate some time wasters to find 30 minutes a day. Make exercising a top priority. Do you really mean it when you say you have all you can do just to struggle and get by each day? The truth is that as you squeeze a more active lifestyle into your life you'll become more fit and add to your efficiency at doing other things because you are more energized. Exercise helps you to better meet the sometimes hectic demands of everyday life. Food for thought…The real question is not can you afford the time to exercise…but rather **can you afford *not* to exercise.**

• *"I'm too overweight to exercise"*

The truth is being overweight and being physically fit are two entirely different things. Each is totally independent of the other. Overweight individuals can be very physically fit and you will find as you exercise, your weight problem and lean body weight will automatically improve as well. As a general rule, individuals who want to lose weight do more cardio work (i.e. exercise bike or walking) whereas individuals who want to bulk up do more muscle-strengthening.

• *"I'm too tired to exercise"*

Does your battery need to be recharged ? Individuals are usually too tired to exercise precisely because they don't exercise! Think about it for a minute. Are you tired of being tired? What it takes to break this vicious cycle of fatigue and inactivity is commitment to a regular time for exercise and persistence through the initial adjustment break-in period. Jump start and revive your energy level today with 30 minutes of invigorating, rejuvenating exercise! Develop the mindset that you've replaced your sedentary patterns with active lifestyle patterns. *Be the most positive, energetic and enthusiastic person you know!*

• *"Someday I'm going to…"*

Someday I'll… means it's never going to get acted upon. I'm going to try to… means there's no commitment and no passion. Let there be no doubt about it. You must have complete confidence that you'll exercise regularly or you'll sabotage your program with easily found flimsy excuses.

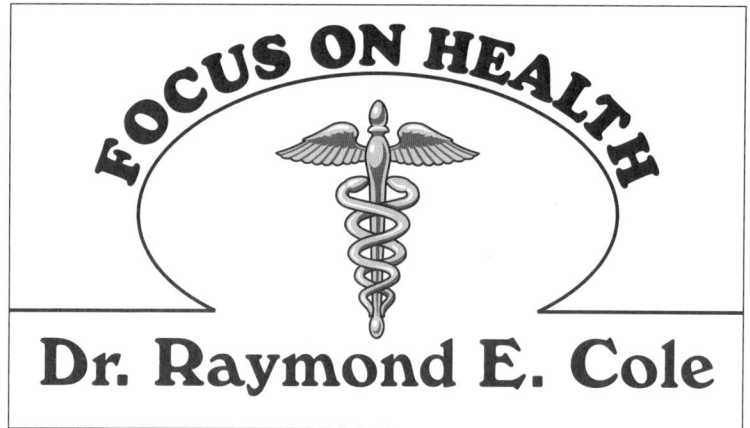

FOCUS ON HEALTH

Dr. Raymond E. Cole

Choose to think differently about your health. Choose to **Focus on Healthy Living rather than getting by** in life. Could it be that now is the time for you to live your life as an exclamation, not an explanation?

• *"I don't want to get bulky and muscle-bound"*

Some individuals think that weight training will make them bigger. Not so. Muscle takes up less space than fat. You will not become muscle-bound if you exercise for fitness. Those Gold Gym body builders lift extremely heavy weights and work out for long hours pushing their bodies to the limits. This is not for you, you are exercising to become more physically fit and to finish feeling good, refreshed, and energized. By exercising 30-45 minutes a day several times a week your muscles will not become too big, only more firm, shaped, and toned. Fitness enhances a woman's femininity and a man's masculinity. A fit and toned body on a woman tones and firms the natural feminine curves and creates a more natural female proportioned appearance. Toned muscles in a man oozes male masculinity in our culture. Fitness is a no-lose situation for both.

Fitness Increases Femininity   *Fitness Increases Masculinity*

• "I have a heart condition"

Begin in a supervised cardiac rehab program under the auspices of a cardiologist. But now for the interesting twist you may not know. *Individuals who have known heart disease statistically live longer than the normal population.* Sounds incredible! Why? Because people who stare death squarely in the face usually reverse their destructive lifestyle habits and take better care of themselves. They decrease their cholesterol and fat and lose weight. They eliminate their destructive lifestyle habits such as smoking, alcohol abuse and of course…they exercise!

Individuals with heart disease can benefit dramatically from a moderate exercise rehabilitation program. Most hospitals have a cardiac rehab program designed specifically for this. These rehab programs are great starting points and a long term, continuous follow up program can be individually designed to fit your needs. Keep in mind that cardiac rehab programs are going to stress cardiovascular fitness and may do little for musculoskeletal fitness. A light weight muscle strengthening program with dumbbells of moderate intensity under a physician's supervision fits the bill to meet these needs.

"*I had a heart attack Thanksgiving Day in 2000. After I came out of the hospital I got started in cardiac rehab. I definitely recommend it to anybody who's had a heart attack.*

I warm up, stretch, and walk on the treadmill about a half-hour 4 to 5 days a week. If I don't exercise, I can really tell it and I feel worse. Exercise is really good for you!"

**Roger Robertson
– Age 70**

• "It's hard for me to exercise in the winter"

A recumbent exercise bike or a treadmill, as well as a pair of 5-pound dumbbells and 5-pound ankle weights is the solution for the snowy cold winter months at home. And of course, do not forget about your **local fitness center.**

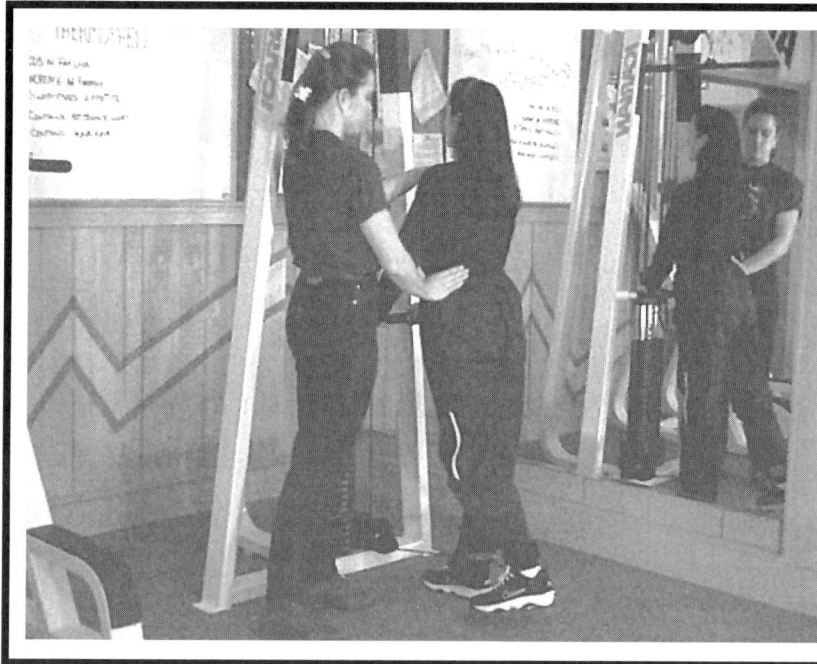

Correct Form

Kris Beyer, Certified Personal Trainer and Owner of The Physical Evidence Health Club in Brooklyn, MI, teaches correct form.

Going to a fitness center three days a week provides a conducive atmosphere, comradeship, emotional support and emotional bonding with others who have a common goal.

• "My motivator has difficulty motivatin"

Is your motivator not motivatin'? If this is the case then consider exercising with your spouse or significant other. Having an exercise partner provides emotional support and positive encouragement. At times when the spirit may be weak you can provide support for one another and an environment that supports success. The power of two is greater than the power of one. You may find it helpful to sign a written exercise contract to exercise together with your spouse, significant other, or friend on a regular basis.

If a family member, significant other or friend or neighbor exercises with you, the companions hip makes exercising more interesting and fun and strengthens your commitment. Also, have a regular exercise time that is planned into your busy schedule and stick to it.

Remind yourself with a sticky note or sign on your desk that you won't settle for mediocrity and getting by but are going to **thrive and feel your best!**

For All Procrastinators:

Commit now in writing to begin a moderate fitness program for 30 minutes 6 days a week or 60 minutes three days a week (i.e. walking and light moderate muscle-strengthening workout) for the next 30 days!!! WHY 30 DAYS? Because psychologists have found it takes 30 days of practice to unlearn an old habit and replace it with a new habit. So it may take 30 days to unlearn being a couch potato and learn to incorporate regular active exercise into your daily lifestyle. After 60 days, the new habit is well solidified in your psyche, after 90 days it is ingrained in you. After one year it becomes such a natural part of you that who knows, maybe it's coded into your DNA!!! (Just trying to be funny!) But don't miss out. Getting Fit is an opportunity to change your life positively forever!

GO FOR IT!

Chapter 4

COMMITMENT TO YOUR FITNESS PROGRAM

Within 30 days from today you could be living your dream and enjoying the benefits of an active lifestyle. Feeling self-mastery, more confident, competent, a reborn energized you. Imagine yourself 30 days from now experiencing the benefits of living your dream…now try to imagine the alternative…living as you are now.

It's simple…commitment spells the difference between failure…and success. The body image and optimal physical well-being you've been wanting is just weeks away. Don't let anything keep you from getting it. **Commitment…makes the difference…and gets results.**

That's the key in a nutshell. There's no use in beginning without complete and dedicated 110 percent commitment. Lifelong commitment! If you can't actively say out loud and put into writing your commitment of time and effort to a regular exercise program, then don't even begin. Without this firm dedication providing a firm footing to exercise, you'll find 101 excuses when your body aches or time is scarce, or on and on… not to exercise. How bad do you want it? Are you totally convinced of the benefits of fitness and willing to put in the effort to realize your goal of a fit body? How great is your desire? Your reason to exercise sparks your motivation. Your passion for exercising determines your future success in sticking to your program.

How much do you value fitness?
Be honest!!!!!!!!!!!!!!!!!!!!!!!!!!!!!!!!!!!

Is Fitness A Priority In Your Life?

I sit down every New Year's and write out my Values, Goals and Plans for the coming year. I write out and prioritize my values and then set goals for the long-term, year-end goals and short-term 6 and 1 month goals in accordance with my priorities. Then I write out my plan of action for accomplishing each goal. There was a time in my life when regular exercising was seventh on my list of values, and I found as a result I consequently found lots of excuses not to exercise. I had placed other things ahead of it in priority. Now, I am much more aware of and have experienced the dynamic benefits of a fit body and mind and have subsequently moved Exercise and Fitness up to third on my priority value list with only two other values ahead of it. To succeed in sticking to your fitness program, exercise must be one of those things you value and therefore do without question.

Do I Truly Value Exercising and Getting Fit?

What are your top five values in life in priority of importance?

1) _____

2) _____

3) _____

4) _____

5) _____

So exercise is one of your top five values? If it is, then continue. If not, then don't kid yourself and begin a fitness program. Here's why: If you really don't deeply and truly value fitness, then you'll drift into self-defeating behavior. If you haven't made the firm decision to make exercising a priority in your life, you won't stick to a regular program. Without a firm commitment you'll find a host of ways to sabotage yourself and take the easy sedentary road rather than persevere and take the road less traveled when time is scarce. Long-term adherence to exercising for fitness requires lifelong commitment. It requires strong motivation because you value it and have strong personal reasons for sticking to it.

No one starts out with intentions to take the easy way out and give in to excuses not to exercise. All individuals who begin to exercise start out with good intentions to follow a regular exercise program religiously. But hold on to your britches! Two out of three individuals are no longer exercising after 30 days and only 10 percent are exercising after one year. A lot of people sprint out of the starting blocks exercising furiously and intensely…but never finish! But just like the sports axiom says, "It's not important who starts the game…but who finishes the game." Fitness requires a lifelong commitment of regular time and effort. Design your exercise program to last a lifetime! *Fitness is not something you do as a short term gain for the day, but rather it is a long-term investment in your health.*

If exercise is up there as a priority value, and you are passionate about changing your life forever and are willing to take the steps to make regular exercise an indispensable part of your daily life like grooming, eating and sleeping, then continue…:

What are the five reasons you want to change your life by exercising?

1) _____

2) _____

3) _____

4) _____

5) _____

For me, I wanted to feel better, be more energetic, firm up my pot-belly, develop more muscle mass and strength and less fat, be of ideal weight and live longer.

Before an artist can create a masterpiece, he/she must have a vision of what they want to create. You must first know what you want before you can bring it into your life and make it your reality. So…

What are the actual specific goals you want to accomplish for yourself by exercising?

1) _____

2) _____

3) _____

4) _____

5) _____

For me, I wanted in twelve weeks, to be less than 190 pounds, have a flat stomach, be aerobically fit, have a firm more toned and defined muscular physique, develop better agility, flexibility and balance, develop improved posture as part of my daily life and have less than 23 percent body fat.

Now that you know what you want to do, you need to find out how you are going to do it. So now list…

How are you going to accomplish your specific goals?

1) _____

2) _____

3) _____

4) _____

5) _____

For me it was aerobic cardiovascular exercise for a minimum of 90 minutes a week in at least three 30-minute sessions on alternating days (Monday, Wednesday and Friday at 5:30 a.m.), and muscle-strengthening, balance, posture exercise for at least 90 minutes a week on two alternating days (Tuesday & Thursday at 7:30 p.m.) of 45 minute sessions each or thirty minutes Tuesday, Thursday and Saturday after aerobic exercise.

What do you anticipate may be the major obstacles or behavior patterns that may prevent you from exercising?

1) _____

2) _____

3) _____

4) _____

5) _____

For me it was the interference of hospital or other social activities, because exercising too late can energize me and keep me up, lack of sleep can make me too tired to get up in the morning for exercise. Sometimes it was a lack of motivation. It was easy to find excuses not to exercise.

How can you prevent the above five potential obstacles from blocking you and turn them into an opportunity you can easily hurdle?

1) _____

2) _____

3) _____

4) _____

5) _____

For me the answer was exercising in the morning or evening of the interfering activity or if necessary doing a longer or double exercise routine the following day; exercising in the evening at 7:00 or 7:30 p.m. and not beginning later than 7:45 p.m.; going to bed by 10:30 instead of 11:00 or 11:30 p.m.; visualizing myself exercising and already experiencing the benefits of exercising; developing an observing self and exposing the excuses.

Now focus inward and picture yourself at your endpoint, having accomplished and achieved your goals, having changed your life. Picture yourself feeling the change that has occurred. See yourself being that person, feel yourself energized, stronger, toned and in total mastery and control of your physical body. Let there be *no doubt* in your mind that you're there. Know that you possess it. Be 110 percent sure and totally confident. Experience reaping the benefits of good physical fitness as a daily part of your life. (You will find it helpful in the beginning to cultivate and reinforce your desire by putting these five values, five goals and the five ways you are going to accomplish your fitness goals up on your refrigerator, at your bedside or framed on your desk or wall. Review and read them out loud each morning and evening.)

Now, you're ready to begin! List your Start Date and Time:

Day_____Date_____Time_____

For me, it was that day at 7:30 p.m.

Now, don't stop here! A successful exercise program begins with taking your actual first step. The first small step you take is a giant step in the right direction…

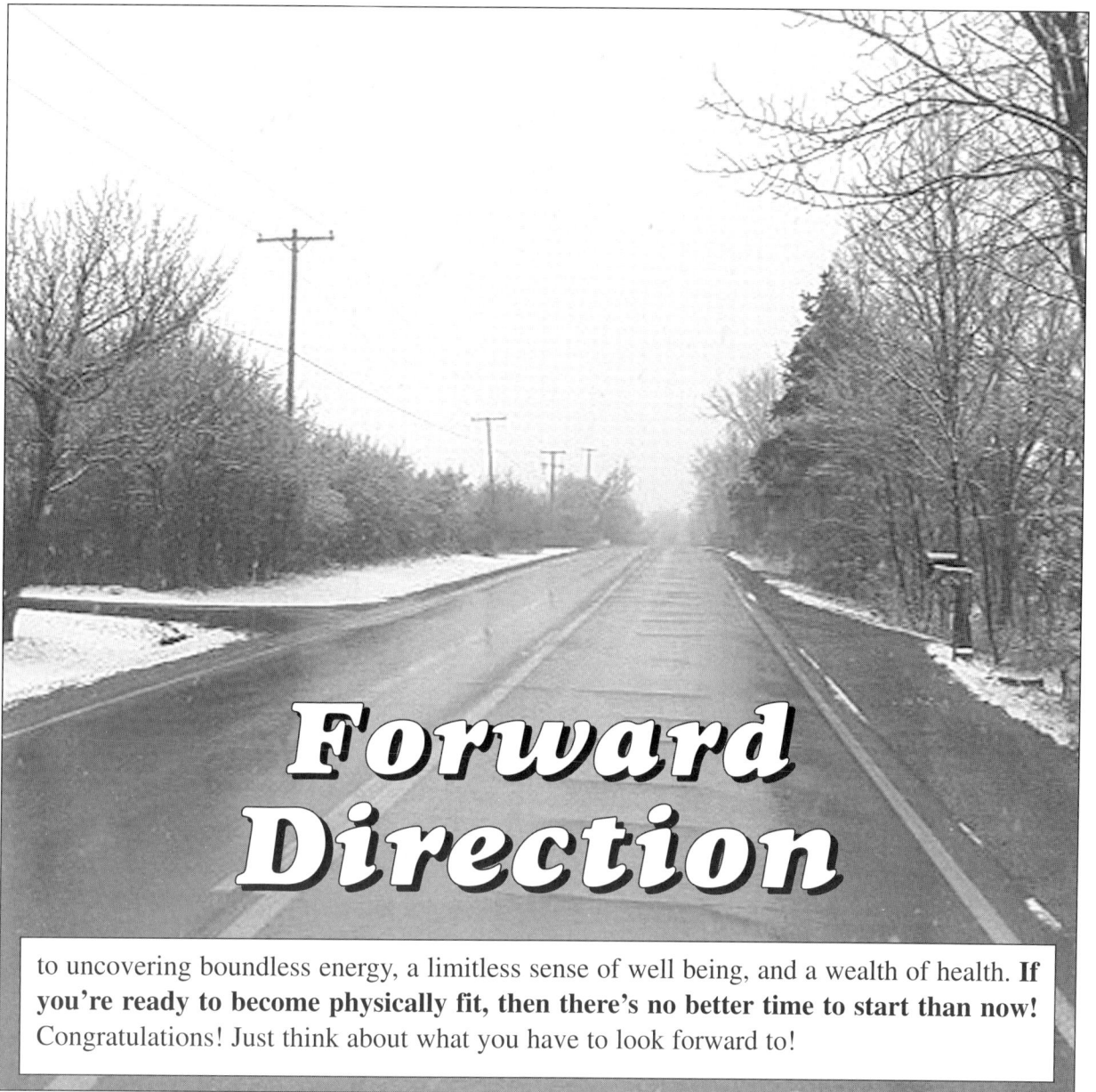

Forward Direction

to uncovering boundless energy, a limitless sense of well being, and a wealth of health. **If you're ready to become physically fit, then there's no better time to start than now!** Congratulations! Just think about what you have to look forward to!

Chapter 5

BEFORE BEGINNING YOUR FITNESS PROGRAM

Before beginning a regular exercise program, find out if there are any conditions which could limit your activity or any problems which might cause a regular exercise program to be harmful to you. For most people exercising is safe, but for some a vigorous program may be contraindicated or a risk for aggravating a pre-existing condition.

Before racing your car engine out on the open highway, it's a good idea to check it and know that it is running OK. The heart is the engine of the body. If it's broken, we don't run and certainly don't want to have it suddenly break down on us because of a hidden defect.

The American Heart Association has found that 1 percent of men under the age of 35 and 10 percent of those over 35 have hidden heart disease. (Hence, the reason for yearly sports physicals as a requirement for participating in grade school or high school athletics.) Although most of these conditions should not rule out exercise, it makes good sense to know as much as possible about your current physical condition. *The American College of Sports Medicine Guidelines recommend a maximal exercise stress test for all seemingly healthy men over age 45 and women over age 55 before beginning an exercise program in which the individual exercises at 60 percent or more of their maximum capacity.*

"Two years ago I was mowing the yard and thought I had heartburn. My wife, Pat, got worried and said I'd better go see Dr. Cole. I had a stress test, Dr. Cole insisted I have a heart cath and they found I had 90% blockage of two arteries of my heart and 80% blockage of two others. I had 4 bypasses. If it wasn't for Dr. Cole I probably wouldn't be here. Dr. Cole saved my life because I probably would have had a real bad heart attack and died!

People should have their hearts checked. There wasn't anything wrong with me. I had a lot of energy and wasn't even breathless. I think everyone should get a regular check-up on their heart!"

Bob Jackson
– Age 68

Before Starting a Vigorous Exercise Program Consult With Your Physician

Consult your physician or professional health care provider and have an assessment of your cardiovascular and musculoskeletal fitness before beginning an exercise program if you have a family history of heart disease or hypertension, or if you have heart disease, hypertension, chest pain, shortness of breath, emphysema, chronic obstructive pulmonary disease, asthma, severe breathlessness after mild exertion, elevated cholesterol or triglycerides, extreme obesity, extreme inactivity, a smoking habit, diabetes, bone or joint problems such as arthritis, musculoskeletal problems, balance problems, osteoporosis, are unaccustomed to moderate exercise or have any other potential risk factors because of which an activity program may pose a risk to your

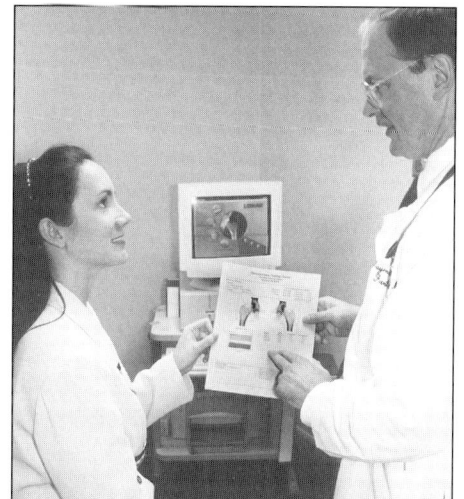

health. A health risk appraisal can be a valuable tool to assess if certain exercises may aggravate or exacerbate a pre-existing condition. For example, if you might have severe osteoarthritis of your hip or a knee, or severe degenerative disc disease in your low back with nerve root impingement from arthritic foraminal narrowing of the L5S1(fifth lumbar-sacral one) disc space, then this must be considered in developing a lifelong exercise program for you.

Your physician may want to perform a comprehensive history and physical examination, blood pressure check, complete blood count and comprehensive medical profile of tests, lipid (cholesterol and triglycerides) profile, urinalysis, EKG, chest x-ray, exercise tolerance test, echocardiogram, bone mineral density test, and possibly other lab tests or back or extremity x-rays depending upon your medical history and his/her findings.

If you have any history of or symptoms of dizziness, fainting or blackouts, you should see your physician for an evaluation and have a carotid ultrasound to check for plaque (arteriosclerosis) in the main arteries of your neck (carotid stenosis). Carotid plaque could decrease the flow of blood to your brain and cause you to experience a lightheaded feeling when you perform exercise movements, resulting in a possible fall with serious consequences such as a fractured hip, spine or wrist.

Risks   Benefits

Exercise Health Risk Assessment

For almost all individuals, the benefits of a moderate regular fitness program far outweigh any minimal health risks.

Chapter 6

SIMPLE REQUIREMENTS

A simple but complete fitness program that you can do regularly in your home requires only:

Walking Shoes
&
Pair of Dumbbells
&
Pair of Ankle Weights

(Available at any local sports store)

WALKING SHOES

You will need a comfortable pair of walking shoes that fit well. Particularly if you are over age 30 make sure you buy a pair with a good longitudinal arch support. Ask anyone in their sixties and they will tell you the obvious. As we get older our feet tend to get wider. This is because with increasing age and mileage there is a natural tendency for our longitudinal arch to fall. Is it no wonder Dr. Scholl's®, arch supports and orthotics custom made by podiatrists are so popular? You can pay a little now or pay a lot in many ways later. So don't skimp on a good pair of walking shoes like New Balance®. If you can't seem to find a pair that feels exactly right for you consider a good pair of walking shoes and buy an athletic shoe arch insert. These are available at all cobbler shops, most good shoe stores and many large department stores such as Meijer. Keep in mind that walking shoes are different from running shoes. When you think about it it's clear. Running shoes are designed so that the weight distribution is first on the ball of the foot and then is gradually distributed posteriorly for the natural stride of running. Walking shoes are designed so that the weight distribution is first on the heel and then moves gradually anteriorly for the natural stride of walking.

DUMBBELLS

Small, adjustable-weight barbells (bar with adjustable weights on the ends secured by a collar) or dumbbells (weight cannot be changed) are relatively inexpensive and easily purchased at any sports equipment store for less than a dollar a pound.

These are used for your upper body muscle groups. Small barbell weight increments may adjust from 2 to 20 pounds. Most women require 2-, 3-, 5-, 8-, and 10-pound dumbbells, but as you

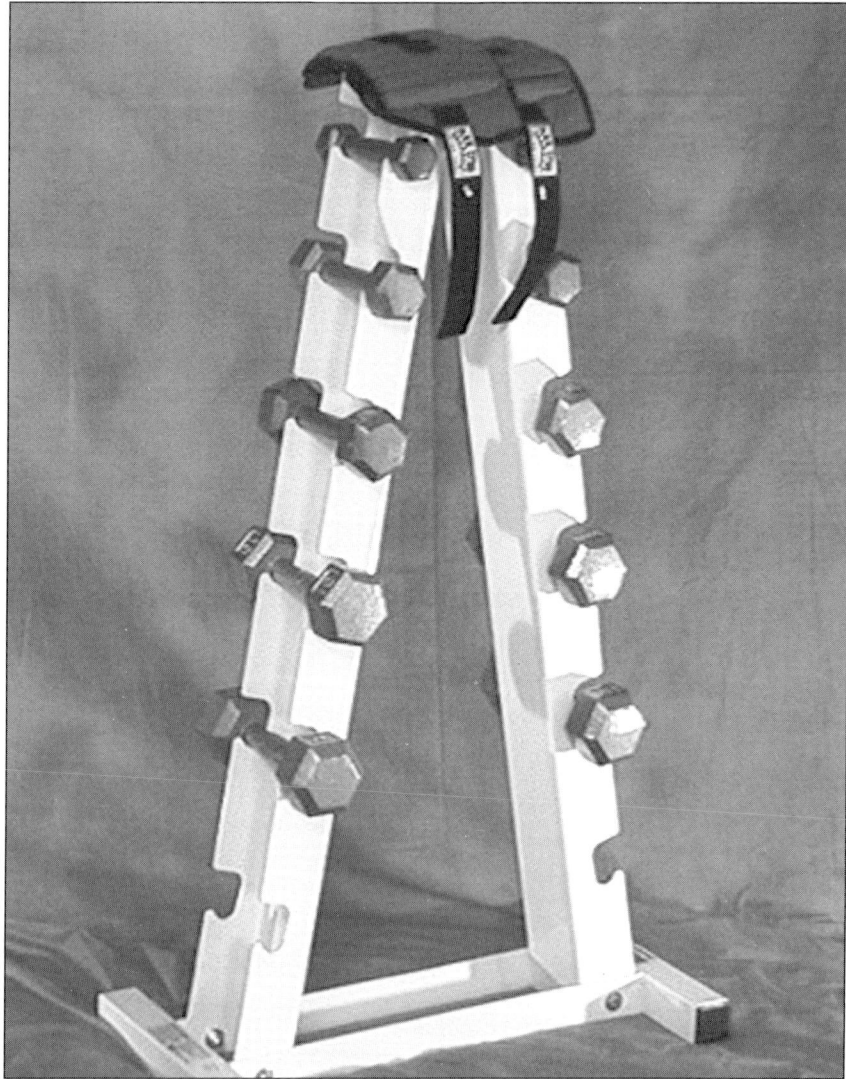

progress in muscle strengthening, you may want to increase to 15- and occasionally 20-pound dumbbells. These can be more expensive if you purchase them in chrome with a storage rack. I prefer hexagonal dumbbells over the round chrome plated adjustable barbells because they will not roll when you put them down. This is particularly important if you use a table for storage rather than a rack with notches to hold them in place.

A method of storage such as a vertical rack is recommended for two reasons. First, it keeps the dumbbells in a single secure place rather than possibly being scattered and tripped over. And second, it keeps them about two feet off the ground so that there may be less chance of injury when you first pick them up to do a muscle-strengthening exercise. There is a tendency for many individuals when first beginning an exercise program to not fully stretch and warm-up and then to bend over from the waist rather than to bend the knees to pick up dumbbells from the floor. Most injuries with weights such as dumbbells occur not during the actual performance of the exercise but in not maintaining good form and carefully and properly picking up the weight or putting it back when finished. Many of you reading this are probably more than 50 years old and have had some episode of back pain already if not some degree of low back degenerative disc disease. Ninety-five percent of us will have back pain at one time or another in our lives. So be careful and consider storing the dumbbells on a rack, and of course do not allow small children to get near or play with them.

For convention, all references to dumbbells in this chapter also refer to small adjustable weight barbells. The exercises are all the same and the differences in the two entities is technical rather than a practical point that is important when exercising.

ANKLE WEIGHTS

Adjustable, strap-on (Velcro) ankle weights are relatively inexpensive and easily purchased at any sports equipment store. These are used for your lower body muscle groups. For most individuals it would probably be best to purchase a pair of these with adjustable weight increments for a total of 20 pounds for the pair (10 pounds each leg). They can be adjusted by removing weight from 2 to 10 pounds per leg. You may be tempted to buy a lighter set with fixed light weights from $2\frac{1}{2}$ to 5 pounds, but consider the 20 pound total pair adjustable set unless you are elderly and somewhat frail. While these lighter weights may increase the intensity of an aerobic exercise such as walking, running, or aerobic dancing (Not generally recommended as ankle weights for walking or running as they throw off the natural gait), you will find they are not heavy enough for a muscle-strengthening program as you progress and your muscles become stronger.
Buy them with one velcro strap not two as one strap ankle weights are much easier to quickly get on and off.

One Strap Ankle Weights are quick & easy to get on and off.

I personally have three sets of ankle weights. One pair of 5 pounds per leg, another adjustable up to 10 pounds per leg, and a third adjustable up to 20 pounds per leg. When exercising with ankle weights you will need to wear long legged exercise pants or high socks. If you strap your ankle weights on bare skin, they may rub and cause a rash or break the skin and cause an abrasion. (Note: I know from personal experience that these abrasions seem to take forever to heal, because you are eager to get back to exercising with the ankle weights again.)

OTHER CONSIDERATIONS

A sturdy chair without arms, a mat for floor exercises (if you choose to do these), and a towel may be considered as well.

A wide diversity of equipment is available at sports stores for in-home use and a larger array is available at various exercise facilities. Various free-standing exercise strength-training gyms are available. These vary from one or two exercise stations to room-sized, multi-station personal fitness systems costing $1,000 to $10,000.

Kris Beyer, Certified Personal Trainer and Owner of The Physical Evidence Health Club in Brooklyn, Michigan

Fitness centers and health clubs are located in every city and provide a diverse choice of various equipment for a good muscle-strengthening program. Most provide a personal fitness trainer who can help tailor a program to your needs. When you first walk into a fitness center you will probably feel a little awkward, like a duck out of water. I know. It happened to me even though I'm familiar with equipment and an ex-football player. I felt like all eyes were upon me, the newcomer or rather misfit, and I wanted to turn around and walk right back out of this unfamiliar territory. But once you take a few abdominal breaths, calm your palpitations, and go through your fear by stepping forward and going to the reception desk and addressing the friendly, helpful personal trainer, you'll soon find yourself calm, at home and glad you went in.

Chapter 7

WHERE TO EXERCISE

Any room will do where you can keep dumbbells off the floor and keep an exercise treadmill or exercise bike (That is unless you do your walking outside). Children must be kept away from the dumbbells so they do not hurt themselves by having the dumbbells fall on them. On the other hand, keeping them on the floor is not ideally recommended as many individuals particularly in the beginning of exercising lift them up with cold muscles and often use poor form in bending over to pick them up and strain their muscles or back.

I recommend a TV with remote control up off the floor so the viewing screen is slightly above (about 15 degrees) eye level. This helps with good posture when you are on the treadmill, bike, or lifting weights.

I exercise in the basement walk-out area of our home which we have finished off with carpeting, drapes, and painted walls. Our dumbbells range in weight from 3 to 20 pounds and ankle weights of 5 pounds per leg, 10 and up to 20 pounds are stored at the south side of the room. We have a 25 inch TV with VCR and remote control for the TV on the treadmill located in the left corner of

25 inch TV with VCR and remote control for the TV on the treadmill located in the left corner of the room on a special elevated stand so the viewing picture is about 15 degrees above eye level so we must maintain good posture when walking on the treadmill. Occasionally I'll listen to music on the radio or from a CD.

We have two treadmills facing the TV one for my wife and one for myself. It's more fun and easier to exercise together and is good quality time to talk together. To the side of the treadmills we have a Schwinn Airdyne® (exercise bike with working arms) and a recumbent exercise bike.

We placed mirrors on the North wall so we can always watch for loss of correct form. In the southeast corner we keep a gym ball which I frequently use to practice correct posture and breathing, particularly when using the dumbbells. This helps develop better core stability of my trunk, balance and posture.

If possible, the ideal way to begin a fitness program is at your local fitness center under the supervision of a Certified Personal Fitness Trainer.

Chapter 8

WHEN TO EXERCISE

There is no fixed time to exercise that is best for everyone, but whatever time you choose, make it a habit.

MORNING
You might set your morning alarm for 30 minutes earlier and perform moderate exercise as you watch the morning news and the hot water is being heated for morning oatmeal or coffee. Just 15-30 minutes of light exercise in the morning gets your body's metabolic engines up and running and makes you feel energetic and alert for the entire day.

AFTERNOON
You might find it best to exercise in the late afternoon an hour or so before supper – just what the doctor ordered to relieve tensions bottled up during the day, revive your energy and make you feel relaxed, rejuvenated and alive again.

EVENING
You might find it best to set your wrist watch alarm to alert you to exercise at 7:30 p.m. on designated weeknights, coordinating it regularly with your favorite TV program.

If you exercise for 30 minutes, then you might coordinate it with watching your favorite half-hour TV show or talk show like Oprah, Rosie, etc. After eating it's best to allow two hours for digestion before exercising. Do not exercise within one hour of going to bed or you may experience trouble getting to sleep.

Useful Information Concerning When To Exercise and Weight Loss
If you want to lose weight then you may want to consider doing your aerobic exercise first thing in the morning on an empty stomach. Our body requires glucose as its gasoline to run on. The glucose in the bloodstream and carbohydrate reserves will be depleted for aerobic metabolism in about ten minutes of vigorous exercise and then our body looks around for another supply of glucose to use. It finds it in the stored fat in our "love handles," middle age spread, and other fat stores. It mobilizes this depot fat and burns it anaerobically for energy.

To lose weight and decrease our stored fat, it's best also to not eat for one hour after exercising. This is due to the **EPOC** (Exercise Post Oxygen Consumption) effect. Exercise increases the mobilization of fat and this continues at a fairly rapid rate for up to one hour after exercise to replenish the energy requirement stores. Most weight with intensive aerobic exercise is lost not to the calories used in the actual exercising but rather due to the mobilization of fat stores immediately after the exercising to replenish the glucose energy requirements. Approximate calories burned per mile of brisk walking can be calculated by multiplying your weight in pounds by .77. (For example, in you weigh 200 pounds, 200 x .77 = 154 calories burned per mile.) These calories are the ones actually burned in the performance of the exercise, but there is an additive benefit of calories burned if you activate the EPOC effect.

If you want to lose weight, then after exercising in the evening do not eat again or drink anything but water before you go to bed. Since no glucose is obtained from digestion the body burns up fat stores overnight to obtain glucose for its metabolic engines to run on. Now just imagine the increased benefit from replenishment of glucose from our storage fat and the EPOC effect. Makes sense.

Here's an interesting, eye-opening tidbit! How many fad diet or diet products have you seen that tell you not to eat after supper or within two hours before going to bed? Is it really their diet or product or is it…Makes you stop and think, doesn't it?

Chapter 9

HOW MUCH TIME DOES IT TAKE TO EXERCISE

Recommendations by The President's Council on Physical Fitness and Sports
The President's Council on Physical Fitness and Sports recommends these amounts of exercise as a <u>fitness minimum</u> for the average person:

> At least two 20-minute sessions per week of muscle-strengthening exercise with weights
> and
> at least three 20-minute sessions of continuous aerobic exercise per week such as walking or cycling
> and
> at each session a 5-10 minute warm-up, 10-12 minutes of stretching (flexibility) after a warm-up or during a cooldown, and 5-10 minutes of cool-down combined with stretching.

Please note that if one is exercising for a <u>total time of 30 minutes</u>, the actual aerobic exercise or muscle strengthening may only be twenty minutes. Although the individual's total exercise time is 30 minutes this includes 5 minutes of warm up (at a slower rate than brisk walking) and 5 minutes of cool-down (at a slower rate than brisk walking) and stretching. The actual time counted as aerobic or muscle strengthening exercise would only be twenty minutes in this common scenario.

My own opinion is that The President's Council on Physical Fitness and Sports recommendations are good…and do not go far enough in their recommendations. They address aerobic, muscle-strengthening, and stretching (flexibility), but do not address balance and posture. This I'm sure is because they have to be very general and generic in their recommendations to fit a wide   variety of people. Their recommendations are, in my opinion, geared toward younger individuals.

My recommendations here, however, are directed toward individuals over age 35, middle age and elderly. Young people are so resilient they can usually get by. But as we get older poor balance and poor posture from the effects of aging increase.

Did you know that approximately 25 percent of individuals over the age of 65 fall each year? In fact, 33 percent of individuals over the age of 70 and 50 percent of the elderly over the age of 80 fall each year and poor balance contributes to most of these. Almost 60 percent of the elderly who fall will fall again within the year and 1-1.5 percent of the elderly who fall will experience a fracture. Almost 300,000 hip fractures occur each year in the U.S. as a result of falls and more than 65,000 people die each year from the complications of fractures as a result of a fall.) If facts like this intrigue you, consider that 50,000 people die each year in the U.S. as a result of traffic accidents. How much attention is given to wearing our seat belts? How much energy is spent preventing motor vehicle injuries and deaths from accidents? Including balance exercises in your fitness program is a simple and effective means of decreasing injuries and deaths from falls as well and possibly saving just as many lives. Both decreasing balance and poor posture needs to be addressed for optimal fitness in middle-age and older individuals.

"I try to walk everyday...it helps me with my back pain. I also do stretching exercises and several times a week weight exercises with 5 pound dumbbells. When I started exercising I found I had more energy, motivation and lost weight. I'd like to tell people to exercise because it's healthy for you, gives you a good positive attitude, builds strong bones, and it'll keep you alive a lot longer!"

**Barbara Wright
– Age 47**

An Investment of Approximately Three Hours a Week

The truth is no matter how you look at or compartmentalize it, a good fitness program requires approximately three hours per week of time: approximately $1\frac{1}{2}$ hours of moderate aerobic exercise, and approximately $1\frac{1}{2}$ hours of moderate muscle-strengthening exercise. (Included in each of these sessions is approximately 10 minutes for stretching [flexibility] exercise, balance and posture exercise.)

These can be broken up, for example, into:

30 minutes total exercise a day for six days a week (alternating each day aerobic with muscle-strengthening exercise

or

60 minutes (one hour) of total exercise three days a week every other day (i.e. Monday, Wednesday, Friday) including 20-30 minutes of aerobic and 20-30 minutes of muscle-strengthening each time as well as warm-up and stretching, balance, and posture exercises.

or

30 minutes a day aerobic exercise (ie. walking or bicycling) for three every other days (i.e. Monday, Wednesday, Friday) and 45 minutes of muscle-strengthening two days a week (i.e. Tuesday, Thursday).

or

other combinations, etc.

Sure you're strapped for time but create time to exercise because…Wow…***What an investment opportunity when you consider the rewards!*** Three hours per week is a relatively small investment of time to ensure a lifetime of optimal physical and mental health!

Chapter 10

INDIVIDUALIZING YOUR PROGRAM

An exercise prescription must be individualized to you and your particular needs, limitations, and goals.

For example, if you are an athletic 5'4" 120-pound 35 year-old healthy woman your exercises might be fairly intense with brisk walking and aggressive weight training.

On the other hand, if you are a 5'2" 180-pound, 55 year-old, inactive, postmenopausal woman with secondary degenerative osteoarthritis of your knees and chronic low back pain from degenerative disc disease of your lumbar vertebrae, your program would be much less intense and tailored differently to avoid further damage to your knees and back. For you, an intense walking program may be impossible, only leading to more problems with your knees and back. You may have to forgo actual weight-bearing exercise in favor of a recumbent exercise bike. You may need to perform your weight training upper body muscle exercises while sitting so as not to further hurt your back and knees and you may find it beneficial to pay more attention to the back strengthening exercises to help alleviate your back pain.

Finally, If you are a 5'1" inactive 100-pound 72 year-old white female with a prominent dowager's hump, 3" lost height from kyphosis and scoliosis, lumbar compression fracture, inactive and practically homebound, poor balance, and hip Bone Mineral Density (BMD) T-score of -3.4 SD, your exercise would be entirely different as well. You have minimal aerobic endurance, minimal muscle strength, and limited muscle mass from muscle wasting. Your exercise prescription would involve more stretching balance, and posture exercises with emphasis on maintaining and gradually increasing mobility.

"Three days a week I do 30 minutes on a treadmill at 3.5 mph or exercise bike and then I do weight training. It makes me feel better and gives me more energy. When I first started lifting weights I'd get sore afterwards but that has gone away. I recommend that everybody do some type of exercise...there's a program for everyone even if they're not in the best of health!"

**John Hills
– Age 59**

The variability of these three different exercise prescriptions is quite diverse in regards to program type, aerobic intensity, muscle toning and strengthening. Also keep in mind that when beginning an exercise program your current activity level, health and age will determine the intensity of your starting workout. Three important elements to consider in individualizing your program are Frequency, Intensity and Time (FIT). Frequency is how often you exercise, Intensity is your degree of effort and Time is the duration of your training.

It's a lot like cooking, where you follow a recipe but vary it somewhat to your liking. You may follow a general recipe (guidelines) but modify it to fit your particular taste.

Chapter 11

WHAT IF YOU MISS A WORKOUT OR WHAT IF YOU ARE SICK OR INJURED

WHAT IF YOU MISS A WORKOUT

Missing an occasional workout is unavoidable. Things happen. For me it's a hospital meeting, Kiwanis activity, an activity with the kids, etc. Sometimes in the early morning I shorten the program from 30 to 15-20 minutes if necessary. If I miss a day I'll try to add it on to the next fitness program. Sometimes I'll get considerable physical activity during the day and use this as fulfillment of part of my fitness exercise.

I like to exercise at least 10-15 minutes in the morning because it "gets my motor going" and gets me warmed up and energized for the day. Sometimes I'm too busy or activities interrupt my program so I just complete as much as I can and try to increase my activity level during the day and/or complete the program in the evening.

Sometimes the weather may interfere with a planned exercise activity. If this is the case you might consider plan B such as walking at the mall or an indoor sports activity at your local community center or YMCA.

"At my home three days a week I use a Nordic Track and two days a week I walk two miles...I do stretches, back exercises, and weight lifting. If I didn't exercise for a few days I'd notice it. I think exercise is important to feel better both mentally and physically. It makes you feel better all around as a person!"

Roger Rutan
– Age 58

WHAT IF YOU ARE SICK

If you are sick, rest and get yourself better. That's it, plain and simple. Don't overstress your body's defenses when it's fighting off an infection, although light activity will increase your circulation and aid your body's defenses. Get at least seven to eight hours of sleep a night. When recovered, get back into your exercise schedule as soon as possible or there may be a temptation to slack and let it slide.

WHAT IF YOU ARE INJURED

Of course, safety-consciousness is always a prime consideration but sometimes injuries just seem to occur. *Injury is a message that something we did wasn't quite right.* It is our body's cry for help that we tried to do too much or didn't maintain proper form. Tune into it because it is a wonderful "steppingstone of opportunity to learn." What is the reason for the injury? What caused the imbalance that made you susceptible to it? What corrections can be made so it does not happen again? Just like an airplane is constantly making corrections to get back and stay on course, so is injury a time to make corrections and get back on course.

If you do experience an acute tendon strain, pulled muscle, etc., as soon as possible take an anti-inflammatory such as ibuprofen, 400-800 mg., apply cold and rest the injured part. The anti-inflammatory and cold prevent the release of enzymes called kinins which cause inflammation, soreness and swelling. All too often individuals begin to exercise and get so excited about the positive changes in their body and how much better they feel, that they want more quickly and push too hard creating an injury.

Most injuries however, are more insidious. Like the automobile accident in which you tell the policeman you're fine and then as the night goes on you get more and more sore and stiff and wake up in the morning in excruciating pain, hardly able to move. Just today a 46-year-old woman presented to my office with chest pain. Her EKG was fine and upon questioning I found out she had gone to the Y two days ago and begun on her own to lift weights. Diagnosis: Pulled muscle.

Injuries take time to heal. Think about this. If you cut your skin it takes at least 7-10 days for the skin to heal together again. That's why sutures are left in for 7-10 and occasionally up to 14 days. When you tear deeper connective tissue fibers by means of a muscle or tendon strain or a ligament sprain, it's also going to take a similar amount of time for the tissues to heal. A muscle or tendon pull is simply a tearing of the muscle or tendon fibers. **Always strive for pain-free and injury-free workouts.**

Chapter 12

VARY YOUR PROGRAM

After a few weeks of the same program, your muscles "learn" the program and adjust to it so that maximum previous benefit is no longer attained. Your routine must be changed periodically for maximum benefit by changing the type of exercise, intensity or duration so the body doesn't become comfortable in an "attenuated learned muscular response." In my experience, I have found that younger individuals tend to embrace changing their programs whereas older individuals tend to be more rigid and want to follow a fixed regular routine. Changing their programs produces mental tension and anxiety. I know you may be "married to your program" but individual programs should be varied periodically, such as every two weeks, so one's body doesn't become attenuated to one exercise routine only.

Variation of your program also helps to prevent boredom and helps keep your interest. Why? Because our psychological make-up is designed such that despite liking and loving a regular routine, we are attracted to contrast.

"I work out four days a week...Mondays I work my legs, Tuesdays I work my chest, Wednesdays I work my arms, and Thursdays I work my shoulders and back. I rollerblade and bike ride also...it makes me feel great and increases my energy level!"

**Charles Davis
– Age 54**

HEALTH AND FITNESS

Key Components of a Fitness Program

Chapter 13

ABDOMINAL BREATHING ESSENTIAL TO LEARN FIRST

Abdominal ("Belly") Breathing is an essential prerequisite for an optimally successful exercise program. The yogis have known the value of proper breathing for centuries, and this is why abdominal breathing is the first thing learned in a yoga or meditation class. Musicians who play wind instruments, singers, and long distance runners all know the value of abdominal breathing.

Take a deep breath!... STOP... now examine your breath with your observing self. Did you take the air in by expanding your chest or by expanding your diaphragm downward into your abdominal cavity? One way to find out is to look at your stomach. If on the inhale you look as if you are three months pregnant, you are using the abdomen properly. Breathing is not something that takes place solely in the chest but involves the entire abdominal cavity as well. Beginning to breathe through the abdomen may at first seem like trying to write with the left hand (or vice versa if you're left-handed). But as you persist, it will come more and more naturally to you.

You might begin by imagining air coming into your lungs and inflating an imaginary balloon in your belly. Or you might actually visualize your diaphragm muscle pulling downward and as it does so actually pulling air into your abdomen.

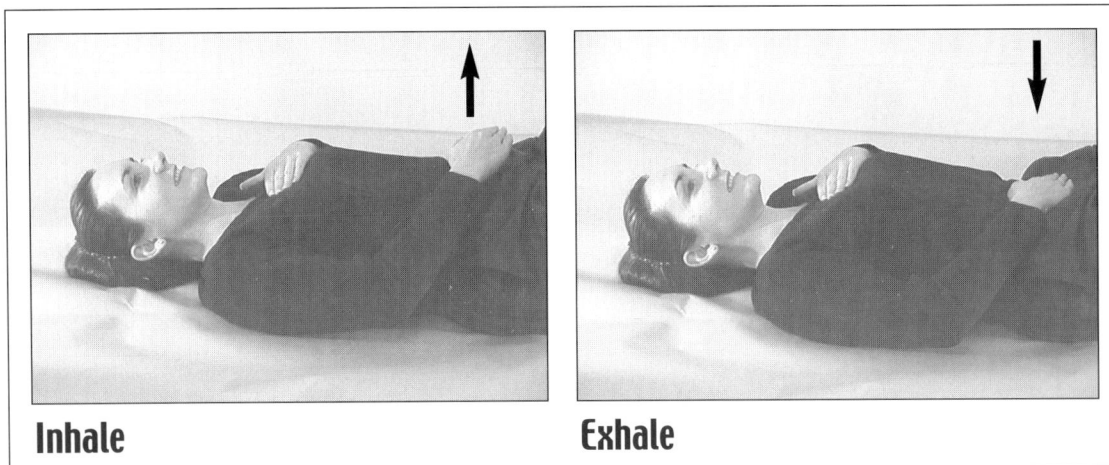

Inhale   **Exhale**

*The main advantage of abdominal breathing is the vastly **increased capacity to take in oxygen.*** The expansion of our rib cage actually accounts for only 10 percent of our lung's capacity, while the expansion of the abdominal wall (diaphragm muscle) downward accounts for 90 percent. It takes a lot of energy, relatively speaking, to expand the rib cage since each of the intercostal muscles must be used. The downward movement of the diaphragm, or *belly breathing*, takes much less energy and provides us with slower, more efficient, and more relaxed breathing. We move oxygen through our lungs and to the blood cells most efficiently when we fully use our diaphragm. If you have never been trained in abdominal breathing and can run one mile, chances are you will be able to run three to four miles after learning and practicing abdominal breathing. This is because abdominal breathing is efficient enough to increase your work capacity by three to four times.

*A secondary benefit of abdominal breathing, one that is well-known to those of you who practice yoga, is **relaxation***. People who hyperventilate (rapid, shallow breathing) tend to use only their upper chest. Not only is this an inefficient way to breathe, but it causes and reinforces tension and anxiety. Among people who are anxious, tense or nervous, the practice of slow, relaxed, abdominal breathing brings immediate positive relaxation results. Notice as you relax you breathe slower. As your breathing slows to six to eight abdominal breaths per minute, your autonomic nervous system naturally places your body into a relaxed mode.

How To Learn Abdominal Breathing

It takes practice to integrate abdominal breathing into your everyday life. In my experience, daily practice for two to four weeks will make abdominal breathing your natural way of breathing, so natural you will no longer have to think about it. Once it is firmly established as a part of your life, however, you will find yourself more efficient in all areas of your life. You will have higher energy levels, feel more relaxed in the face of daily problems, and stress will no longer trigger the inappropriate conditioned bodily responses it once did.

Find a quiet place where you can be undisturbed for ten minutes twice a day. Do not practice within one or two hours after eating, as the post-meal alkaline tide will tend to make you too drowsy to practice. Be patient with the process; don't force it.

Preferably, lie on your back. You may learn by sitting comfortably in a chair. Place one hand at your navel (belly button), the other on your chest. Take air into your abdomen. In doing so, your diaphragm will expand downward into the abdominal area. I ask patients to imagine as they breathe in that air is coming in through their nose and going into their belly so that it appears as if they are three months pregnant. Sometimes I tell them to imagine the air is going into an imaginary balloon in their belly.

As you inhale and expand the diaphragm downward, the hand on your belly will rise, and the hand on your chest will not move. The chest will naturally expand somewhat at full inspiration.

If the hand on your chest is rising, then you are using your intercostal rib cage muscles, and you need to practice until you can inhale into your belly without appreciably expanding your chest.

Exhale through the mouth. Let your jaw muscle (masseter muscle) relax and your mouth drop slightly open as it relaxes. It is generally recommended that you inhale through the nose and exhale through the mouth, but this is not essential at this stage. Your main focus at the beginning is in developing a natural rhythm and flow by focusing attention on the relaxed abdominal breathing. I find it helpful to purse your lips slightly as this creates a backflow of air slowing your exhalation. I teach my " chronic lungers" this method, and it's particularly beneficial. Some people find it helpful to pause for a short moment after inhaling, then exhale slowly and completely, pausing again before the next breath. When you are breathing properly with your abdomen, exhalation as a general rule takes twice as long as inhalation. In other words, strive for a two (exhalation) to one (inhalation) rhythm. Get a sense of following your breath rather than focusing your breath into a rigid pattern. Do not force it, but rather let it happen. After a few weeks of steady practice, you will get the feeling you are *being breathed* rather than exerting any effort.

The twenty minutes or so a day you practice abdominal breathing may be one of the most valuable time investments you'll ever make towards better health. In your automobile on your way to work if you're late and the light changes to red in front of you, take a few abdominal breaths and practice relaxing. If your observing self finds you feeling agitated with a family problem or a problem at work, practice three slow, relaxed abdominal breaths before proceeding. You might key yourself when learning abdominal breathing to practice three slow, relaxed abdominal breaths when your phone rings. Take every opportunity to practice. You will find that after two to four weeks you will automatically have incorporated more efficient abdominal breathing into your life as your everyday modus operandi (mode of breathing).

After a few weeks most individuals no longer need to practice regularly but instead use the technique automatically in their everyday lives. As one patient said to me after learning this powerful breathing technique, "I don't know why God didn't make us breathe properly when he made us, but thank goodness this is something we can learn to do." But in fact, we were created to breathe properly. Notice that babies breathe with their abdomen.

Incorporating abdominal breathing into your everyday life will not only help you have better physical health, it will also help you experience better mental health. In spite of living in modern civilization, our human autonomic nervous system is still set up as it was millions of years ago for *fight or flight*. In response to acute stress, the senses heighten, the heart rate quickens, and adrenaline rushes through our bodies to prepare us for every contingency. The fight-flight response is appropriate for life and death situations but inappropriate for most everyday situations. Next time you are late for an appointment and find yourself in a hurry but stuck in a traffic jam, notice what goes on in your body. You probably experience tension at the base of your neck, forehead, and jaw as you slam on the brakes and begin to look for ways to make the traffic move faster. When your efforts fail, your tension and frustration mounts. Your jaw becomes tense, your brow furrows, your neck aches, your upper back (trapezius) muscle tightens, you feel pain in the lower arch of your back and your stomach may even churn a little. As you become more emotionally upset and agitated, notice that you are experiencing rapid, shallow breathing confined to your chest and upper rib cage.

It is only a traffic jam, a very insignificant incident in our lives, yet we are responding to the stressor as if we are facing down a saber-toothed tiger. The tiger is really not there to kill us, but our unchecked autonomic fight/flight response might. Most of us respond to the stresses and frustrations of daily life as if our survival were at stake. Our breathing is that of the fight or flight response because our autonomic nervous system is in a constant state of *red alert* from everyday stresses inherent in modern, fast-paced everyday life.

Learning abdominal breathing and incorporating it into your everyday life as the normal way you breathe is literally a *breath of life*. Learning it before you begin a serious exercise program is akin to tuning up your car before going on a long trip. Although you do not absolutely have to use abdominal breathing when performing aerobic or muscle strengthening exercise, it makes sense to do so. The breath provides the oxygen and thus the energy necessary to condition your body for optimal performance, and is a natural method of properly pacing the tempo of your exercises.

Chapter 14

THE WARM-UP

Have you ever noticed that when you awaken in the morning or when you've been sitting for long periods of time your muscles feel stiff? They are literally cold. **Warming up involves gradually increasing the blood flow to your muscles and getting them used to movement.** This actually does increase the temperature of your muscles. If you exercise when your joints, ligaments and muscles are cold, then abruptly tensing them to their limits may tear some of the fine connective tissue fibers and cause strain, pain, inflammation and possibly serious injury. This damage, which can be seen if the tissue is put under a microscope is analogous to that caused by taking celery and bending so that some of the fibers break.

None of us would ever get into our car on a cold morning and immediately rev up the engine to its maximum and drive away at high speed. Just like our car engine's moving parts needs to be warmed up when cold, so do the moving parts of our body: our muscles, tendons and ligaments. Warming up our muscles before exercising greatly reduces the risk of soreness 12 to 24 hours after exercising and even more importantly, greatly reduces the risk of injury.

Warming up your muscles, heart and respiration consists of a few minutes of light aerobic exercise such as walking with arm motion or a recumbent exercise bike (preferably with arm motion).

Another very fine way to warm up is to go through the motions of your weight exercises without or with very little weights. This not only prepares your body physically for exercising but mentally prepares you for doing the exercises with the proper motion. Some individuals walk in place for two to five minutes to warm up.

Another really fun and very effective way of warming up is to put on your favorite CD and go to your favorite song such as Ricky Martin's "Livin' La Vida Loca" and dance. It's a great, fun way to warm up the heart and lungs and "loosen up" at your own pace and speed.

Chapter 15

THE COOL-DOWN

A cool-down consisting of light intensity aerobic exercise, i.e. slow walking, followed by gentle range-of-motion stretching should be done after moderately intense aerobic or muscle-strengthening exercise. **The cool-down allows your heart and lungs to slowly return to normal and your muscles, ligaments and joints to gradually return to their normal character.** Stretching exercise must be included after any strenuous activity because exercise tends to shorten and tighten muscles. For example, running tends to shorten your lower back muscles, reducing their flexibility.

After exercise, higher levels of the hormone norepinephrine are present in our tissues. A cool down helps remove it, reducing soreness and tissue pain we might feel from vigorous exercise. Precipitously stopping exercise leaves blood pooled in our extremities, our heart racing, our blood pressure elevated, our lungs breathing more rapidly and our body temperature elevated. It also leaves stagnant metabolic waste products including lactic acid in our tissues. (When a muscle is exercised so that oxygen needs cannot keep up with its need for energy, nonoxidative (anerobic) metabolism to produce energy takes place and one of the major metabolic waste products of this is lactic acid, which is thought to contribute to muscle soreness. A slow cool-down enables our heartbeat and respiratory rate to gradually slow, our blood pressure and temperature to lower gently, and lactic acid and other anaerobic waste products to be removed.

Chapter 16

THE FIVE KEY COMPONENTS OF A COMPLETE FITNESS PROGRAM

A moderate aerobic exercise (walking) program, in combination with moderate muscle-strengthening, flexibility (stretching), balance and posture exercises three to five days a week should be a **universal prescription for fitness.**

Aerobic (uses oxygen, improves heart and lungs) exercise exerts its most dramatic effect upon cardiovascular health but has limited effect on muscle mass, strength, and bone density. When you are aerobically fit you experience the optimal ability to acquire, transport and use oxygen. Aerobic (cardiopulmonary) exercise enables our heart to function at improved efficiency by pumping more blood with each beat and therefore it can operate at a lower rate. Our lungs operate at an improved efficiency for oxygen and carbon dioxide exchange for maximum oxygen transport to our muscles, brain and all the tissues of our body.

**Muscle Strengthening Exercise**, on the other hand, has a powerful positive effect on muscle mass, strength and increasing bone mineral density but less of an effect on aerobic cardiovascular fitness. As we age our muscle mass and strength decreases. Those who maintain muscle strength and muscle endurance are much better able to maintain an active, independent lifestyle and enjoy their "Golden Years".

Flexibility (Stretching) is the freedom of motion of our muscles and joints. Every movement we do during the day enhances or decreases our flexibility. From repetitive mundane activities, i.e. sitting, standing, computer typing, our joints and muscles become stiff and tightened and their freedom of motion restricted. Some muscles become chronically tense while others become weak from disuse, atrophy. With advancing age there is also a tendency to become more rigid, less supple, and stiff. _**Move It or Lose It!**_ Many individuals in their 70's and 80's tell me "I'd feel fine if my joints weren't so sore and stiff." "The consequence of rigid joints affects all aspects of life; including walking, stooping, sitting, avoiding falls and driving" says the President's Council on Physical Fitness and Sports. Some people are genetically more flexible than others by virtue of their being born with naturally longer ligaments. Women also genetically seem to be as a whole slightly more flexible than men. Joints and muscles that are not flexible limit movement, cause soreness and pain, and increase the risk of strain and injury.

Balance Exercises help prevent falls. How do most people fracture their bones? By falling, of course. Falls cause 90 percent of all fractures. While some aerobic and many muscle strengthening exercises using light weights improve balance, some exercises work specifically to improve this. Improved balance reduces your possibility of falling and breaking a bone. There is lessening of the risk of falling by improvement in muscular strength, improvement in flexibility, mobility, agility, loss of sway, balance, and neuro-muscular coordination.

Posture Exercises decrease the possibility of deformity from thin or brittle bone. A kyphotic (stooped over, Dowager's hump) posture exerts considerable compressive force on the anterior (front) bodies of your vertebrae and frequently causes compressive deformities and fractures. This force is particularly magnified if you flex (bend forward) your spine. Thoracic vertebral compression fractures can not only cause chronic pain, loss of height, and severe kyphosis of your spine, but cause anatomical chest deformities with decreased chest expansion, secondary shortness of breath, and subsequent easy fatigability. A lordotic (extended backwards) posture in the low back can magnify compressive deformities of the low back and with little added force to thin or brittle bone subsequently cause compression fractures of the lumbar vertebrae. This can be a cause of low back pain and lead to progressive immobility and a subsequent cycle of increasing bone mineral density loss. Men and women alike who develop a "gut or belly" or "middle age spread" of the abdomen are particularly prone to this. Weak abdominal muscles frequently contribute to the problem in combination with poorly developed lower back extensor muscles.

THE OPTIMAL FITNESS PROGRAM INCLUDES THESE FIVE KEY COMPONENTS:

1). *Aerobic Exercise*

2). *Muscle-Strengthening Exercises*

3). *Flexibility (Stretching) Exercises*

4). *Balance Exercises*

5). *Posture Exercise*

Chapter 17

AEROBIC EXERCISE
KEY #1

Aerobic weight-bearing exercise three to five times a week not only strengthens our heart and lungs, but strengthens our bones, increases muscle strength, improves balance and improves our mobility.

Weight-bearing exercises such as those involving various loading stresses seem to work the best to strengthen bone — in other words, exercise that forces us to work against gravity, such as walking, slow jogging, hiking, stair climbing, and dancing. Non-weight bearing exercises such as swimming and bicycling, while having excellent aerobic (cardiovascular) benefits, do not seem to give the same bone-building benefits. The reason weight bearing exercise is emphasized over non-weight-bearing exercise is that it puts considerable mechanical stress on our hip and subsequently has dramatic influence on increasing BMD at the neck of the femur. Since breaking our hip is the most dangerous of fractures (remember that 65,000 women die a year from hip fractures), it makes sense that this would be the most important bone in the body to strengthen. While breaking our wrist, ankle, ribs and vertebrae may be debilitating and painful, these fractures are usually not fatal. Weight-bearing exercise such as walking demonstrates positive increases in BMD in the hip and spine and subsequent decreases in both hip and vertebral fractures. Moderate exercise stimulates osteogenesis (the formation of bone). When a muscle exerts tension on a bone, the bone formation cells are triggered to stimulate the formation of bony matrix. This builds bone. Sometimes we forget that bone is a living tissue just like the other tissues of our body such as the muscles, connective tissues, heart, lungs, etc. Just as muscles are strengthened through exercise, bone is strengthened by exercise.

Some individuals are adamant about achieving aerobic *target heart rate*. Aerobic physiologists have determined that there is a *training zone* based on heart rate in which there is enough activity to produce aerobic cardiovascular fitness but not so much as to exceed a safe level. This training zone has been determined to be between 70 and 85 percent of our maximum heart rate. Your approximate training zone can be determined by this formula:

(220-age) x 70 percent = Lowest training heart rate

(220-age) x 85 percent = Highest training heart rate

For example, If you are a 50-year-old woman:

(220-50) x 70 percent = 119 beats per minute = Lowest training heart rate

(220-50) x 85 percent = 144 beats per minute = Highest training heart rate

If you are sedentary, not in good physical condition and beginning an aerobic exercise program, then begin at 60 percent of maximum heart rate for the first few weeks. Again, if you are a 50-year-old woman, that would be:

(220-50) x 60 percent = 102 beats per minute = Beginning training heart rate

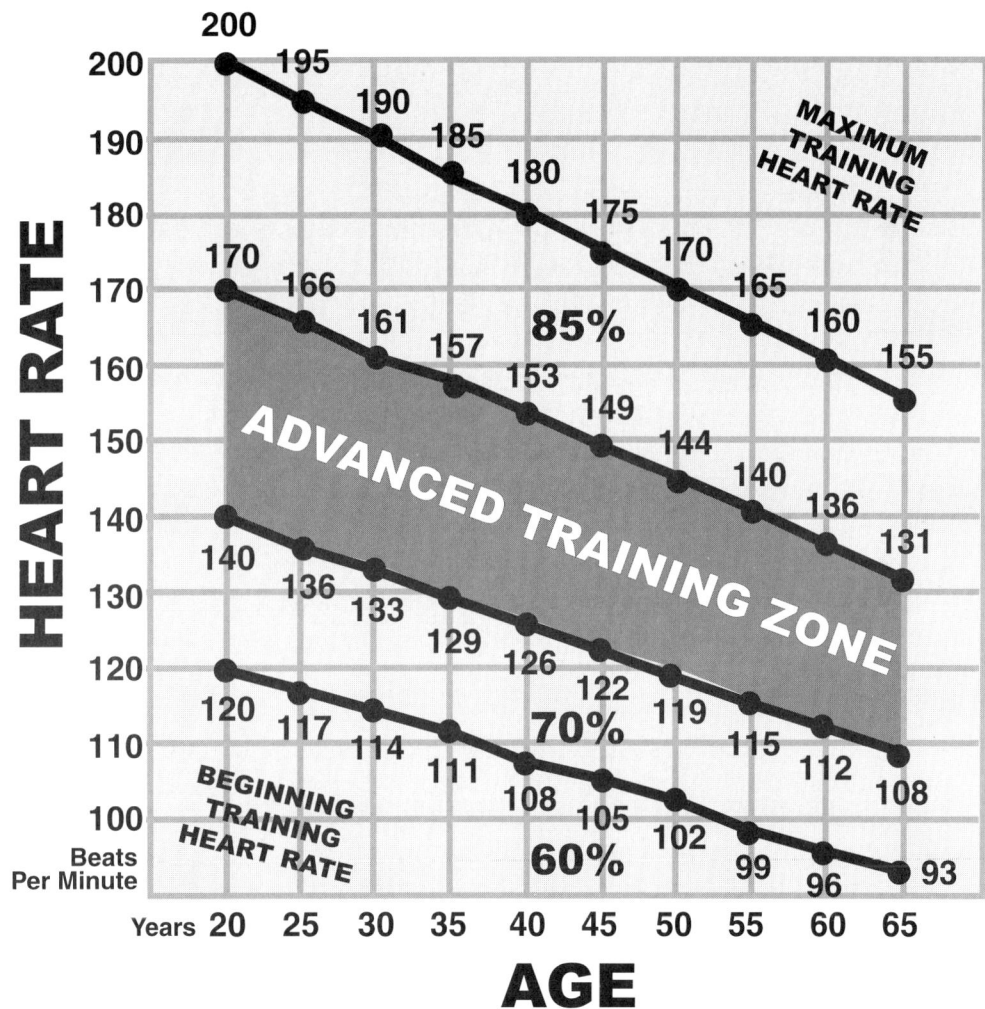

To take your pulse at your wrist, place your first two fingers just below the base of your thumb inside the wrist and slightly above the tendons running up the top of your wrist. Press lightly and move your fingers around until you feel the pulse of your radial artery.

To take your pulse at your neck, place two fingers on either side of your Adam's apple and move your fingers around until you find the pulse of your carotid artery.

Many of you reading this are, like myself, over the age of 50. I firmly believe that individuals over the age of 50 would probably find it in their best health interest not to take up impact exercises such as jogging, running, rope-skipping or high-impact aerobics. In fact, it is my opinion that individuals beyond their natural physical peak at approximately age thirty to thirty-five should think twice before engaging in these activities on a regular basis. The reason…injury!

Impact activities such as running on a regular basis place severe stress on the balls of your feet, ankles, knees and, of course, the low back. I speak from first-hand experience. I used to regularly run six miles every other day and had this activity abruptly halted due to chronic pain in the ball of my foot (anterior metatarsalgia). It developed one winter when our Michigan snows forced me to run inside on an electric treadmill one February. The treadmill's elevation could be adjusted to increase the intensity of the workout and as I did so, the pain developed. All my medical knowledge, medications, physical therapy, orthotics, injections, two orthopedic specialists and a podiatrist specializing in sports injuries could not provide lasting relief. Over the next few years I would get it feeling better and then as soon as I'd start running again, it would flare up with intractable pain. The sports podiatrist summed it up best when he said, "Give up running. As you're getting older, your feet can't take the constant pounding."

Over my 25 years of medical practice I've seen patient after patient with similar scenarios: knee pain, pain in the forefoot, heel spurs, pain in the medial arch, pain in the ankle, hip pain and low back pain. By far the most common chronic painful joint I see in the office in the older individual with a history of impact exercise activity earlier in life seems to be knee pain. The pain is usually located on the medial aspect of the knee in the major weight-bearing area (medial tibial tuberosity) and there is joint space narrowing from wear and tear of the cartilage.

So having been there, done that over the years, I've developed a broader perspective as regards exercise. I believe that not only must we *Eat Fit for a Lifetime,* but we must *Exercise Fit for a Lifetime.*

Exercise Fit For a Lifetime

In my opinion, the short term benefits of daily high impact aerobic activities are not worth it when considering the wear and tear on the body over your lifetime. Rather, you must look for the long-term benefits of moderate exercise activity as a means of exercising for a lifetime. *Remember... think of exercising as a long term investment for your health, rather than just a short term gain for the day.*

WALKING

Walking seems to be the easiest and best aerobic (cardiovascular) weight-bearing exercise for most individuals to incorporate into their daily lives. Walking is one of the most natural exercises we can do. Sixty million Americans walk regularly for recreation and their health.

Walking allows you to get your aerobic weight-bearing exercise while holding a conversation with your spouse, significant other or friend; it enables you to think, take in fresh air and enjoy the scenery.

Walking is inexpensive, requires no special equipment, can be done almost anywhere, offers little risk of injury (unless you jaywalk or walk on a highway!), can be done any time and almost any place and can be done without necessarily getting smelly and sweaty. Walking is suited for people of all ages, particularly if you are over thirty-five, if you are obese, as well as if you are thin. And walking can easily be done even if you have been inactive for a long time. Even in inclement weather, you can walk in an enclosed shopping mall or at home on a manual or electric treadmill.

Take Steps To Care For Yourself

Walking is an incredible exercise and you can vary it in intensity and length of time to fit your individual needs, from a brisk paced, four-m.p.h. one-mile, fifteen-minute "quickie", to a leisurely two-m.p.h. three-mile stroll. Walking is also a way to relax, burn off stress and clear your mind. Walking around the house picking up after the kids or walking at work from your desk to the coffee machine or water cooler is not considered effective aerobic exercise as it does not offer measurable aerobic weight-bearing or cardiovascular conditioning benefit.

When beginning a walking exercise program you must consider your present level of fitness, your physical capabilities (i.e. weight, osteoarthritis) and your goals. Each trainer has their own preference of a starting program for individuals who need more rigid structure. The bottom line is take that first step and begin… just do it! Start low and go slow.

If your're older, in poor physical condition or overweight, you might begin walking slowly for 10 minutes. Don't risk an injury. Go slow rather than pushing it. Give your heart, muscles, tendons, joints and bones time to adjust. The first 30 days of a beginning exercise program are equally important for developing the exercise habit as for getting fit. You might begin by walking 5 minutes, rest 2 to 3 minutes, then walking another 5 minutes. After two weeks increase your walking time to 15 minutes, then gradually increase to tolerance every 2 weeks to 20, then 25, then 30 minutes. Then as you become acclimated to this, gradually increase your speed.

A middle-age reasonably healthy individual might begin with a more advanced and demanding program. For example he or she might begin with 15 minutes of walking at a moderate speed, and progress in time and speed (duration) at a more advanced pace. Keeping in mind, however, that developing the exercise habit is just as important, if not more important in the first 30 days as the exercise program itself.

WALKING IS A STEP IN THE RIGHT DIRECTION FOR HEALTHY LIVING AND AN ACTIVE LIFESTYLE

Walking is an exercise which practically everyone can do and is a step in the right direction for better health.

Chapter 18

MUSCLE-STRENGTHENING EXERCISE
KEY #2

Women and men of all ages, even in their nineties, can safely build strength using light-weight muscle strengthening exercises.

Strength training is a potent stimulator to improve bone mineral density, muscle mass and muscle strength. It also improves balance, leading to less falls and thereby less potential for fractures. Muscle strengthening improves mobility, agility, coordination and posture. Again, moderation must be emphasized. Light-weight strength training is for fitness, not for body-building. Leave body-building to the Olympian athletes. For them the axiom may be true: No pain, no gain. But this does not apply to the rest of us doing moderate exercising with light weights for fitness. It's okay to feel challenged during muscle-strengthening exercises but not pushed to or going beyond your limits. Exercising for fitness should be invigorating and when you finish exercising you should feel good, not exhausted from pushing your body to its limits of physical endurance.

The muscle-strengthening program should concentrate on the **three large muscle groups of your body**:

Arms – <u>upper</u> extremity muscle groups including:
    1) biceps (front arm – flexes arm)
    2) triceps (back arm – extends arm)
    3) deltoid (shoulder) and teres major, minor, etc. (rotator cuff)
    4) pectoralis (anterior chest)

Abdominal and back – <u>mid</u> muscle groups including:
    1) rectus abdominis, obliques (flexes forward abdomen—tightens and flattens stomach), transverse abdominis
    2) erector spinae (extends lower back), trapezius, latissimus, rhomboids, (upper back muscles)

Legs — <u>lower</u> extremity muscle groups including:

1) quadriceps (front thigh – extends knee)
2) hamstrings (posterior thigh – flexes knee)
3) tibialis (front lower leg)
4) gastrocnemius and soleus (posterior lower leg – Achilles)
5) gluteus maximus (major buttock or "butt" muscle extends hip backward)
6) iliopsoas and rectus femoris (flexes hip forward)
7) gluteus medius, minimus and tensor fascia latae (abducts out the the leg)
8) adductor magnus longus, brevis, pectineous and gracilis (adducts in the leg)

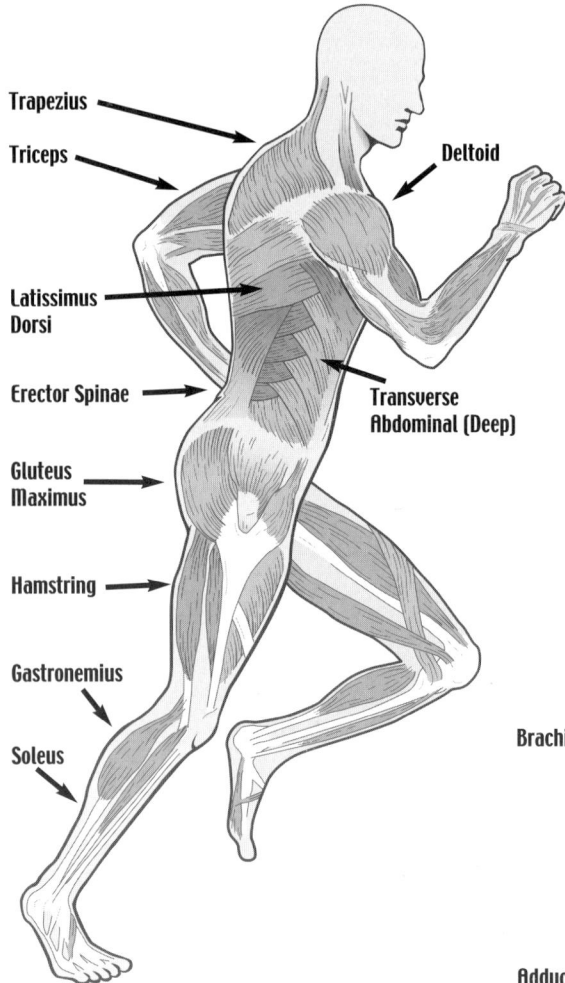

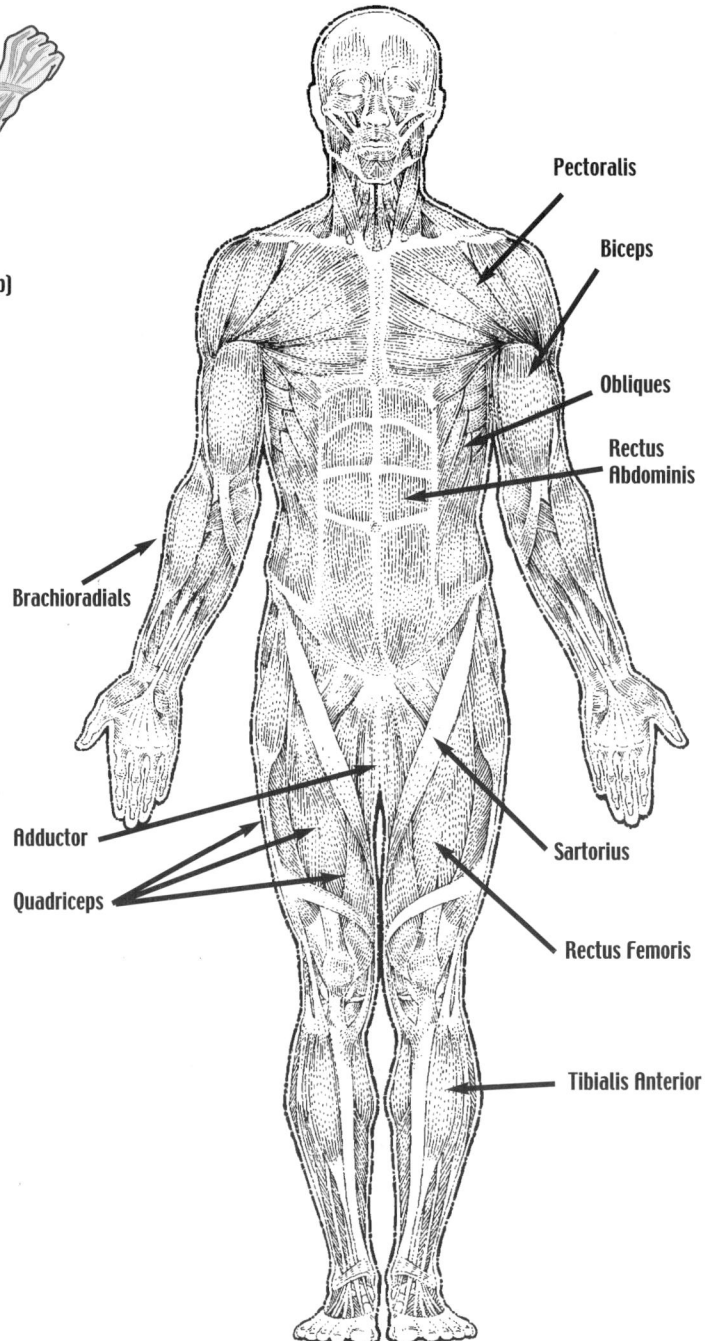

Trapezius

Triceps

Deltoid

Latissimus Dorsi

Erector Spinae

Transverse Abdominal (Deep)

Gluteus Maximus

Hamstring

Gastronemius

Soleus

Pectoralis

Biceps

Obliques

Rectus Abdominis

Brachioradials

Adductor

Quadriceps

Sartorius

Rectus Femoris

Tibialis Anterior

A Sample Muscle Strength-Training Program

A typical total body program might include two 45 minute full-body exercise sessions per week to include approximately:

    5 minutes warm-up

    35 minutes 13 muscle-strengthening exercises consisting of 4 upper, 1 mid (abdominal-back), 4 lower, 4 balance and posture.

    5 minutes cool-down and stretching

MONDAY	TUESDAY	WEDNESDAY	THURSDAY	FRIDAY	SATURDAY
Full Body (upper, mid, lower, balance)			Full Body (upper, mid, lower, balance)		

A typical split (half) body program might include four 30 minute exercise sessions per week to include approximately:

    5 minutes warm-up and stretching

    20 minutes muscle strengthening exercises, alternating days of exercising the upper and lower major muscle groups

    5 minutes cool-down and stretching

MONDAY	TUESDAY	WEDNESDAY	THURSDAY	FRIDAY	SATURDAY
Upper & Balance & Posture	Lower & Mid	Rest	Upper & Balance & Posture	Lower & Mid	

Always allow a day of rest, or in other words at least 48-hours, before rechallenging the same muscle with another intense workout with weights to allow for full recovery of the muscles. This is called the **48 hour recovery principle**. This principle applies for intense training with weights. This does not apply to stretching, or aerobic exercise such as walking, or to isometric exercises like the abdominal curl. These exercises can be done daily or even several times a day if desired.

Strength trainers refer to a complete movement as a **lift. Reps** (short for repetitions) are a repeated number of lifts. **Sets** *are a certain number of reps*, usually eight to 12, but sometimes six when first beginning a program and for more advanced muscle strengthening exercisers up to 15. Usually there is at least 15 seconds but sometimes up to 90 seconds of rest between sets. Rest until your muscles feel rested. There is no need to use a watch and no specific rest time is "fixed in stone" between sets. For example, you might perform one set of 10 reps of biceps curls, rest for 15-90 seconds and then perform a set of 10 reps of triceps extensions. Do not perform more than 15 reps as this has been found to tire the muscles too much and results in diminishing returns in muscular strength and muscular endurance. When you are advanced in muscle-strengthening increase to two sets of each exercise. As weeks progress and your lifting becomes easier as you become stronger, increase the weight two or three pounds each time of a specific exercise. All beginning exercisers should do only one set of each exercise, otherwise the exercise routine will get too long and you'll get discouraged and possibly stop the program. As you progress you may increase to two and then possibly even three sets of each exercise. Your strength-training program should begin with lighter weight and a full range of motion, gradually increasing in weight as the weeks progress.

When increasing weights to build muscle mass, the goal is to be challenged somewhat by the last two reps. If the last two reps are very easy, then consider adding small increments of weight next time.

You might begin your first workout doing one set of 10 reps, then after a few sessions as the last two reps become challenging do two sets of 10 reps, then after a few sessions do three sets of 10 reps. Increase the weights as the ninth and tenth reps of the third set are no longer challenging. If you find yourself jerking the dumbbells, you are using too much weight.

If you are just beginning an exercise program, then start with one set of exercise for each of the major muscles in the three major muscle groups: (1) upper body, (2) mid body back/abdomen, (3) lower body. The reason for the emphasis on one set is because you have time to flow through your whole program this way. This is satisfactory for producing your goal of a moderate increase in muscular strength and endurance for physical fitness. If you really want to tone, shape and build a large muscle or group of muscles, then multiple sets up to three of 15 reps each of a particular exercise would be indicated. But if you want moderate muscle toning and strengthening for fitness, then one challenging set is adequate. The weight can be increased with increasing fitness. Remember, for lifelong fitness you are focusing on moderate muscle-strengthening, not body building.

An average free weight lift such as a biceps curl is done slowly, focusing on the isolated muscle being exercised typically:

> 1-2 seconds to contract the biceps muscle and slowly raise the weight
> (called concentric phase)
>
> Brief pause up to 1 second (called isometric phase, muscle is held at peak contraction)
>
> 2-4 seconds to relax the biceps muscle and slowly lower the weight
> (called eccentric phase, muscle contraction is slowly released)
>
> Brief pause up to 1-2 seconds to relax then repeat

If your muscles become fatigued and you start to lose form, its time to stop and rest. A loss of good form creates an improper movement pattern which can lead to injury.

Breathe out with slightly pursed lips when contracting the muscle to lift the weight and breathe in with a deep, slow, relaxed abdominal breath when returning to the relaxed starting position. Develop a rhythm with your abdominal breathing and the lifts. If you find yourself holding your breath as you exercise, then notice this and focus on a slow relaxed abdominal breath as you let the weights down to relax and return to the starting position. Focus upon a rhythm of exhalation through your mouth with slightly pursed lips as you raise the weight and focus on a slow-relaxed abdominal breath in as you relax the weight. After a short pause, begin the cycle of muscle contraction and slow exhalation again. *Exercise in rhythm with your breathing* because it brings oxygen into the lungs and increases oxygen-rich red blood cells to your tissues, but also because it slows down the repetitions which creates a better exercise routine. During the 15- to 90-second rest time between reps is a good time to practice slow, relaxed, abdominal breathing because this type of breathing is maximally efficient and the oxygen replenishment to your tissues will be much more rapid and effective.

Most individuals have a tendency when beginning to exercise to do the reps too fast. *By slowing the pace of your repetitions in rhythm with your breathing you challenge a muscle with more constant resistance and obtain a better workout of the muscle you are isolating.* A slow deliberate repetition with letting the weight down about twice as slow as it took you to contract the muscle, with pauses at the beginning and end, challenge the muscle with more constant resistance.

Please note, however, that many Fitness Trainers recommend emphasis on a brisk natural fluid motion rather than a slow deliberate motion with pauses between reps. (Critics of this argue that although there is nothing wrong with this more fluid workout, you are only getting half the benefit of the exercise as you are not reaping the benefit from the slow eccentric relaxation of the muscle.) As with many things in life both have merit depending on the end result you want: to challenge the muscle more versus to increase fluidity of motion. Through practice you will find a rhythm that feels right and is correct for you, but always remember, do not rush the movement.

You must **always control the movement.** As you raise and lower the weight you must always control the weights and not let them control you. The movement should be done smoothly and slowly and always with you in full control of it. The control of movement should be through the full range of motion. Never let the momentum of the weights control you.

Exercising in rhythm with slow, relaxed, abdominal breathing reduces the speed of your exercise and automatically gives you the proper pace for your exercises.

> **If too much carbon dioxide (CO_2) is blown out of the lungs, then the pH of the blood becomes alkalotic and this causes a lightheaded, dizzy feeling. Remember: breathe slowly!**

If you find that you simply cannot get the hang of abdominal breathing when you exercise, at least *do not hold your breath* but rather breathe freely. Holding your breath momentarily causes increased air pressure in your chest and abdomen which raises your blood pressure and prevents blood from returning to your heart. (Note: This is easy to demonstrate. Just stand in front of a mirror, hold your breath and notice that the veins of your neck dilate and the veins on the back of your hands become more prominent). If you hold your breath as you do the exercise, then as you breathe out again your blood pressure abruptly falls which can cause a serious strain on your heart and may even cause a blackout. *Counting the reps out loud as you do each one prevents you from holding your breath* and is a simple way to be sure that you are breathing freely.

I personally use and am a strong proponent of slow, relaxed, abdominal breathing. I recommend using the rhythm of slow, relaxed, abdominal breathing to obtain a better, more oxygen-efficient work-out. I also highly recommend incorporating it into your everyday life as your preferred method of breathing for better overall oxygenation of your tissues, improved energy and better health.

I can't stress enough that in the beginning less is better and increase slowly.

Start Low and Go Slow

When performing an exercise, *for maximum benefit focus your attention on the specific muscle you are contracting*. As you contract the muscle you might visualize in your mind the muscle contracting and moving your bones. When performing an exercise, only the muscles you are exercising should be worked. This is called **muscle isolation**. All your other muscles, particularly the forehead, jaw, upper back and lower back muscles should be relaxed. If you notice any of these other muscles tightening up, let go of the tension and see the tightness leaving with your next breath. As you breathe out, see the tension leave the muscles and exit your body with the exhaled air.

When you let the weight back down, never allow it to fall down abruptly or bounce at the end of your lift. This is a good way to cause injury. As you lower the weight back down, there is a slight resistance so there is not a jerky movement.

It is preferable to design your program so that succeeding exercises work on different muscle groups so that a long rest is not required between exercises. If doing a second or third set of the same exercise, you may need to take a longer rest between sets. This may be particularly true if you are not physically conditioned.

When beginning an exercise, use the pneumonic **PTA** to help maintain good form.

P **is for Posture:** Step 1: Begin in a neutral posture with shoulders back, spine straight and pelvis in mid neutral position.

T **is for Transverse abdominal:** Step 2: Begin with contracting the transverse abdominis (TVA) muscle for trunk and core stability. A simple way to do this is to suck in your belly button towards your back.

A **is for Abdominal breath:** Take air into your lower abdomen until the lower part of your abdomen above the pelvic bone expands.

And then *begin the weight exercise on the expiration*. In other words, breathe out when you lift (contract) the weight and inhale into your abdomen as you lower (relax) the weight.

A Sample Muscle-Strengthening Program

A <u>basic</u> muscle-strengthening program to maintain fitness and improve health consists of a simple 4-1-4 program.

    4 upper-body exercises
    1 mid (abdominal-back) exercise
    4 lower-body exercises

Begin with eight repetitions (reps) of each exercise and then over the next few weeks increase the number of reps to 10, then 12, then 15. Increase the weight as you feel challenged but not strained. After several more weeks as you become more advanced you may gradually increase to two sets of eight reps and then again over the next few weeks increase the number of reps to 10, then 12, then 15.

These exercises can just as well be done on exercise weight machines (commonly called Nautilus machines although there are several manufacturers such as Cybex, Body Masters, etc.) at your local fitness center. If you have the money to purchase one of the multistation units for your home, this can be used to perform the exercises and it can be used in combination with dumbbells or other free weights as well. Some of the exercises may be done on the multistation weight machine and some with free weights . The key point is to isolate and exercise specific muscle groups and there is no one method of doing this that is suited for everyone.

The exercises are shown here for demonstration using simple, inexpensive ankle weights and adjustable weight dumbbells and a chair. Comparative exercises can be done at your local fitness center or on a more expensive home exercise multistation unit.

CAUTION:

The exercises illustrated in this book are representative of many that can be performed. Discuss these exercises with your physician, physical therapist, personal trainer or other qualified health professional who is familiar with your medical condition to determine if they are right for you before performing any of them. Any of these exercises should be performed only under the direction and supervision of your health professional.

Each of these upper extremity muscle group exercises may be done in the standing or sitting position.

4 Upper Extremity Muscle-Strengthening Exercises

1) Arms Forward (Press) with dumbbell in each hand. This strengthens the deltoid (the shoulder muscle) and somewhat the rotator cuff muscles; the trapezius (upper back and lower neck muscle); and the biceps (the muscle in front of your upper arm).

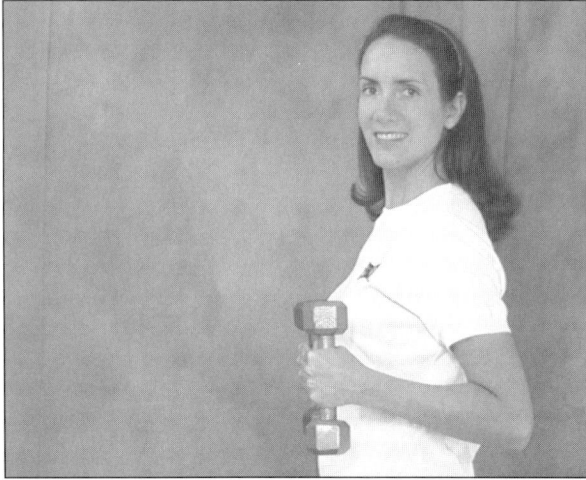

Forward

2) Arms Back (Triceps) with dumbbell. This strengthens the triceps (muscle in back of your upper arm) and somewhat the rotator cuff; trapezius (upper back and lower neck muscle).

Backward

3) Arms Out (Lateral Side Raise) with dumbbell. This strengthens the deltoid (the shoulder muscle) and somewhat the rotator cuff (four muscles that keep your arm in the shoulder socket). Keeping the elbow slightly bent reduces stress at the elbow .

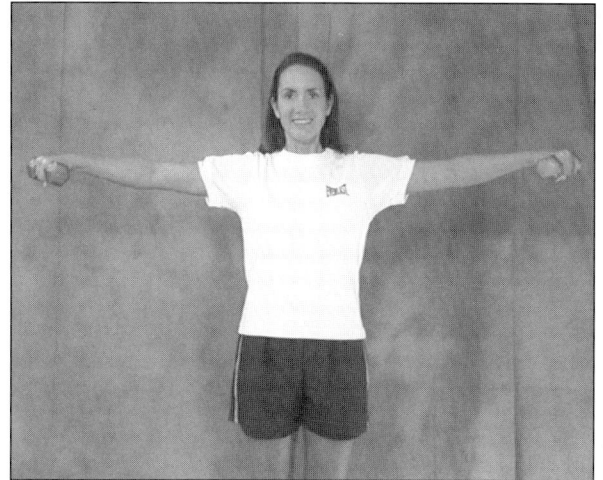

Out

4) Arms Up and Down Biceps Curl (alternating arms) with dumbbell. This strengthens the biceps (muscle in front of your upper arm) and the forearm. Both arms may be exercised at the same time for simultaneous curls if you desire, as long as it does not adversely stress your low back.

Up and Down

Standing Abdominal & Low Back Pelvic Tilt Exercise

This exercise might more appropriately be called a standing tummy tuck pelvic tilt. The basic exercise consists of flattening your abdomen (sucking your belly button in) and contracting your low back muscles (flattening the arch of your low back).

The motion of this exercise is begun by exhaling and contracting the transverse abdominis muscle known as the TVA. This is done by "tightening the abs" sometimes known as "sucking the stomach in" as in a tummy tuck. A good way to do this is to imagine your belly button being sucked in as far as it can go toward your back and contracting your gluteal (butt) muscles together known as the "standing butt squeeze."

Then progressively contract your lower back muscles so that your low back is flat and the arch of your low back is flattened. The top of the pelvis naturally in this movement rocks back. The exercise is completed by tilting the top of the pelvis toward your back. This action is called the pelvic tilt.

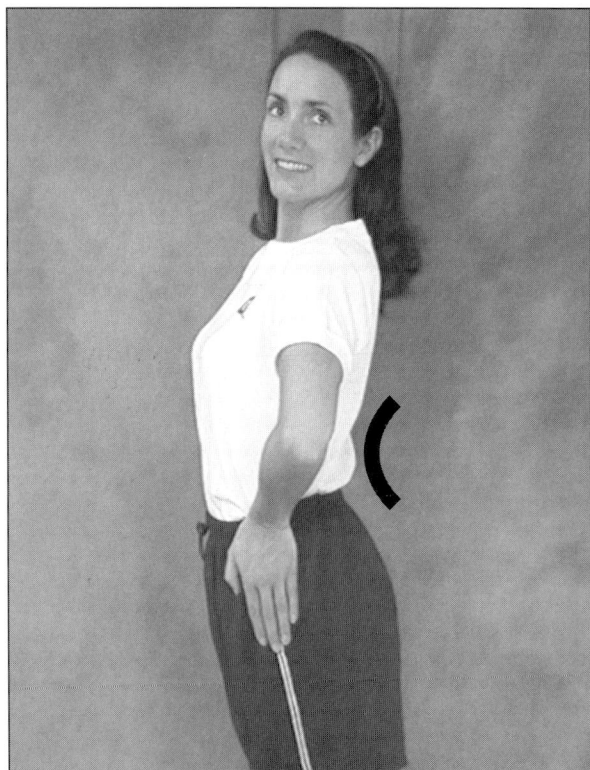

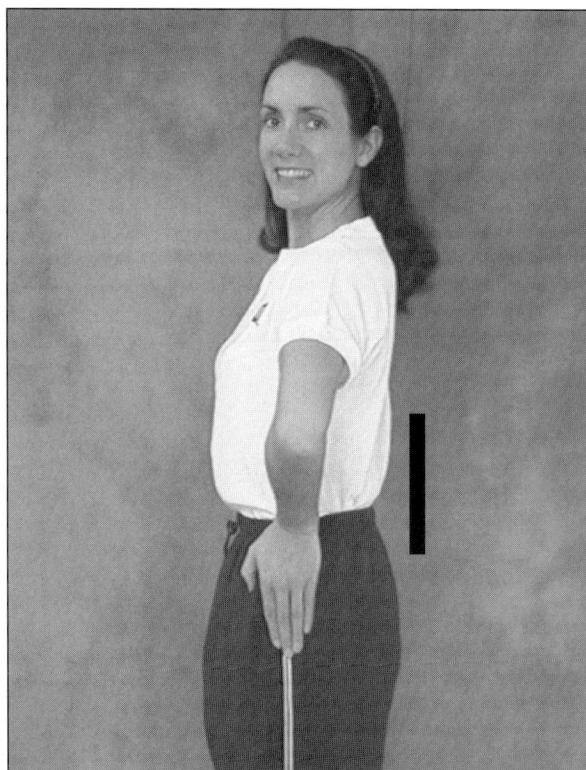

Perform this exercise in rhythm with exhalation. With each exhalation progressively contract your abdominal muscles and then your low back muscles so that your tummy is tightened and the arch in your low back is flattened. On inhalation relax the abdominal and low back muscles.

Perform the exercise so that you hold for a short while (i.e. five seconds) at the peak of the contraction movement and then relax slowly, pause and repeat the movement.

This is primarily an abdominal and low back exercise and primary muscular effort in the performance of the exercise should come from isolation of these muscles. This exercise strengthens the rectus abdominis (front abdomen), transverse abdominis (TVA), tightens and flattens the tummy and is a great low back exercise for strengthening the erector spinae muscles (low back). The pelvic tilt flattens the low back also known as decreasing lumbar lordosis.

There is a tendency to want to hunch the shoulders forward on exhalation at the peak of the contraction of the abdominal and low back muscles. Be aware of this and keep your shoulders and head back and maintain good form and posture.

Since this is an isometric exercise and does not use weight resistance for effort, a second set may be considered for a better work-out. Because weight resistance is not used, this exercise can be done daily without a day of recovery between. The 48-hour muscle recovery rule does not apply to isometric exercises.

The exercise can be done with arms on your hips, at your side or holding dumbbells. This exercise can also be done sitting or lying on your back with your knees flexed. There are many variations of the basic pelvic tilt exercise. They all have in common flattening the arch of the low back and strengthening the abdominal and extensor muscles of the low back.

Weak "Abs" are one of the most common problems with aging. It is as if weight seems to gravitate to the mid-section. Weak, flabby abdominal musculature contributes to an anterior pelvic tilt (increased) arch in our low back which causes back pain. Strengthening the "Abs" not only creates a more chiseled mid-section, but takes pressure off the spine by holding our back in proper alignment. Just about every exercise magazine has a section each month on "Hard Abs" or "Awesome Abs" or Rock-Solid Abs." The standing Abdominal Isometric/Pelvic Tilt Exercise is very basic and utilized because it can be done in the standing position and by just about everyone. **Please note that all exercises presented in Best Body Best Bones can be done in the standing position because I have found that most elderly individuals will not get down on the floor to perform exercises.** If one has no contraindications to performing and is willing to lie on the floor to do exercises, there are many great abdominal-strengthening exercises which can be done while on your back such as; abdominal crunches with legs up, twisting crunches with legs up, abdominal crunches with knees flexed, bicycle, bent-knee raises, and many more.

4 Lower Extremity Muscle-Strengthening Exercises

1) Leg Forward with ankle weights. This strengthens the quadriceps (large muscle in front of your thigh).

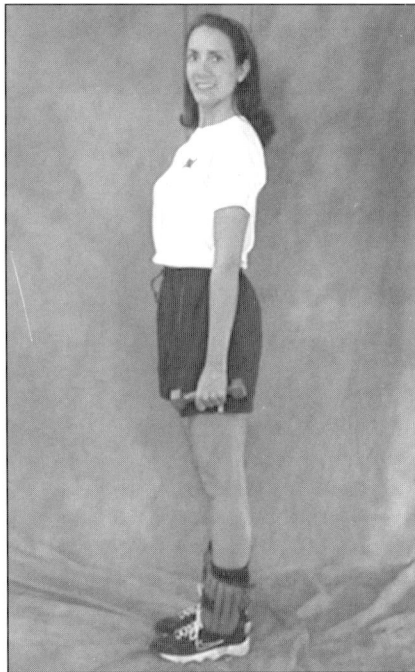

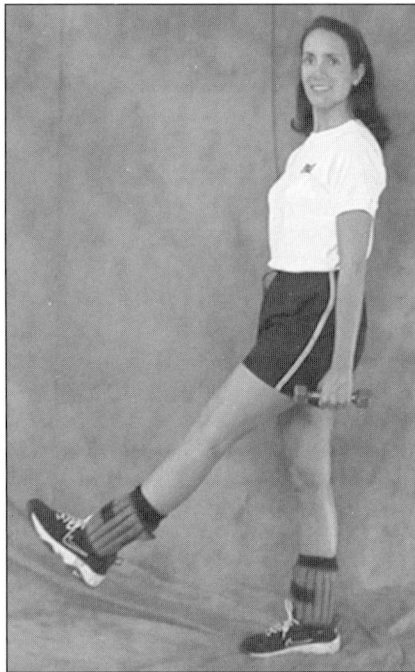

Forward

2) Leg Backward with ankle weights. This strengthen the gluteus maximus (muscle of your buttock) and your hamstrings (muscles in the back of your thigh).

If the hip extension exercise feels uncomfortable or hurts your back do not do it.

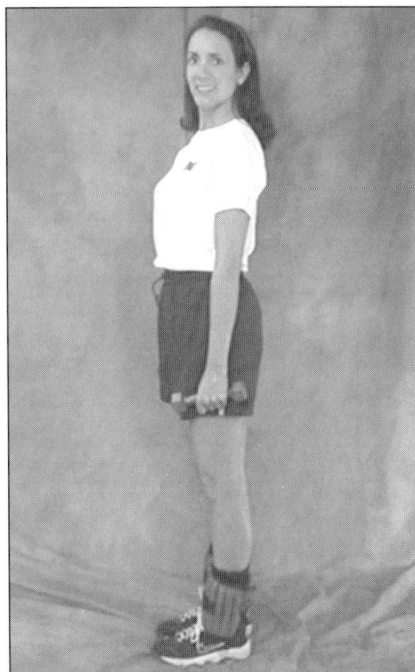

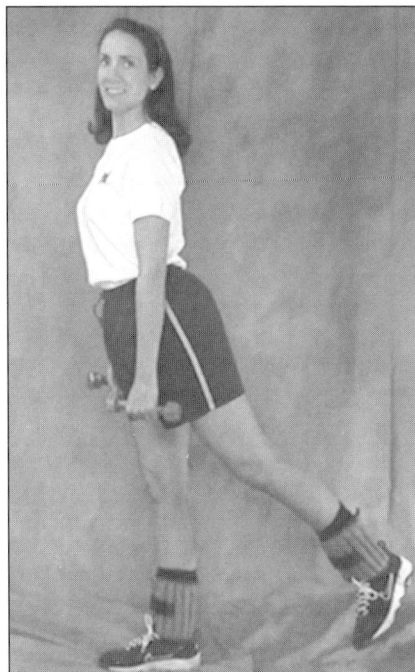

Backward

3) Leg Out (Lateral Hip Raise) with ankle weights. This strengthens the hip abductors (muscles located along the outside of your thigh).

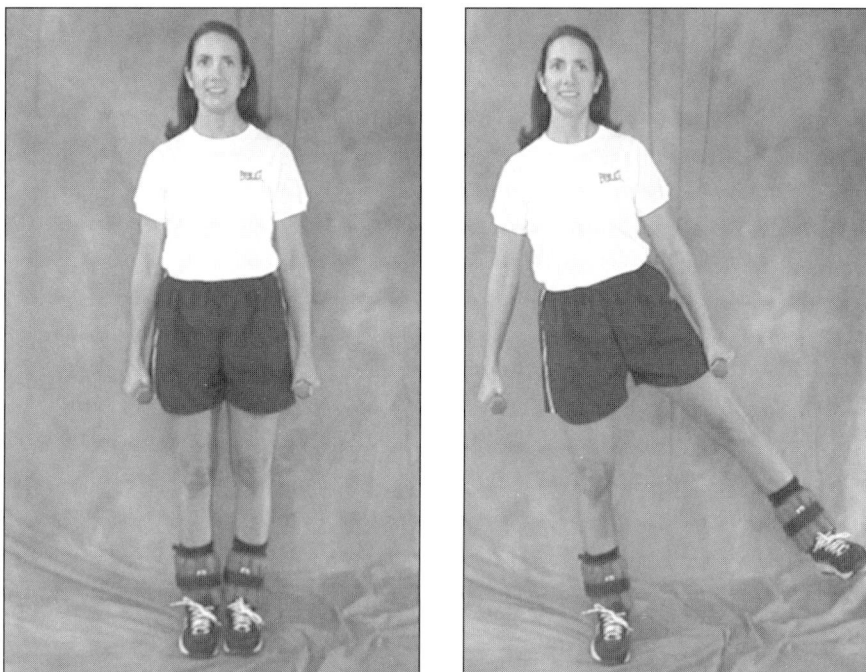

Out

4) Leg Up (Hip Flexion) with ankle weights. This strengthens the hip flexors, the muscles in your anterior thigh that cause the thigh to move forward and up. Also secondarily helps strengthen the abdominals and somewhat the quadriceps.

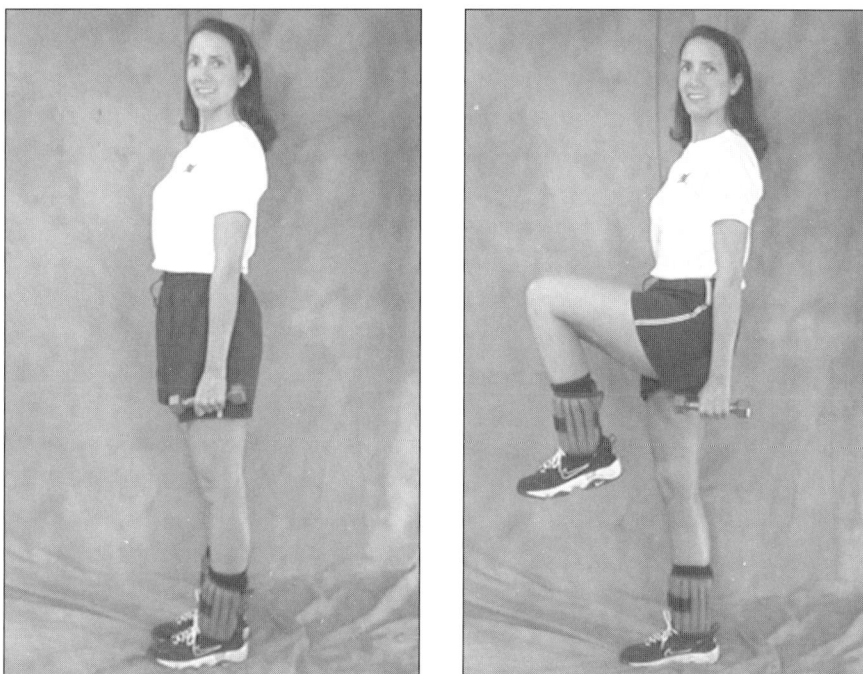

Up and Down

For specific programs of exercises and more in-depth muscle-strengthening information, the exercise and fitness section at your local bookstore will have rows of books on the subject.

Chapter 19

FLEXIBILITY (STRETCHING)
KEY #3

Stretching improves the flexibility of our muscle fibers. It improves the range-of-motion of our joints, loosens them up, makes them more pliable and improves mobility so that when we exercise more vigorously they will not be damaged.

Correct stretching takes our joints, ligaments and muscles through their full range-of-motion to improve flexibility in a mildly tense, yet relaxed way. Stretching should never be jerky but rather slow and gentle and last just until tissue resistance is met. You should ease into the stretch and hold the motion of a sustained stretch position for 10 up to 30 seconds with your attention centered on the muscle(s) being stretched. Move slowly and easily through your range of movement without jerking, bouncing (as in calisthenics) or straining. You want to elongate the muscles and ligaments while still feeling relaxed. Movement should be through but not beyond the range of motion or to the point of pain. The intent is to stretch all the muscles of our body.

If a ligament, tendon or muscle is stretched too fast or too far, a stretch reflex causes the muscles to automatically contract to prevent serious injury. Too much force and fine tears of the muscle fiber can occur, causing pain and even scar tissue if the injury is severe or the tissue repeatedly injured. It's analogous to the skin being cut or torn. The skin heals but leaves a fine scar. Correct stretching does not hurt. Your muscles should not be sore afterwards (only more pliable), feeling good and ready to do work.

When you're young and resilient and have the feeling of being invincible it's often hard to see the value of stretching. If you don't think that's the case, just try and convince your 18 year old to stretch regularly. But as you get older you eventually painfully realize its importance. You realize you are not invincible and can break.

If you like to stretch before lifting weights, as many do, you might do gentle warm-up stretches as part of your warm-ups, holding each up to 10 seconds. But remember, warm-up stretching does not replace flexibility-enhancing stretching which needs to be done _after lifting weights_ to maintain full active range of motion and reduce muscle soreness.

The following samples are simple yet effective stretching exercises: Hold each one you perform for 10-30 seconds. Do not hold your breath while stretching, but breathe freely with slow relaxed abdominal breaths.

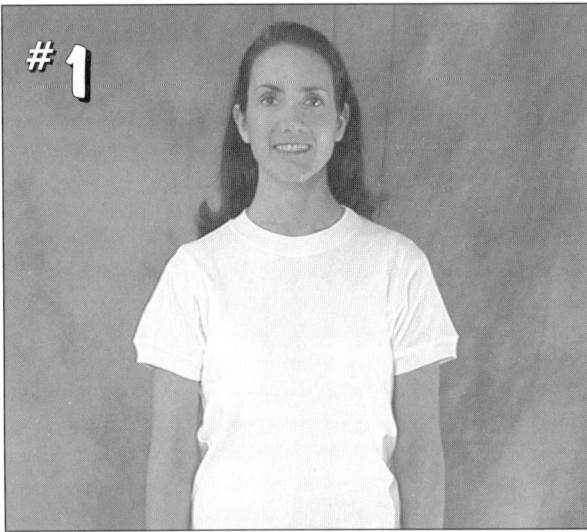

#1

Begin Upper Extremity Stretches

Upper Extremity Stretches

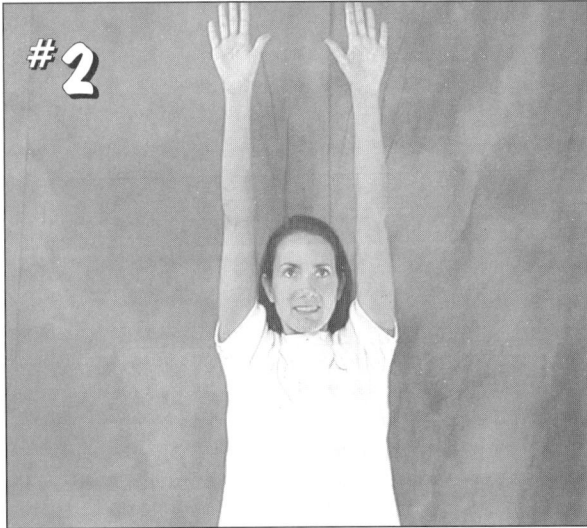

#2

Overhead Stretch

#3

Hand Stretch

#4

Right Side Stretch

#5

Arm on Hip

Arm Down Leg

Repeat Overhead Stretch

Repeat Hand Stretch

Left Side Stretch

Arm on Hip

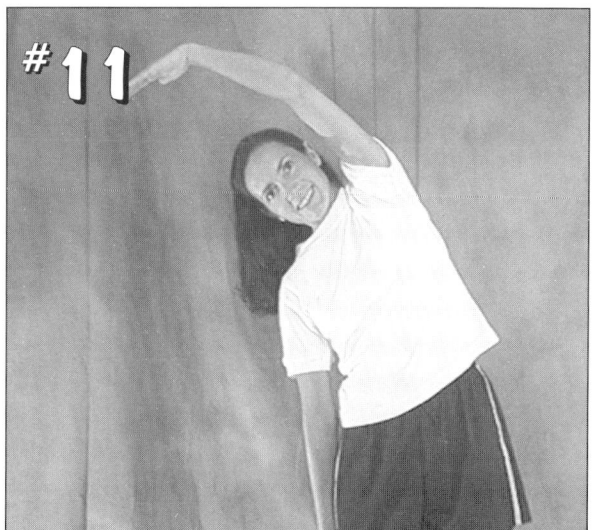

Arm Down Leg

The Four Policeman Posture Stretches.

1) "Stick em up" Back Extension Stretch

Arms up with palms forward, as if you were surrendering

Contract your shoulder blades together extending your elbows back. Hold for 3-5 seconds, relax and return to starting position

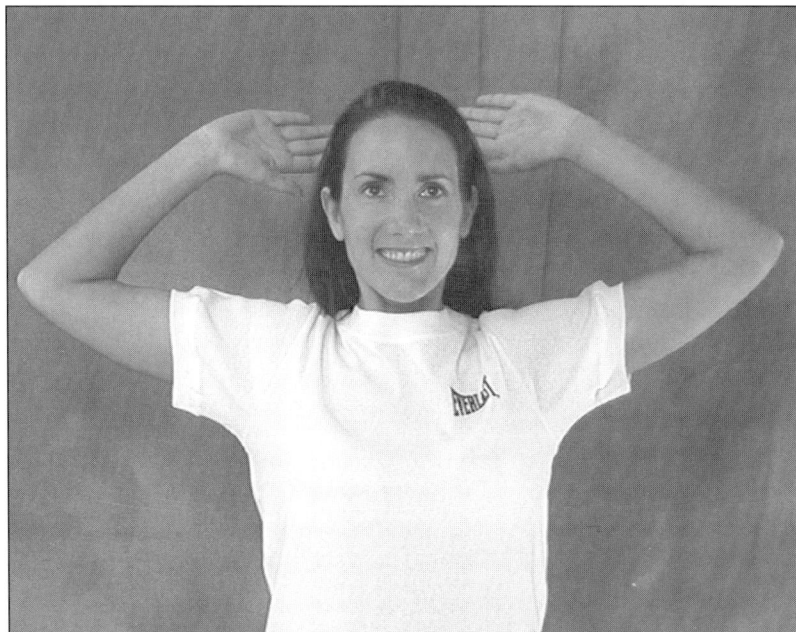

Primary action for each of the Policeman Posture exercises comes from contraction of the muscles between the shoulder blades

Flatten your stomach and project your upper chest forward and up as you pull your elbows back

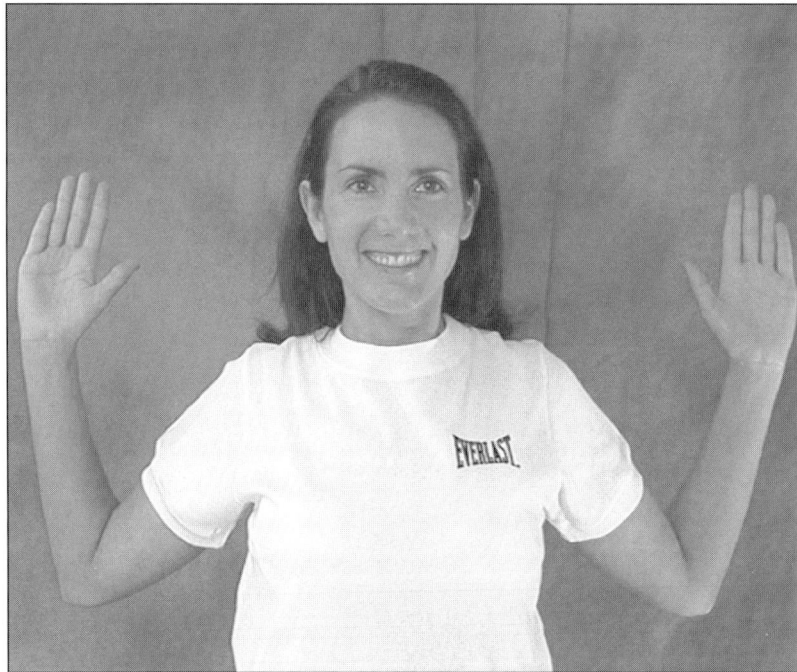

"You're Under Arrest"

Maintain proper posture with head up. *(Caution: Do not arch your low back).*

2) Arms Behind Head Back Extension Stretch

Contract your shoulder blades together extending your elbows back. Hold for 3-5 seconds, relax and return to starting position

"Put Your Arms Behind Your Head"

3) *Arms Tucked Into The Side Back Extension Stretch*

Contract your shoulder blades together extending your elbows back. Hold for 3-5 seconds, relax and return to starting position

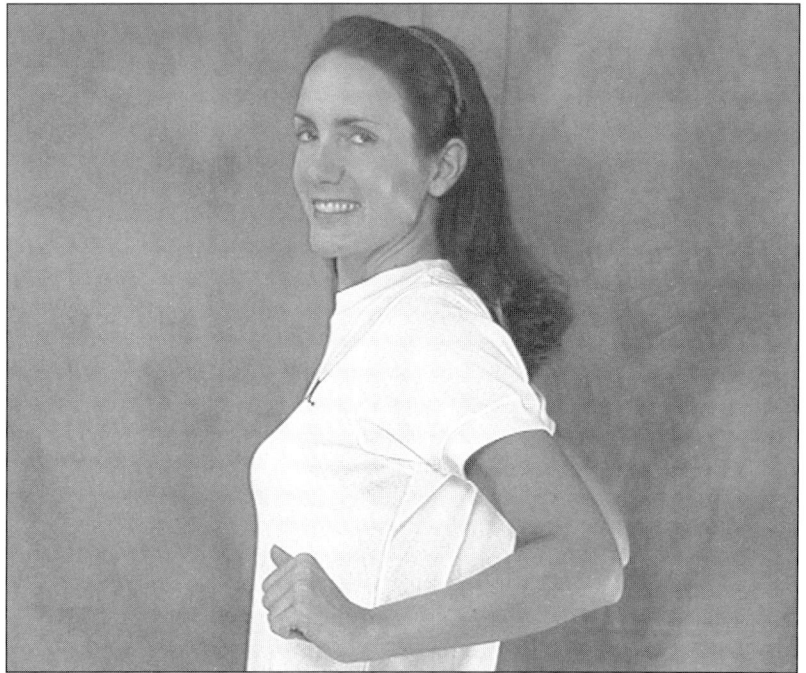

"But Officer I didn't do anything"

4) *Arms Outstretched and Down Back Extension Stretch*

Contract your shoulder blades together extending your elbows back. Hold for 3-5 seconds, relax and return to starting position

When advanced, may clasp outstretched fingers together and gently pull extended arms up and back

"You're under arrest, I'm going to cuff ya"

Mid-Body Stretch

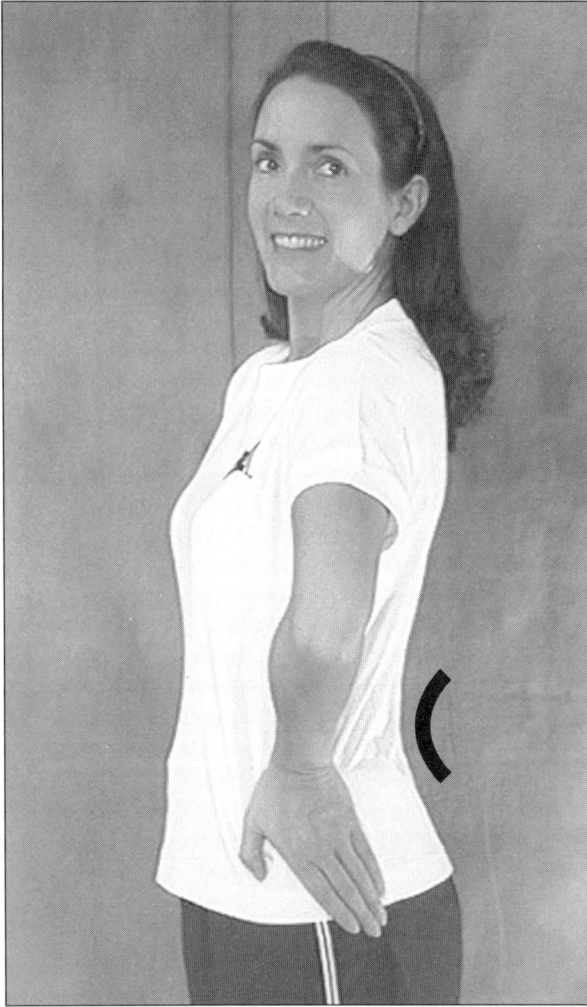

Neutral

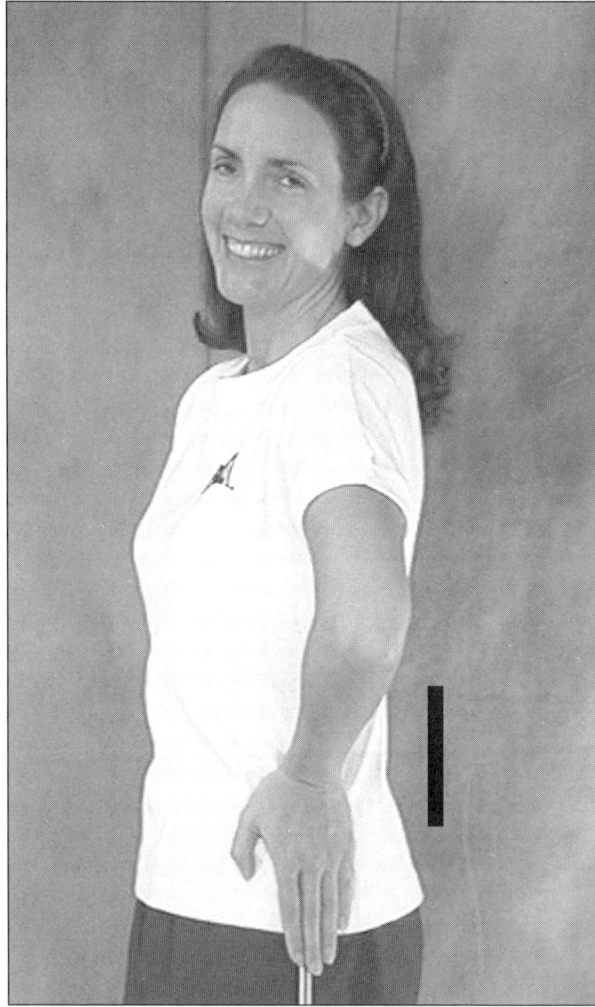

Abdominal/Pelvic Tilt

Lower Extremity Stretches

Adductor Right Stretch

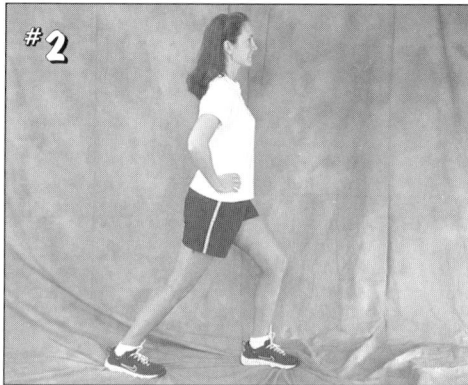

Achilles (back heel on ground)

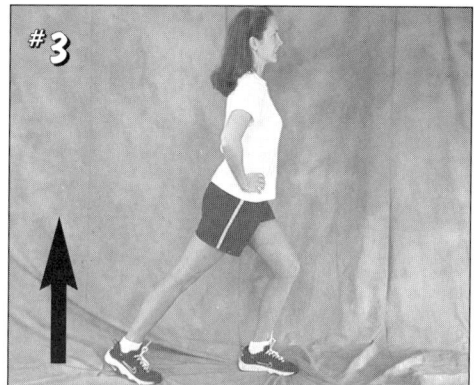

Hip Flexor (back heel off ground)

Adductor Left Stretch

Achilles (heel on ground)

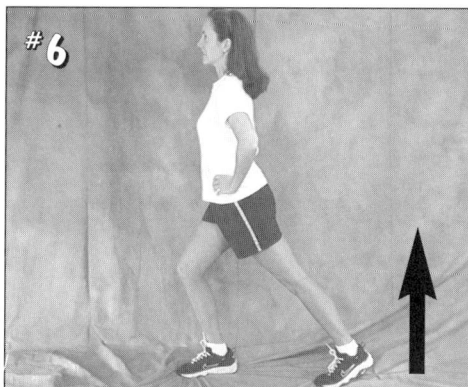

Hip Flexor (Back heel off ground)

Finish

In Summary:

Try to stretch all your muscles. Allow your slow, rhythmic, abdominal breathing to relax you and allow each stretch to be effective yet effortless without strain. Hold each stretched position for 10 to 20 seconds, up to 30 seconds if you desire. Feel your muscles elongate. Then slowly relax with a smooth motion. Take a complete breath and then go on to the next stretch. If you desire you may repeat a particular stretch. Allow the movement of your stretched muscle to follow your breath. Obtain a complete slow stretch but without strain each time. Remember to focus your attention on the muscle(s) being gently stretched.

Stretching improves our flexibility. Flexibility is the range of motion of our joints. In simple terms it is the range of motion through which our arms, legs and spine can move. Range of motion (ROM) is affected by many things such as tightness of the muscle, excessive body fat, shortened tendons, skin, connective tissue, diseases of the joints such as Rheumatoid Arthritis which may restrict movement, etc. The range of motion increases when joints, tendons and muscles are warmed. Hence, the warm up before strenuous effort. If a joint is forced beyond the ROM through which it is capable, injury consisting of tearing of the fibers will occur.

After exercising, stretching of tightened muscles helps maintain the active range of motion and reduce subsequent muscle soreness. Hatha yoga positions are wonderful examples of relaxing flexibility exercises.

You may want to tailor your stretching to your type of exercise activity, age, posture and fitness. For example, after walking your back, calf, groin and hamstring muscles may be tight. Stretching them can be the difference in whether or not the post-exercise recovery period will be relaxing and enjoyable or sore and painful. For a detailed program, refer to *Stretching* by Bob Anderson (Shelten Publications). I highly recommend that you purchase this book. He gives specific stretching exercises for many types of exercise and sports activities.

Attention! The older we get the more we need to stretch. It's true! Here's why:

When we're young we're very pliable and flexible, almost like rubber. But as we get older our bones, muscles, tendons and joints become more rigid and inflexible and as a result tend to break and tear more easily. In analogy, drop a rubber ball and it'll bounce, but drop a ceramic ball and it'll break. As a young child our bones, muscles and tendons are somewhat pliable and flexible, but as we get older they are more rigid. Bend the limb of a tree sapling and it'll bend easily. Bend an older, mature tree limb and it'll tear like celery does. Bend a very old tree limb and it'll snap and break.

Chapter 20

BALANCE
KEY #4

Balance is the normal state of equilibrium between two or more parts of the body. In terms of the musculoskeletal system **balance is stability**. In everyday life it is our body's ability to constantly maintain the body's center of mass over its support. The result is…we don't fall. When in the condition of balance there is a constant equilibrium of counteracting forces for stability.

Dynamic balance is our ability to maintain equilibrium during vigorous movement. Take a basic task like walking. When we walk we are actually balancing on one leg 80 percent of the time. The body maintains balance so we don't fall by: visual input and by proprioceptive input from muscle by muscle spindle sensory receptors, proprioceptive input from the tendons by Golgi tendon organ sensory receptors, proprioceptive input from the joints by joint receptors known as articular mechanoreceptors and proprioceptive input from the vestibular apparatus in the inner ear.

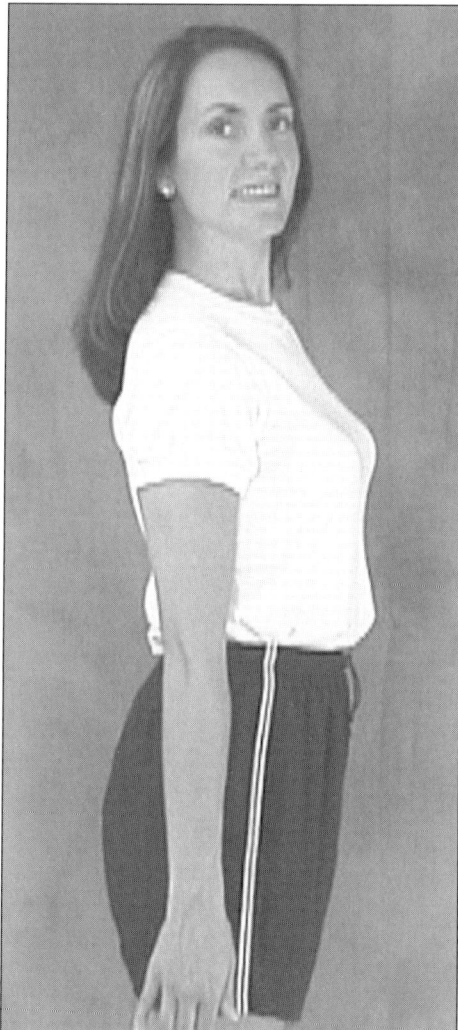

Balance can be improved by specific exercises. There are many others designed to do so as well. For elderly individuals who have considerable problems with balance, I would recommend a specific balance exercise program designed and begun with your local physical therapist.

Keep in mind that balance is different from coordination. *Coordination is the smooth flow of movement in the performance of a task.* For example, the golf swing involves a harmonious movement of many body parts. When each movement is executed in smooth union with the other, the swing is smooth and appears coordinated. If for instance, the arm motion is jerky, the movement appears uncoordinated. Coordination is achieved through practice. When a child learns to walk it takes practice and trial and error before the child learns the skills of walking. The same is true with the learning of other task-specific coordinated skills such as tennis, basketball, etc.

THE 4 BALANCE EXERCISES

1) Toe stand with or without ankle weights and with or without dumbbells. This strengthens the gastrocnemius and soleus (muscles in the back of your leg, sometimes called calf muscles). In the beginning, may be done with hands on a wall or holding onto a high-backed sturdy chair in front of you for balance, but as better strength, posture and balance is achieved, done without the hands on the wall or chair and then as you advance, holding light dumbbells. As you progress, you may perform the exercise with one foot on the floor and the other flexed (bent at the knee) and then perform it on a step using a handrail for balance.

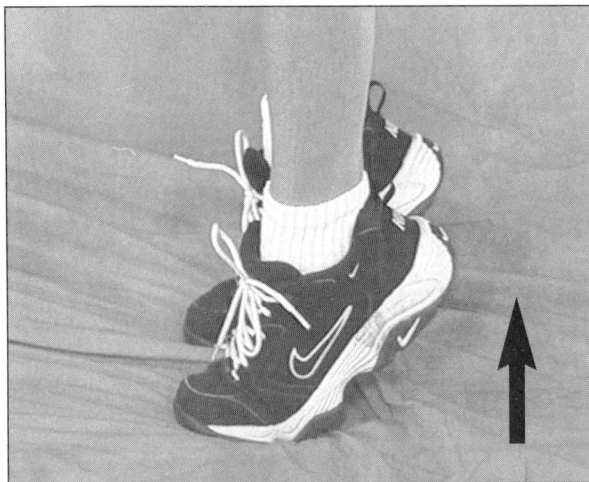

Forward (raise up on toes)

2) Heel stand with or without ankle weights and with or without dumbbells. This strengthens the anterior tibialis muscle (front of your lower leg). In the beginning, may be done with hands on a wall or holding onto a high-backed sturdy chair in front of you for balance, but as better strength, posture and balance is achieved done without the hands on the wall or chair. As you advance, you may do it holding light dumbbells.

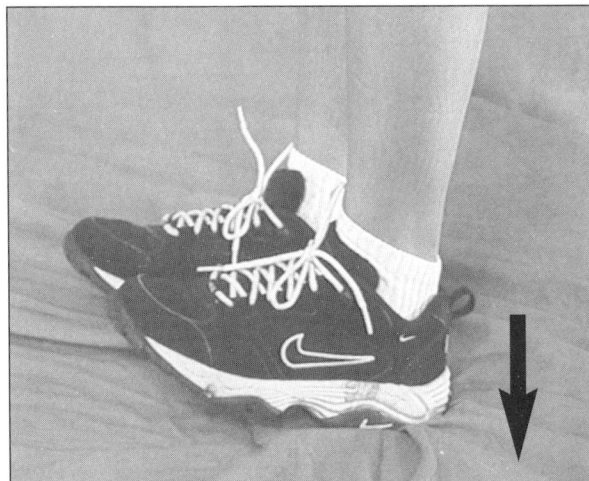

Backward (go back on heels)

3) Lunge with or without ankle weights and with or without dumbbells. Strengthens the quadriceps (muscle in front of thigh), hamstrings (muscles in back of thigh), gluteals (butt) and gastrocnemius and soleus (muscles in back of lower leg also known as calf muscle).

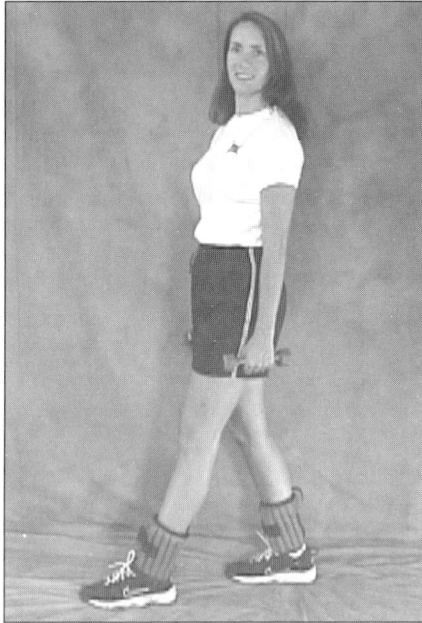

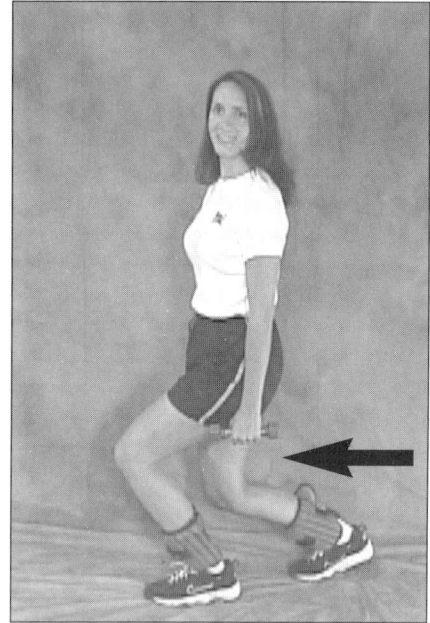

Out to side (Stationary Lunge) — Do left & Right sides

The lunge may be done keeping the feet stationary with one in front of the other and if done this way is called the stationary lunge. I recommend the stationary lunge for most individuals as foot position and knee alignment is maintained. With the stationary lunge good form and posture is more easily maintained as well.

The exercise is performed by standing with your feet naturally apart as wide as your shoulders, your back straight, head and eyes forward and with your weight a little back on your heels, hands on your hips. Keeping one foot in place lunge forward with the other foot about one stride (24-30 inches) bending your legs approximately 45 degrees. Keep your knee in line with your first two toes. As you lunge, the heel of your back foot will come off the ground. Do not step too far forward such that you cannot keep your balance or allow your front knee to move forward past your toes. Keep your head up and your eyes focused on a point in front of you because if you look down you may have a tendency to lose your balance and fall forward. The lunge is a controlled, fluid movement, not quick and jerky. For the stationary lunge, keeping one foot in front of the other, return to a standing position. If you are going to do the step forward-step backward lunge, lunge, step back, pause, then repeat.

If you have very serious problems with balance or falling, do not do this exercise. Young individuals under the age of 35 may want to do a full lunge by bending the knees to 90 degrees. But for most individuals this is not recommended as it places too much strain on the knees and older individuals may not be able to get themselves back up. Extreme flexion of the knee under weight-bearing also places the knee in a mechanically unstable and weakened state and may result in injury to the knee's ligaments. The reason the knee should not be moved past your toes is because this also places the knee in an unduly stressed position as it moves the knee out of its neutral position into a position that severely stresses the knee joint, supporting ligaments and muscles.

4) Squat with or without ankle weights and with or without dumbbells. This strengthens the quadriceps (muscle in front of thigh), as well as back thigh muscles, buttocks (gluteals), abdominals and lower back muscle groups.

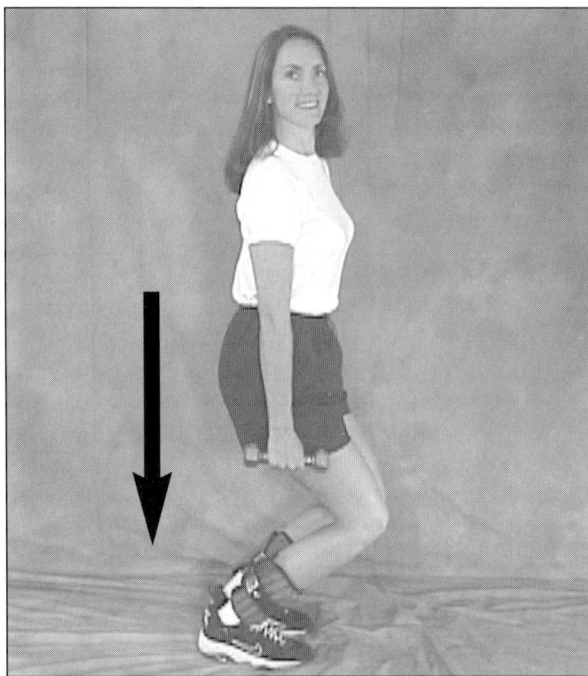

Up and Down (Squat)

There is an excellent exercise which strengthens multiple muscle groups and may be done with many variations. For example, may be done as a half-squat in which the thighs are bent at approximately a 60-degree angle and may be done with a narrow stance or wide stance (note: a wider stance is better for balance but also creates more stress at the sacroiliac joint). It may be performed with back against a wall for balance, or may be performed getting up and down from a chair with arms crossed or with arms outstretched or holding, may be performed standing behind and holding onto the back of a sturdy chair for balance or holding onto a walker may be performed with or holding light dumbbells and can be done standing on one leg to improve balance.

To perform, stand with your feet shoulder-width apart, your toes slightly outward, your back straight and head and eyes straight ahead. You begin the squat motion with your butt moving slightly backwards as you bend your legs to 45 degrees.

To perform against a wall, stand with your back against the wall and your feet 8-12 inches away from wall. Keep your back, head and stomach (low back) flat against the wall. Bend your knees and slide up and down against the wall. When down, you should be in a sitting or "chair" position. As a variation you may hold the down position for up to 30 seconds for a better workout. Move your feet closer to the wall for an easier exercise and slightly farther away from the wall for a harder exercise. For an easier exercise perform with hands flat against the wall, for intermediate exercise with arms crossed over your chest and for an advanced exercise with your arms outstretched forward.

Chapter 21

POSTURE
KEY #5

Good posture

Good posture allows for optimal functioning of our muscles and bones by providing ideal skeletal alignment. **Good posture provides optimal distribution and production of forces for maximum efficiency and minimizes the risk of injury.** When we have good posture control our posture muscles are coordinated for maximal stability which creates good balance.

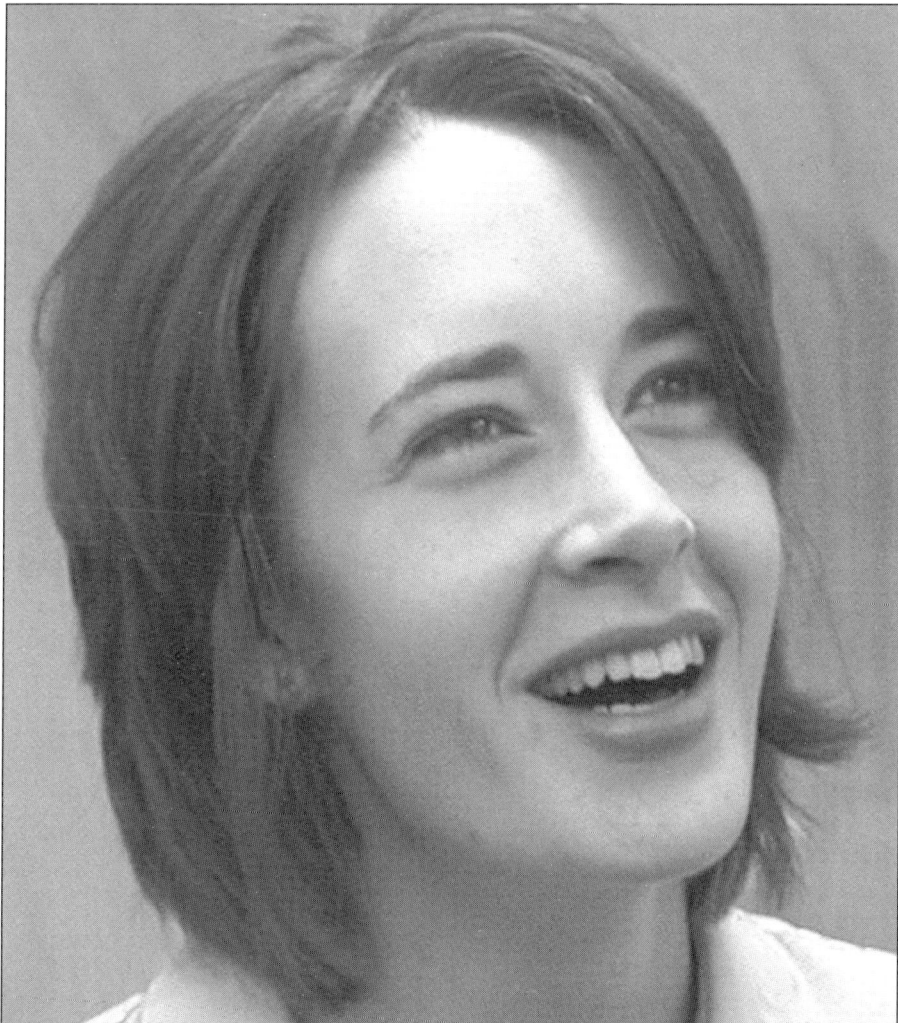

"Several times a week I do resistance exercises, stretching and some aerobics either on a treadmill or exercise bike. It makes me feel better and I've developed better posture."

Candace Hackborn

Someone who has good posture has a **neutral alignment** in which the ears (head) are directly over the shoulders, the shoulders back and over the hips and the pelvis in a neutral position. As we get older there is a tendency to hunch or move the head forward, to round the shoulders forward and to develop an anterior pelvic tilt (increased arch in the lower back, "pot belly" or middle age spread of the abdomen and slight hip flexion). These posture aberrations need to be first recognized, addressed and steps taken for their correction before proceeding to other exercises.

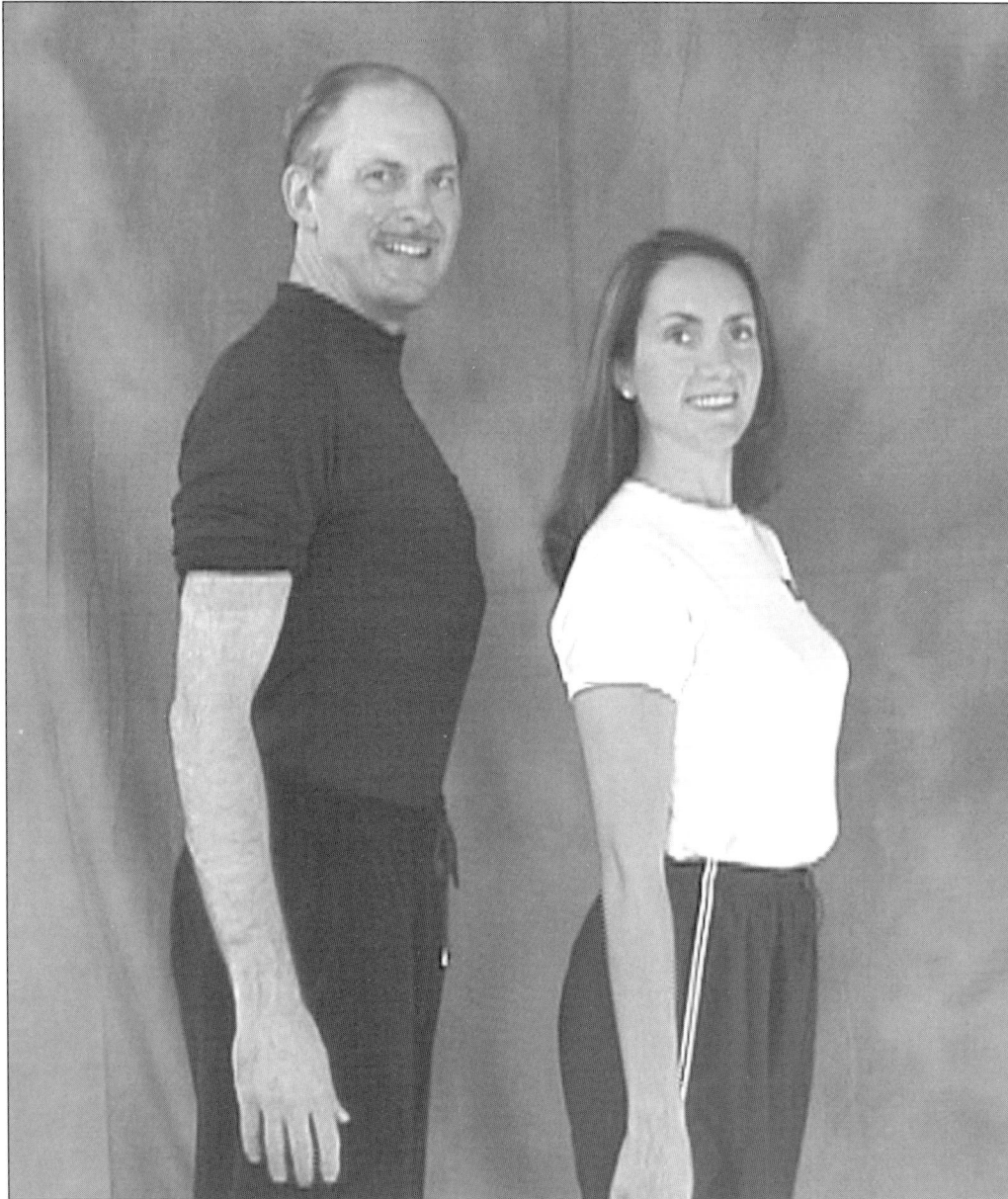

Core Stability

Good posture is the key to a stable shoulder, spine and pelvis. The shoulder girdle, spine and pelvic girdle (lumbo-pelvic-hip complex) and its muscles make up the core. When these are aligned and strong it is called core stability. It is best to develop good stabilizing posture muscles before working on the muscles of the arms and legs. Why? The deep stabilizers of the trunk provide a firm basis of support and work in unison with the outer muscles. Most movements with weights actually originate in the trunk's core stability muscles and emanate outward to the extremity muscles. In fact, when lifting a weight with the arm or leg, the deep abdominal wall stabilizing muscles are activated 30-110 ms before the arm or leg muscles are activated.

The Transverse Abdominis or TVA muscle is one of the most important of the core stabilizing muscles to be aware of. This deep horizontal-running abdominal muscle on either side of the abdomen functions like a girdle does to provide belt-like resistance to increased intra-abdominal pressure. This function provides considerable support for the spine and trunk. A good way to contract the TVA is to first obtain good neutral posture and then to contract your abdomen inward. *Imagine your belly button being pushed in to your back.* Be careful. There may be a tendency to move your shoulders forward in a sort of C curve. Notice this if you do it and correct it. Your belly button and corresponding abdomen moves in, but no other part of your posture should change.

Once you have mastered the neutral posture and then the ability to tighten your TVA and thereby provide for core stability of your trunk, you then need to practice abdominal breathing while maintaining contraction of the TVA. This can be difficult and I had a lot of problems mastering it in the beginning. I could only do so by finally imagining I was taking air into not my abdomen, but rather deeper down into my pelvis. Practice! Practice! Practice! If you find you cannot maintain good posture, contract your TVA and breathe abdominally, then probably it would be best to make an appointment with a certified fitness trainer at your local fitness center and have him or her work with you on it for a few visits.

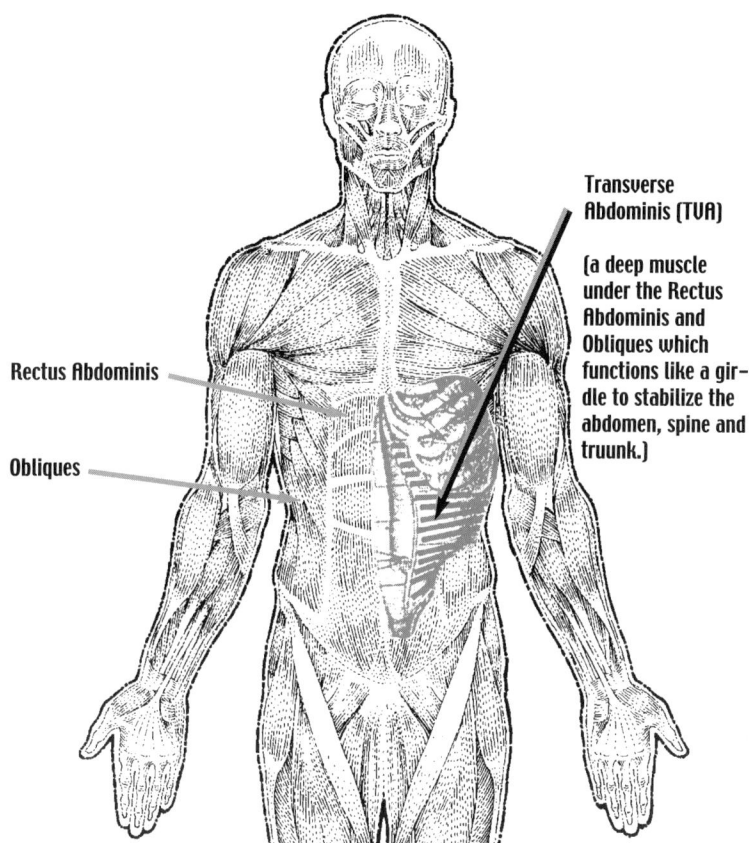

Rectus Abdominis

Obliques

Transverse Abdominis (TVA)

(a deep muscle under the Rectus Abdominis and Obliques which functions like a girdle to stabilize the abdomen, spine and truunk.)

(Note: Other core trunk stabilizing muscles in case you want to know and look them up are: internal obliques, multifidus, thoracolumbar fascia, paravertebrals, external obliques, rectus abdominis, erector spinae and numerous muscles of the pelvis, hip and shoulder.)

Once you have mastered good posture, stabilizing your core trunk muscles and all the while being able to do abdominal breathing, then you can move on to strengthening your arms, legs and other muscles with weight exercises. Always remember when performing an exercise; *Stability before Mobility! Proper posture with core stability must be maintained when performing any exercise.* Excellent exercises during which you can practice proper posture are in the performance of the 4 Balance Exercises in the preceding chapter (see Balance pages 82 - 84).

A favorite means of working on core posture stability I like to do is to practice the upper extremity exercises while seated on the gym ball.

This is good for the development of core stability because you have to maintain stability of the trunk on the ball first and hold it while performing the exercises with proper form. A great way to exercise but not for everyone, particularly not recommended for the beginner or the elderly.

CAUTION:

The exercises illustrated in this book are representative of many that can be performed. Discuss these exercises with your Physician, Physical Therapist or other qualified health professional who is familiar with your medical condition before performing any of them to determine if they may be appropriate for you. These exercises should be performed only under the direction and supervision of your health professional. No exercise should hurt when you perform it. If it hurts… then stop it immediately. The exercises may cause some minor muscle soreness but should not cause muscle achiness for more than 24 hours after you perform them

Chapter 22

WRITE DOWN YOUR DAILY PROGRAM

Write down the exercises you do *every time* you do them. This is vitally important particularly in the beginning. Keep a record. This serves as a visual stimulus to continue your program and a permanent log to chart your improvement. It will indicate your progress in distance and time of walking, tell which muscle groups exercised, give the number of reps and sets, indicate change in weight and give any other personal endpoints of improvement you may wish to note.

Daily Exercise Record

Date _____   Day of Week_____

Warm-up _____min.

Walking _____min.   Distance_____miles

Muscle-Strengthening Exercises	**Weight**	**Reps**	**Sets**

Upper Extremity

1. _____
2. _____
3. _____
4. _____

Abdominal/Back

1. _____

Lower Extremity

1. _____
2. _____
3. _____
4. _____

Balance & Posture Exercises

1. _____
2. _____
3. _____
4. _____

Stretching & Cool-down _____min.

Notes:

Daily Exercise Record

Sample

Date **2/15/01**   Day of Week **Monday**

Warm up Time **5** min.

Walking Time **30** min.   Distance **1.55** miles

Muscle-Strengthening Exercises	Weight(lbs)	Reps	Sets
Basic four exercises with dumbbells for arms			
1. Dumbbells forward	5	10	1
2. Dumbbells back (Triceps)	5	10	1
3. Dumbbells out to side (Lateral side raise)	5	10	1
4. Dumbbells up (Biceps)		10	1
Standing abdominal/pelvic tilt		10	1
Basic four exercises with ankle weights for legs			
1. Leg forward (flexion)	5	10	1
2. Leg backwards (extension)	5	10	1
3. Leg out to side (lateral side raise)	5	10	1
4. Leg up and down (leg raise)		10	1
Four Balance & Posture Exercises			
1. Forward on toes (toe stand)		10	1
2. Back on heels (heel raise)		10	1
3. Out (standing lunge)		10	1
4. Up and down (squat)		10	1

Stretching & Cool-down Time **10** min.

Notes: Becoming too easy. Will challenge muscles with 8 lb. dumbbells & increase ankle weights to 8 lbs. next routine.

A *Prescription* For

Good Health

The Actual Exercise Program

Chapter 23

THE BEST BONES BEST BODY FIT FOR LIFE PROGRAM

HOW TO BEGIN

A BASIC BEGINNING PROGRAM:

30 minutes of walking three alternating days a week (i.e. M-W-F)
and
30 minutes of muscle-strengthening, balance and posture exercise with dumbbells and ankle weights and finishing with stretching.

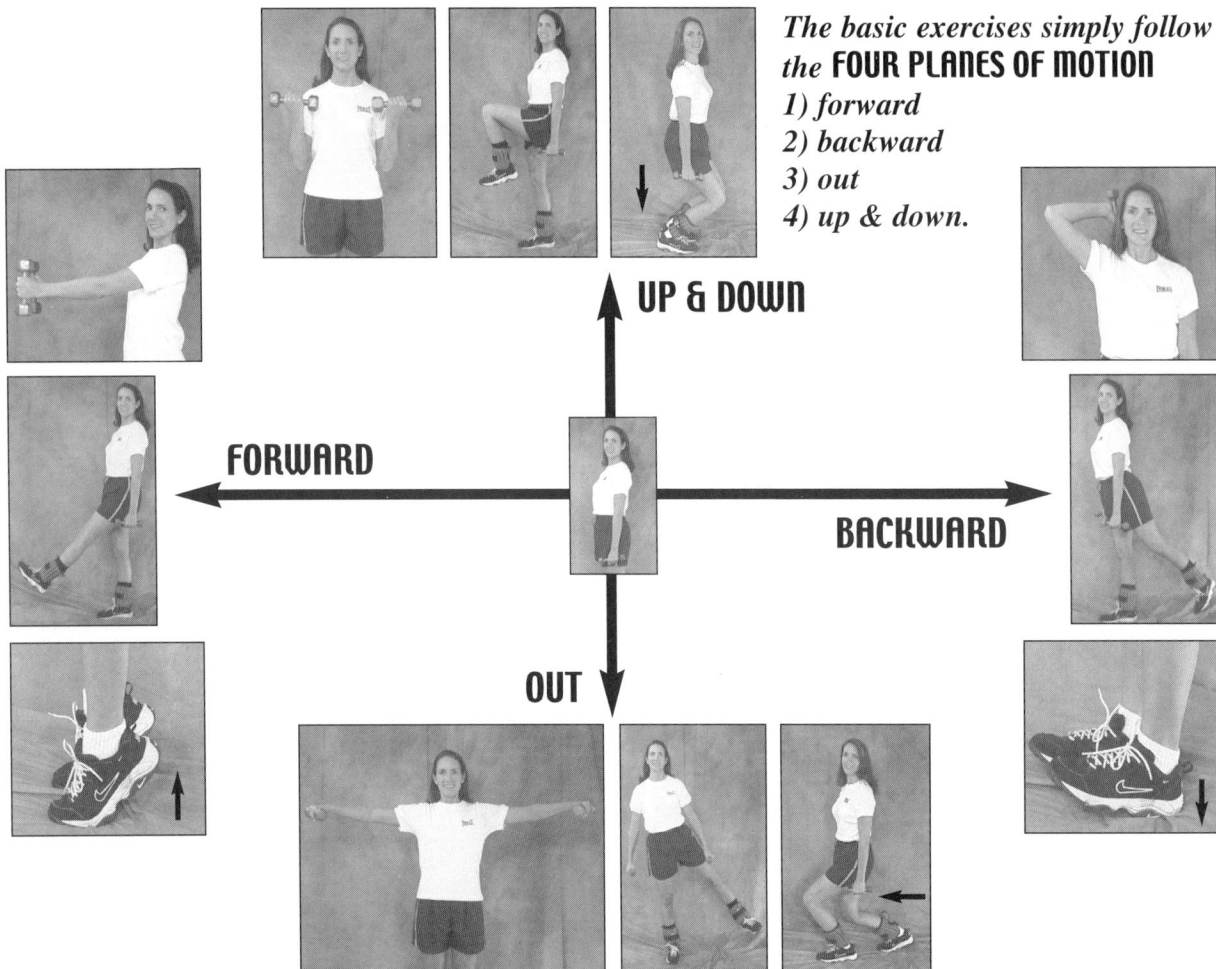

The basic exercises simply follow the **FOUR PLANES OF MOTION**
1) forward
2) backward
3) out
4) up & down.

UP & DOWN

FORWARD

BACKWARD

OUT

The 13 step basic weight program is:

Basic four exercises with dumbbells for the arms
1. Dumbbells forward
2. Dumbbells back
3. Dumbbells out to side
4. Dumbbells up and down

Basic one exercise standing abdominal pelvic tilt for the midsection

Basic four exercises with ankle weights for the legs.
1. Leg forward
2. Leg backwards
3. Leg out to side
4. Leg up and down

Basic four balance & posture exercises
1. Forward on toes
2. Back on heels
3. Standing lunge out to side
4. Squat up and down

AN ALTERNATE BASIC BEGINNING PROGRAM:

30 minutes of walking three alternating days a week (i.e. M-W-F) and 30-45 minutes of muscle-strengthening balance & posture exercise with dumbbells and ankle weights two days a week (i.e. Tu-Th).

AN ADVANCED BEGINNING PROGRAM:

30 minutes of walking six days a week. (i.e. M-Tu-W-Th-F-Sa) and 30 minutes of muscle-strengthening balance & posture exercise with dumbbells and ankle weights three days a week (i.e. M-W-F) or 45 minutes two days a week (i.e. Tu-Th).

If the aerobic and strength training are done consecutively on the same day, as is often the case, it is best to perform the aerobic weight-bearing exercise (i.e. walking) first to further warm up the muscles for strength training. If, however, you are going to be pushing your strength-training to its maximum intensity, then weight training should be done first for maximum energy availability to the muscles. Brisk aerobic walking would deplete the bloodstream of much of its energy-producing glucose.

If strength training is done on consecutive days of the week, do not strength-train the same muscle groups two days in a row but rather alternate them. Allow the muscle groups to rest at least one day between workouts. You might do upper extremity muscle groups one day and lower extremity muscle groups the next day. If you do a full body program, don't lift more than three days a week and leave at least one day of rest between workouts. Individuals beginning a muscle strengthening program might find it suited to them to work on a split (half) routine of the upper and lower muscle groups individually such as upper extremity with mid-body (abdominals and back) and then lower extremity with mid-body (abdominals and back) rather than the full-body program. A full-body workout to begin with may be too much in the beginning and cause discouragement and disillusionment. After four to six weeks of easing into the exercise program on a regular basis, incorporate the whole-body exercise routine. Also, never exercise seven days a week but always allow the muscles at least one day of rest a week for "R & R" and full recuperation.

If you choose to do a complete total-body program (Aerobic, Muscle strengthening, Stretching, Balance and Posture) on the same day:

The following is a sample Monday-Wednesday-Friday program you might begin at 7 p.m. and end at 8–8:15 p.m.:

       5 minutes warm-up (slowly increasing walking speed)
       20-30 minutes walking (brisk)
       5 minutes cool-down (Gradually decreasing walking speed)
       20-30 minutes full-body weight-training
       10 minutes cool-down and stretching

If your muscles are extremely weak and flaccid, you might find it best to begin with a light muscle-strengthening program first to strengthen the muscles and then incorporate the aerobic program into the exercise regimen after your muscles are stronger.

For most individuals, the beginning exercise program should consist of both low-level aerobic weight-bearing and low-intensity muscle-strengthening. The program must start out at a low level and then increase slowly in intensity. For example, it might begin with brisk walking a half-mile and then one mile and then gradually two miles over 30 minutes. It would also start with free-weight exercises utilizing light dumbbells or low level variable/resistance exercise machines at your local fitness center and slowly increase in intensity and duration as weeks progress.

After an individual has been into a regular brisk walking program for eight to 12 weeks, adding light wrist weights might be a consideration to further enhance the aerobic and muscle-strengthening benefits. Ankle weights are not recommended as a general rule for walking or running because they throw off the natural gait and cause a jerky running motion rather than smooth and rhythmic.

Good fitness will give you a better lifeline for a lifetime ! Investing in your health now is the best possible investment you can make for your future!

Terrific Advantages of The Best Body Best Bones Fit For Life Program

It's easy to see how this exercise program distinguishes itself from the pack of other fitness programs by its many special advantages:

- **Can do it at home**
- **Can do it at your own pace**
- **Can do it at any level of fitness**
- **Can do it at any age**
- **Can be done standing, does not require you to get down on the floor**
- **Inexpensive start-up costs (pair of shoes, $10 for pair of dumbbells, $20 for pair of ankle weights)**
- **Requires no special gym equipment**
- **Complete with all five components of a good exercise program (aerobic, muscle-strengthening, flexibility, balance and posture)**
- **Can be done for short or long time**
- **Can be done in morning, afternoon or evening**
- **Can be done daily or every other day**
- **Is fitted to your needs and level of health**
- **Simple and easy to do**
- **Can be done alone or with others**
- **Can be done while watching TV or doing other activities**
- **It's fun!!!**
- **IT WORKS!!!**

T · H · E
BOTTOM
LINE
YOU FEEL GOOD!

Chapter 24

STEP-BY-STEP VISUAL CHART OF THE BEST BODY BEST BONES FIT FOR LIFE PROGRAM

Putting it All Together for a Lifelong Exercise Program

A good safe and simple beginning exercise program for most individuals is

30 minutes of WALKING

then

30 minutes of WEIGHTS

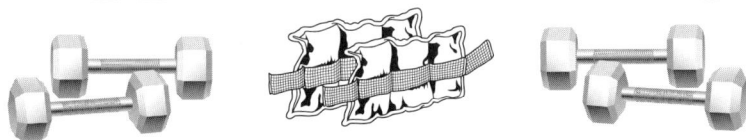

The weight exercises are muscle-strengthening, balance and posture exercises with 5- to 10-lb. dumbbells and 5- to 10-lb. ankle weights (The 4-1-4-4 Program) three times a week on alternating days (i.e. M-W-F). The fitness program always finishes with stretching.

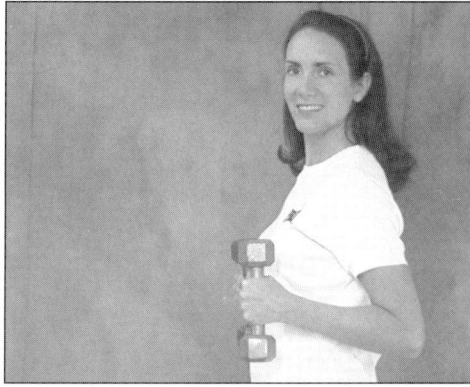 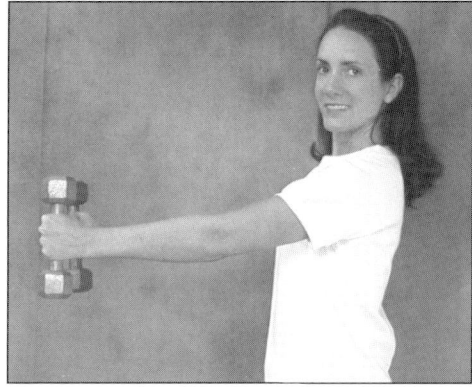

Forward

Backward

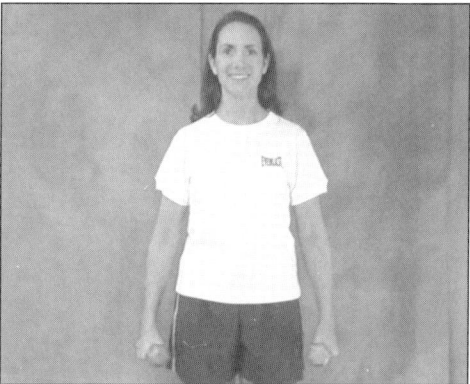 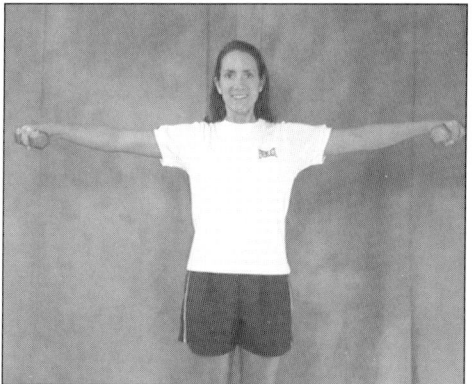

Out

Up and Down

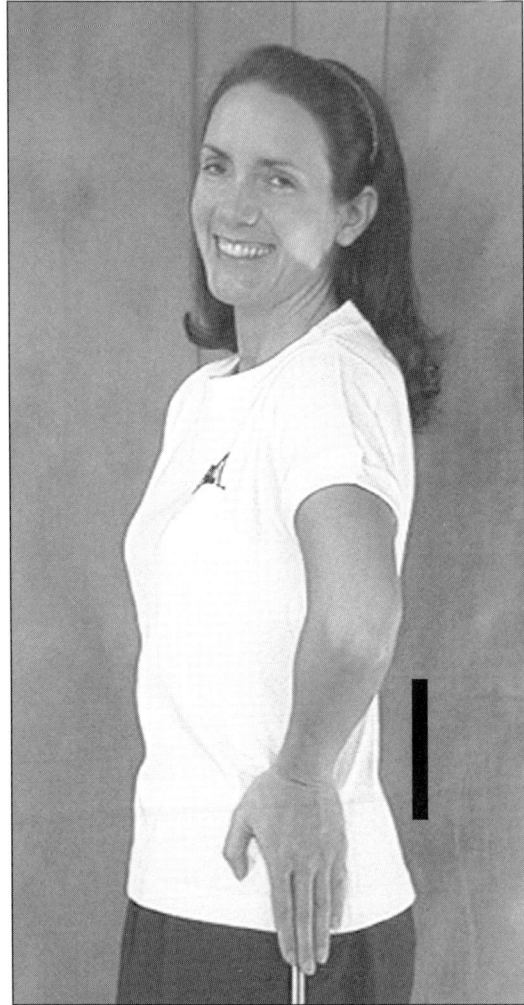

Contract Abdomen and Flatten Back

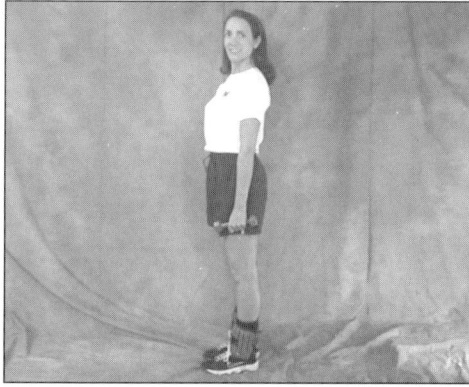 

Forward

Backward

Out

Up and Down

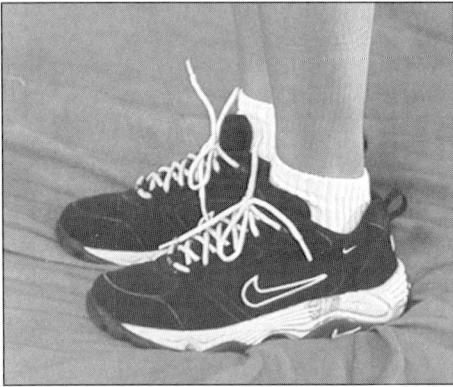

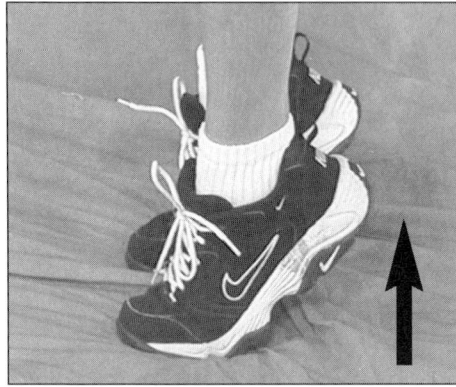

Forward On Toes

Backward On Heels

Out to Side (Stationary Lunge) Do Left & Right Sides

Up and Down (Squat)

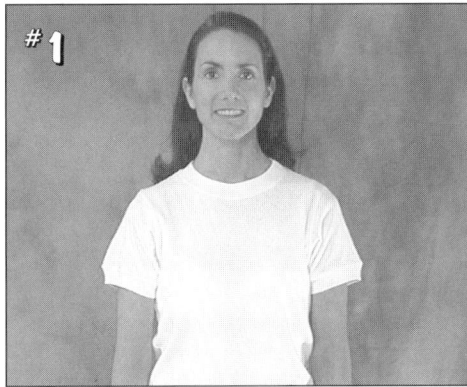
Begin Upper Extremity Stretches

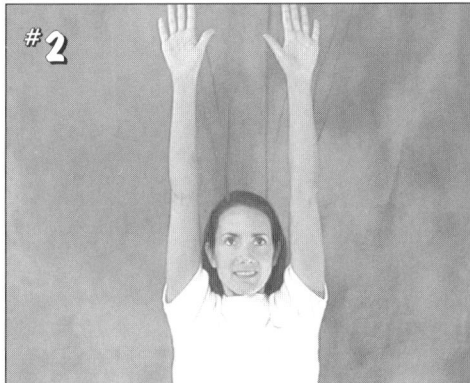
Overhead Stretch

Hand Stretch

Right Side Stretch

Arm on Hip

Arm Down Leg

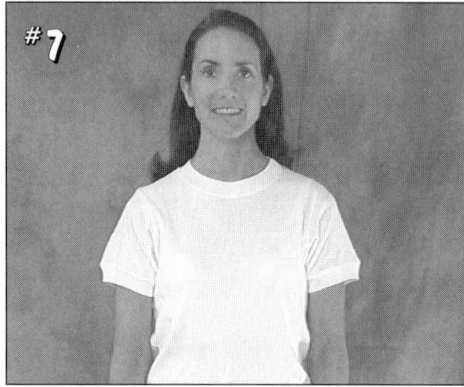

Neutral

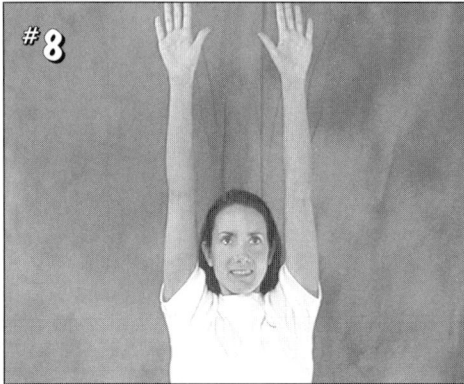

Repeat Overhead Stretch

Repeat Hand Stretch

Left Side Stretch

Arm on Hip

Arm Down Leg

"You're under arrest"

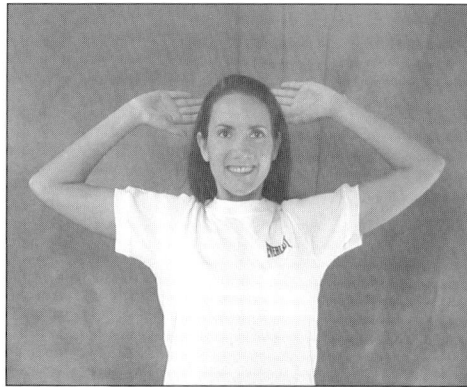

"Put your arms
behind your head"

"But Officer,
I didn't do anything"

"You're under arrest,
I'm going to cuff ya"

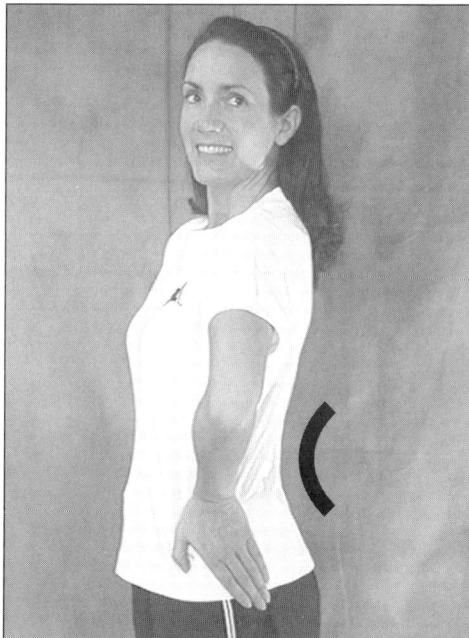

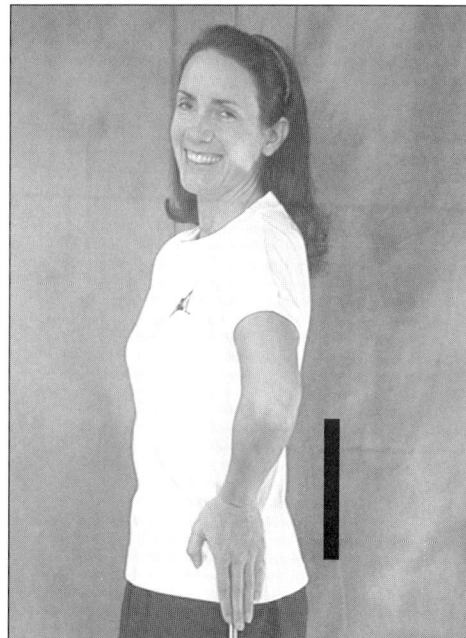

Abdominal Flattening/Low Back Flattening Stretch

#1

Adductor Right Stretch

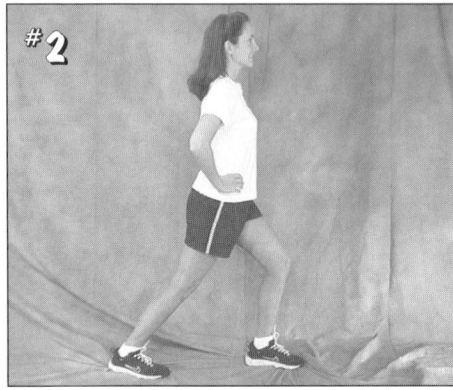

#2

Achilles *(back heel on ground)*

#3

Hip Flexor *(back heel off ground)*

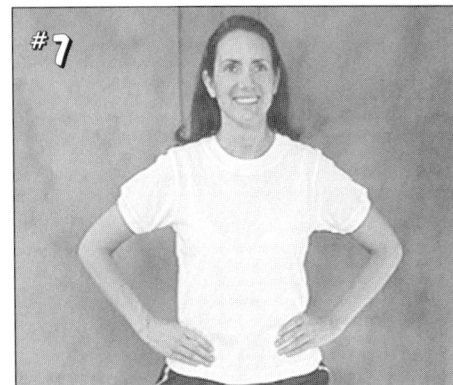

#4

Adductor Left Stretch

#5

Achilles *(heel on ground)*

#6

Hip Flexor *(back heel off ground)*

#7

Finish

Chapter 25

OTHER INTERMEDIATE & ADVANCED EXERCISES TO VARY YOUR WALKING AND WEIGHT PROGRAM
UPPER EXTREMITY

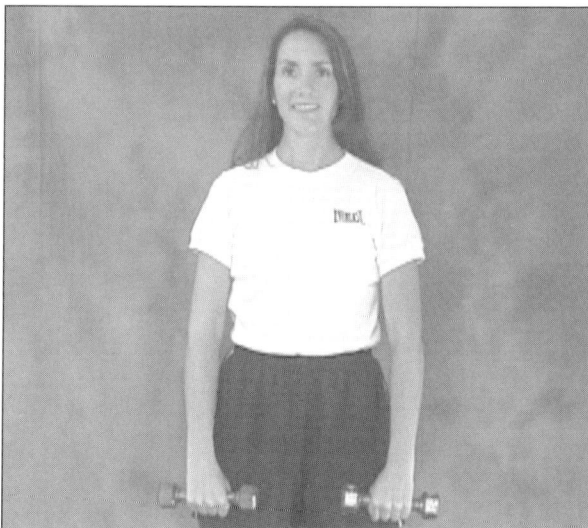

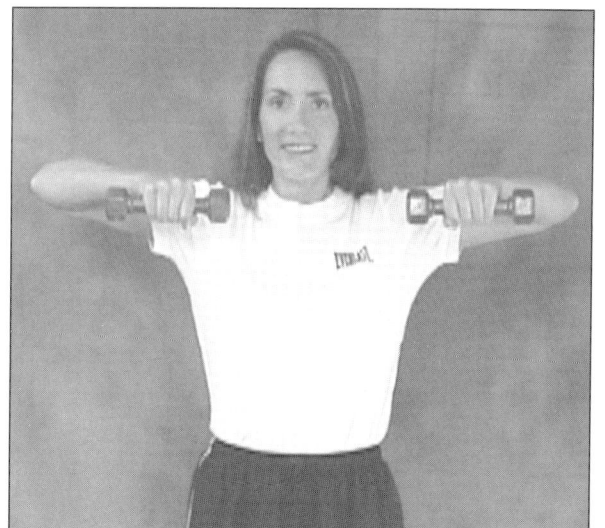

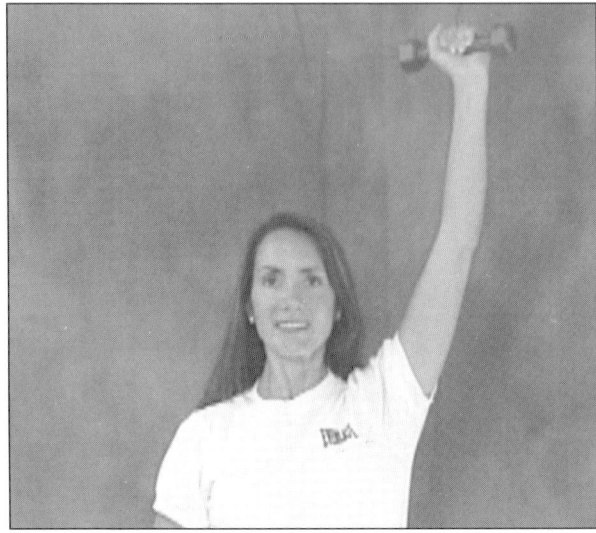

This overhead press may be substituted
for the Biceps Exercise as an Upper Extremity Up and Down Exercise.

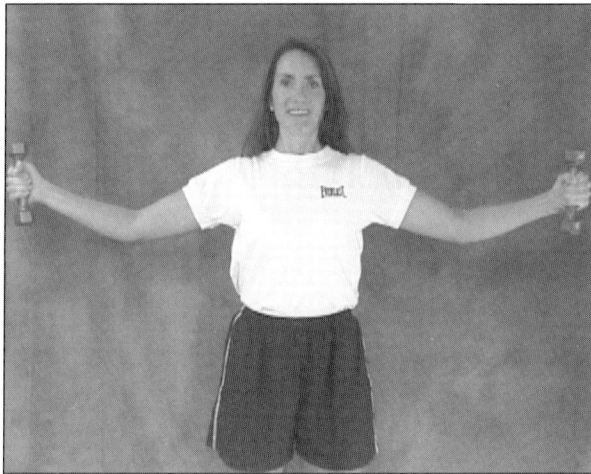 

 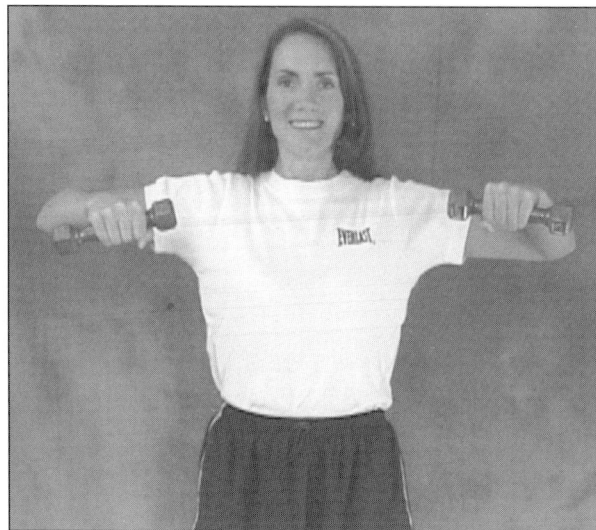

 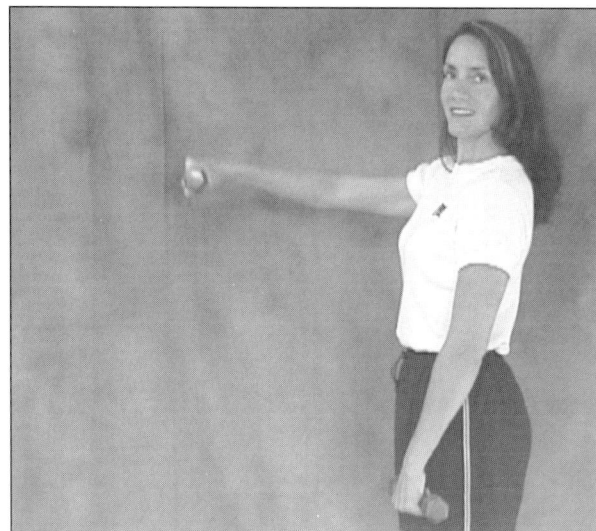

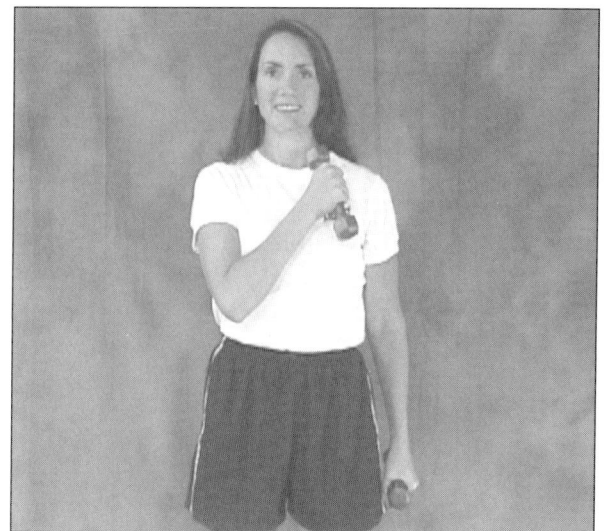

Enjoy Good Health

Tailoring Fitness To You

Chapter 26

MAKING YOUR EXERCISE PROGRAM WORK FOR YOU
Steps To Ensure Success

One thing you can be sure of regarding your exercise program. As enthusiastic as you might be right now, there are going to be times when you are going to find excuses not to exercise. Our deconditioned body may find sore ways to protest, our sedentary lifestyle may seduce us or we may not be able to find the time until finally we realize we are no longer exercising. Here is a revealing statistic: 68 percent of people who begin an exercise program are no longer exercising after 30 days! That's greater than two out of three who quit for one reason or another. What can you do to insure that you will not be one of those 68 percent? You can follow these guidelines.

- Choose an exercise program you enjoy and can do. The commitment to exercise must be a lifelong commitment. No matter how beneficial an exercise program may be for you, you probably will not stick with it long-term unless it feels good. Getting fit should be fun and energizing for you, not dull and boring.

There is no one ideal exercise program for everyone. The specific type of exercise program you incorporate into your daily life to promote your physical fitness will depend not only on the activities you enjoy and your personality but also on what equipment or facilities are available to you, your own physical health, your capabilities and your age.

• Keep in mind that you are exercising for better health and not doing grueling, demanding training for athletic competition or training for the Olympics. You should finish the exercise routine feeling energized and relaxed. Exercising for lifelong fitness should make you feel like you've been plugged into a battery charger. When you finish exercising you want to feel as if your life's energy batteries have been charged, not discharged. You should feel energized not drained of your life's energy. If you finish feeling tired and sluggish or pained and strained, then you are overdoing it and you need to back off somewhat.

"I started running at the age of 30, it was about that time that the running boom was getting started. At the age of 35 I set a goal to run a marathon by the age of 40...and I did. In my forties I decided I wanted to build more muscle, particularly in my upper body so I cut back on my running to 10-15 miles a week and began working out with weights. When I first started lifting weights I knew nothing about them...I didn't want to get hurt so I began with a personal trainer.

I really enjoy it...I have more muscle and more shape now than when I was just running. If more people would realize that they'd feel great and so much better if they'd exercise...The more you exercise the more energy you have..The more I exercise the less I want to eat the bad foods like sweets. Before I started lifting the weights, I noticed I had "grandma arms," but now they've toned. I feel like I'm 30, exercising has helped me feel good physically and mentally. You have to make exercising a routine...You can't skip your routine and say I'll do it tomorrow...You have to make time for it today!"

Cynthia Lycan
– Age 50

- Make exercise a part of your daily routine. The easiest way to insure that you persist with your exercise program is to make it a habit. Choose a time of day to exercise daily and set your wrist watch alarm to alert you to stick to it. Write down your time period to exercise in your appointment book. Some individuals find that they prefer to exercise first thing in the morning and then when they leave for work they feel invigorated and alert. Some prefer to exercise during the early part of lunchtime because it reduces their appetite and gives them far more energy for the afternoon than a big meal would. Others prefer late afternoon after work but before supper. They find that exercise helps them shed tension from work and provides a surge of energy to get them through the evening hours. Still others prefer a walk and light weight routine about an hour or two after supper. They find that this helps them "wind down." Whatever time you choose, make it as much a part of your day as eating, sleeping or working. Exercise consistently on a regular basis. Once exercising is a firm part of your daily life, you will find that if you don't exercise one day, you will feel as if something was missing.

- Write out your specific exercise program including specific exercises and short-term exercise goals. Forget about long term statements like "I'm going to exercise to get in shape" or "I'm going to exercise to improve my health and or get a better figure." Stick with concrete, do-able, specific activities. Write out week-by-week what abdominal breathing, stretching, aerobic weight-bearing and muscle-strengthening exercises you intend to do. Assess yourself every week. How well have you done? Are the exercises accomplishing what you want them to do? Adjust your exercises accordingly.

- Condition yourself mentally. Professional athletes know that conditioning the psyche is as important as conditioning the body. As mentioned above, two thirds of individuals who begin an exercise program fail to get beyond the first month. An excellent way to reinforce your exercise program is through visualization. First, visualize the results you desire. For example, visualize yourself with stronger bones, trimmer, more attractive and energized through exercise. Second, visualize yourself doing and enjoying the process of exercising.

When you visualize, use all five of your senses to experience actually doing the exercises and enjoying the benefits. See yourself exercising. Touch yourself and feel your muscles becoming firm and your bones strong. See your heart becoming more conditioned, your blood vessels becoming more elastic, your resting pulse rate decreasing, your lungs able to take in more oxygen, your mind becoming more alert. Feel invigorated. See increased oxygen being supplied to every cell of your body by efficient, slow, relaxed, abdominal breathing. See the cholesterol and triglyceride levels decreasing in your bloodstream. See yourself eager to exercise, invigorated and maintaining the high of exercise in your daily activities long after you've exercised that day.

What If You Do Not Want To Do (Choose Not To Do) Weight Exercises

Then briskly walk for 30 minutes at least three days a week. And if you feel you cannot squeeze this into your life, then briskly walk for just 10 to 15 minutes (or whatever you can to maintain mobility) at least five or six days per week. Some exercise is better than none.

If You Still Insist On Not Exercising Regularly

If after reading this you still are not motivated to begin a regular exercise program, then I have one thing to say to you: *stay active*. In my 27 years of medical practice I have taken care of several individuals over 100 years of age and many in their 90s. The common thread among these individuals is that they have all stayed mentally and physically active. They have maintained a feisty, vigorous zeal for living, for keeping physically busy, for nurturing active social relationships and for keeping interested in all aspects of living. I have noticed that as individuals age, material accomplishments and possessions are less valued and maintaining active relationships with friends and family such as grandchildren and great-grandchildren become the focus of their lives. While this active lifestyle may not be considered by some to be exercise, *maintaining an active physical, emotional and mental life seems to be one of the keys to long, healthy living.*

Chapter 27

LONGER DURATION
Versus
HIGHER INTENSITY

The controversy between working moderately and longer (for endurance) versus working harder and shorter (for strength) goes back many years and each has its merits and hard-core proponents. Let's discuss the merits and pitfalls of each.

Low Intensity & Longer Duration
(Endurance)

For many, their daily routine is to get into their groove on a daily walk around their neighborhood, briskly walk their German Shepherd dogs for 3 to 4 miles every morning, or get into a steady rhythm on their treadmill and go 3 to 3.5 mph for an hour three to five days a week. They "get into their zone" and chug steadily along for 15 to 20 miles per week. Many also have a regular routine of lifting light weights three days a week for two or three sets of 10 to 15 reps in a regular daily set routine of exercises. They are not interested in obtaining maximum intensity of exercise effort but rather want to get into a rhythm and maintain a plateau of moderate intensity exercise for a longer duration of time.

The proponents of this low intensity longer duration regular routine argue that it maintains moderate fitness, they feel invigorated yet relaxed and fresh when they complete the routine. Also, the risk of acute injury, one of the major reasons for discontinuing an exercise program, is low.

The critics of this program argue that maximum cardiovascular and/or muscle-strengthening benefit is not being obtained unless the intensity is upped. The body "learns" the routine after two weeks and adapts by muscle recruitment to accomplish it with less effort and more efficiency and therefore maximum benefit is not attained. They argue that although the muscle need not be pushed to maximum intensity, some increasing challenge is necessary for substantial aerobic or muscular benefit to be obtained. They also argue that long hours doing repetitive motions may cause chronic damage to joints i.e. degenerative wear-and-tear osteoarthritis of the knees from long hours on the treadmill.

Higher Intensity & Shorter Duration
(Strength)

The proponents of a high intensity, shorter duration aerobic exercise program argue that challenging, maximally intense exercise is required for maximal cardiovascular and musculoskeletal fitness. They argue that more effort must be put into the quality of the workout rather than the quantity. They never become complacent with a plateau of fitness but rather continually strive for higher endpoints of greater intensity and effort. Popular today is to do aerobic exercise of peak intensity for short periods of time. For example, in a 20-minute workout an individual after a short warm-up would increase gradually to near-maximum intensity for a few minutes, then decrease to half-intensity for a short time, then would increase gradually up to near-maximum intensity for a few minutes, then decrease to half-intensity for a short time, then repeat. This type of interval training alternates aerobic and anerobic exercise. At maximum intensity lactic acid builds up from anerobic metabolism which causes the individual to slow down. At moderate or half-intensity aerobic metabolism allows the lactate to clear and the individual can go full intensity again.

It's thought that these short bursts of high-intensity aerobic effort speed up metabolism better than a longer less intense workout and keep it up for a longer time after the workout for a better EPOC (Excess Post Oxygen Consumption) effect which burns up more fat calories. They argue that with this type of exercise the preponderance of calories burned from fat storage depots occurs after the workout (provided one does not eat within the first hour after exercising).

The proponents of a high-intensity, shorter duration strength-training exercise program argue that by stressing and slightly overloading the muscles, microtrauma is initiated at the microscopic level in the targeted muscle tissue. During the resting period the body requires energy for muscle repair so it obtains the energy by mobilizing stored body fat and metabolizing or "burning it" for energy. With high-intensity workouts the 48-hour recovery principle applies. This principle is simply: after a high-intensity workout the muscles of the body need at least 48 hours of R & R (Rest & Relaxation) for repair. For this reason, intense weight-training should occur on alternate days such as Monday, Wednesday, Friday and not consecutive days to allow for adequate recovery time.

When lifting weights if an individual wants to increase the size and strength of their muscles, then they must perform higher intensity (heavy weight) with shorter duration (less reps). This creates greater bulk (size) to the muscles and better definition. This type of training is the "no burn-no gain" approach and requires a hard workout with pushing of resistance training to the limits of maximum intensity. The results are increased muscle strength and size and a "buff" body.

Proponents of the high-intensity program also argue that without high-intensity exercise a training plateau is reached. An individual's body learns a routine and then it takes only a minimal amount of energy to maintain this training level. The proponents of the pushing to higher intensity are usually younger, more aggressive and intent on building a fine muscular physique rather than exercising for a lifetime of fitness.

These individuals also tend to demand high intensity of focus upon the actual weight lifting process. For example, focusing down on the target muscle and stressing it to its maximum fatigue, not just psychological fatigue but rather maximum intensity physiological fatigue. The no pain, no gain attitude. The results these individuals want are larger defined muscles.

Younger individuals tend to be more for a high-intensity, strength and physique minded-program. Reminds me of a Winston Churchill witticism: "If you're 20 years old and not a liberal, you have no heart…And if you're 40 years old and not a conservative, you have no brain." As you get older and wiser, you realize you don't have to conquer the world, only be in control of yourself.

Sometimes there's a fine line between challenging a muscle and causing microtrauma and tearing a muscle and causing major trauma. This applies to the novice exerciser in particular. For many, the only way to know where this line is, is through experience and all too often this could be a painful, exercise-ending experience. The critics of this high intensity program argue that pushing the body to its limits will initially give more rapid success in terms of stamina and muscle strength, but also greatly increase the risk of injury, one of the leading reasons for discontinuation of an exercise program. Middle age and older sedentary individuals are particularly susceptible. They openly commit to and embrace an exercise program only to have it come to a tragic end by doing too much too soon. Individuals over the age of 50 who begin an exercise program should probably be given a T-shirt with their commitment to fitness blazened on its front and then in equal size letters on the back of the T-shirt the reminder "Start Low and Go Slow." It's a lot like the stock market, you are investing in your health but your first rule is to protect your investment. As we get older we realize we're not invincible but often rather vulnerable. The long-term question also looms: what is the effect on the body of a lifetime of repeated maximum intensity (microtrauma) exercise? Is it similar to a car engine that wears out if it's continually revved-up and driven hard? The short-term benefits are substantial, but it remains to be seen if lifelong trauma to the muscles is a solid investment in one's health.

What is Right For You?

As you can see there can be a big difference between exercising for endurance and exercising for strength. Both have their merits. For young "whippersnappers," beginning an intense strength training program with a high-intensity workout may not be a problem, but such a program may lead to serious injury for middle-age or older sedentary individuals. For most middle-age (over 50) sedentary individuals the lower intensity would be best in the beginning and then they may proceed if desired with cautious, moderate progression up to higher intensity, shorter duration. And for the sedentary older retiree (over 65), the lower intensity is the only sane and sound way to proceed. After satisfactory performance, they slowly and cautiously may increase to slightly higher, more challenging intensity with shorter duration.

What may fit like a glove and be right at one time in our lives may not fit at another time in our lives. Our needs and our bodies are constantly changing and what seems right for us today may not be right for us tomorrow.

Most individuals in good health under age 35 seem to prefer and probably should be able to handle the higher intensity, shorter duration workouts. For many of these "fading into the sunset weekend warriors with a small paunch and love handles" (and I was once one of them), the rapid increasing weight loss and better muscle definition of higher intensity aerobic and weight-training workouts with improved physique would be satisfactory.

Most young individuals less than age 35 lean towards the more challenging greater intensity shorter duration approach. Whereas individuals 35 to 50 usually lean towards the greater intensity, shorter duration approach until they injure themselves and then develop a more moderate approach. Most age 50 to 80 and older individuals lean towards the less intensity, moderate duration approach.

I exercise for fitness and I don't believe in punishing or traumatizing my body either by too much intensity or overuse. I want it to last a lifetime! I can't believe that continually pushing to its limits day after day is good for it. Good grief…would your car last very long if you continually drove it to its limits like driving in a race at MIS (Michigan International Speedway). The short-term benefits of high intensity or long workouts take their toll over a lifetime. As I've heard it said so eloquently by many of my patients **"It's not the age, it's the mileage."** *Don't physically abuse and traumatize your body. I believe that if we treat our bodies with reverence, respect and care, they will support and take care of us.*

When I exercise in the morning before going to the office, my intent at the finish of the program is to be energized and to feel good. For this reason I never perform a high-intensity cardiovascular or muscle-strengthening program in the morning. I also tend to do only a maximum of 30 minutes of exercise in the morning due to time constraints. I tend to do high-intensity cardiovascular exercises and more challenging muscle-strengthening exercises in the evening when I have more time and my body has a longer time for recuperation and recovery afterwards during sleep. This routine naturally suits my needs and as a formula for success works for me. It may not be suitable for you, however. Work at the pace and intensity that suits you!

Chapter 28

MY PERSONAL EXERCISE PROGRAM

A sample routine of mine is to get up at 5:30, slip on my warm-up suit and a pair of socks, go downstairs to the kitchen, drink a glass of water, turn on the 4-cup coffee maker which I have set up the night before, go downstairs to the exercise room, put on the walking shoes I keep by the treadmill, snatch up the remote, turn the TV on to CNN and begin:

Monday, Wednesday and Friday at 5:30 a.m.

I warm-up for five minutes at medium intensity on the Schwinn AirDyne.

Then I walk usually on the treadmill for 20 minutes at 3.1 to 3.9 mph. Most days I'll go continuously at one speed and occasionally I'll do waves of moderate increasing – decreasing intensity over the twenty minutes. Then I stretch beginning with the hands over head stretch, left then right upper extremity and neck lateral flexion stretch, then triceps stretch, then lateral spine hand on hip stretch, then lateral spine hand down lateral leg stretch, then "stick 'em up" back extension stretch, then arms behind head extension stretch, then arms tucked into side extension stretch, then arms outstretched and down extension stretch, then mid-section abdominal isometric stretch, then (standing with legs apart) do right and left leg adductor stretches, then place leg forward for gastrocnemius stretch, then raise heel and move forward for a iliopsoas stretch. Finish other leg. My goal is to finish feeling relaxed and energized.

Then I take a shower, get dressed from clothes laid out the night before, come downstairs, make breakfast consisting of 4 eggbeaters, three low-fat sausages and two cups of coffee, put bird feed out and observe all our feathered friends for a few minutes while having breakfast, then I take out my PDA personal planner and go over goals and make my "things to do" list for the day.

Tuesday, Thursday at 7:30 p.m. and Saturday at 4:00 p.m.

On Tuesday, Thursday at 7:30 p.m. and Saturday at about 4:00 p.m. I'll do the same 30-minute cardiovascular routine above and then begin a muscle-strengthening program. If time does not permit for the aerobic cardiovascular exercise (walking), after warm-up I'll go right into the muscle-strengthening program. On Tuesdays and Thursdays and Saturdays (Note: sometimes this program gets moved to Sundays depending on personal activities) I always do at least a 30 minute muscle-strengthening program. I strap on five-pound ankle weights and take five pound dumbbells and do 10-reps of each of the four planes of motion arm exercises, then a 10-rep set of isometric abdominal contraction exercise, then 10-rep sets of the four planes of motion leg exercise, then do 10-rep sets of the four balance and posture exercises. I take off the five-pound ankle weights and put on the 10-pound ankle weights and pickup the 10-pound dumbbells. I then repeat the exercise sequence as a 10-rep set. I then take off the ten pound ankle weights and put on 20-pound ankle weights and pickup 15- to 20-pound dumbbells and then repeat the same exercise sequence above as a 10-rep set. I then do stretching. My goal is to do a challenging routine but not one that leaves me feeling pushed and drained of energy.

This is my basic "bread and butter" exercise program although I vary it weekly. Sometimes I'll add one, two or three other upper-extremity dumbbell exercises, various stretches, various abdominal exercises, use greater weight and do less reps as the weight increases (pyramid system), sometimes add exercises on the personal fitness system, add exercise bike or other aerobic activity such as basketball, etc.

Exercise News You Might Be Able to Use For Personal Insight

When exercising in the morning by myself, once my rhythm is steady and I'm on "automatic pilot" at 3 to 3.5 mph on the treadmill with good posture and slow, relaxed abdominal breathing, I often rest my fingertips on the handle of the treadmill just for balance and close my eyes and go inward. Sometimes I'll focus on one thought and just be with it and see what surfaces. These are precious times and I'm able to tap into an awareness and peacefulness not available to me otherwise. If intrusive thoughts or outside distractions interrupt, I let these float by in my mind like clouds floating by in the sky. Then I gently bring my attention back to the focus of my thought. I never force anything but rather focus like a laser light focuses one wavelength of light rather than the many wavelengths of white light. I let it happen. Sometimes I'll clear my mind in a sense of its clutter and focus/be/meditate in between thoughts. This is mentally very refreshing. Other times I'll review and mentally complete the previous day and/or plan the current day.

I too have days when the spirit is weaker and have noticed that on days my motivator is sputtering it's easier to exercise on the treadmill than on the exercise bike. I'm sure this is because the treadmill has an electric motor which makes you sort of go along with it. The bike, however, requires your own power to go at all. Oh yes, sometimes I'll relax and focus or meditate while on the bike as well. This is a little different, though, in that the treadmill's motor keeps at one speed whereas on the bike I find I often tend to slow as my body becomes more at ease in a relaxed state and its distracting to have to bring my attention back to maintaining the speed.

FITNESS

Other Fitness Considerations

Chapter 29

PREVENTION OF INJURY
"Start Low and Go Slow"

When beginning an exercise program, exercise to tolerance and do not over do it. **If you push yourself beyond the limits you feel capable of, you risk potential serious injury** and then become discouraged and decide exercise is not for you. Nagging injuries can lead to frustration and discouragement particularly early in an exercise program. Exercising should be as "risk free" as possible.

"Exercising to tolerance" is a phrase I find myself using a lot in encouraging elderly individuals to increase physical activity without going beyond their bounds so as to risk injury. Some trainers use the *"Rate of Perceived Exertion" (RPE)* scale in which the individual rates their overall exercise intensity on a 0-10 scale.

If you do experience an injury, listen to what your body is telling you through the pain. If you should have to miss a regular exercise time due to injury or illness, when you begin exercising again, take as much time as you need to get back to your previous exercise level. Remember, gradual progress is still progress. Avoid pushing too hard too quickly and you can prevent a more serious strain or injury which can derail your exercise fitness program for weeks. Be careful not to overtrain and do not exercise more than six days in a week.

Some minor muscle soreness and achiness after exercising is normal when first beginning to exercise, particularly if you are considerably "out of shape". Frequently, one causes injury in the beginning of a program by overdoing the intensity or exercising too long. The injured muscles and tendons become very stiff and sore 12 to 24 hours after, not necessarily at the time of the injury.

You'll notice that if you do injure yourself the pain and soreness will not usually develop until the next day. For example, let's say you overdo it and lift too much weight with the dumbbells. At the time of exercising you may or may not feel a little strain but the next day you'll really know you overdid it because you'll wake up feeling soreness and pain in the strained muscle rather than a good feeling in the muscles, tendons and ligaments. This is because of the injury. Enzymes called kinins move into the injured area and cause inflammation during the first 12 to 24 hours of an injury. They cause swelling and pain. These are the body's defenses. Have you ever been involved in an automobile accident and at the time of the accident you tell the police officer you're fine, but as the night goes on your neck gets stiffer and stiffer and when you wake up the next day you can hardly move it. Or have you ever lifted something a little too heavy and feel a slight twinge in your back but think that it'll go away, but as the night wears on it becomes more and more uncomfortable and when you wake up the next day you can hardly get out of bed. It's because of kinins. So remember "Start Low and Go Slow!"

Chapter 30

SPECIAL EXERCISE CONSIDERATIONS IF YOU HAVE OSTEOPOROSIS

If you currently have osteopenia (thin bone) or osteoporosis (brittle bone), you are at risk for fracture and you need to avoid spine-jarring exercise programs such as high impact aerobics, jogging, running, skipping rope, vigorous dancing and racket sports. These exercises carry a greater possibility of bone fracture. Thin, weakened vertebrae can compress and fracture with very little force.

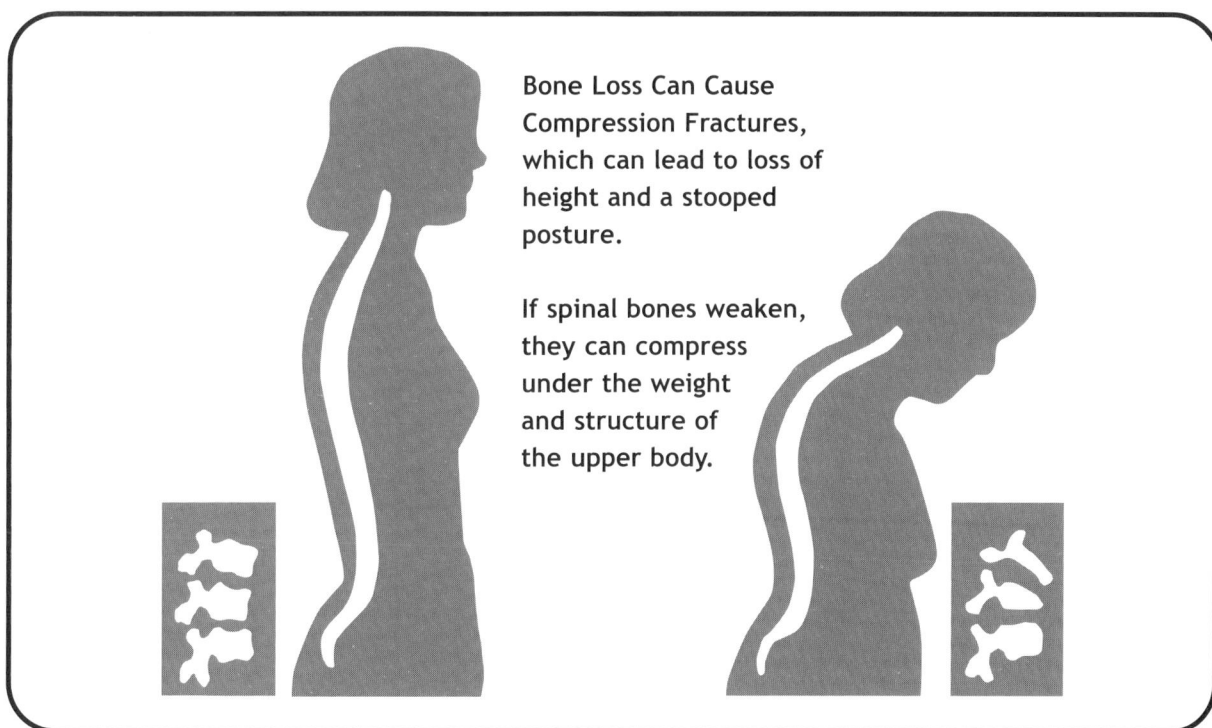

Bone Loss Can Cause Compression Fractures, which can lead to loss of height and a stooped posture.

If spinal bones weaken, they can compress under the weight and structure of the upper body.

Even the impact of jarring the spine from simple bending or twisting or jogging may possibly cause a fracture if you have osteoporosis.

If you are over the age of 50, you should think twice about running, trampolines, jumping rope and high-intensity or impact aerobics since there is a much greater potential for injury with these exercises. Increasing age is an independent risk factor for the development of osteoporosis and subsequent osteoporotic fracture.

If you have thin or brittle bones, forward stooped (flexed) posture, or osteoporotic compression fracture, do not perform any motion which consists of bending forward at the waist with the back rounded. This includes such exercises as sit-ups, abdominal crunches, toe-touches and any exercise machine that requires a bending motion forward. These spinal flexion motions might further compress the bone and result in a compression fracture of a spinal vertebrae. You should consider, however, performing more spine extension exercises which strengthen the back extensor (erector spinae) muscles.

Do not perform exercises which require bending forward at the waist or excessive twisting of the spine.

These could result in crush fractures.

If you have thin or brittle bone of the hip, particularly the neck of the femur, then never perform exercises that demand outward movement (abduction) or inward movement (adduction) of the leg against strenuous resistance. This could result in fracture.

WARNING:

If you have a history of back problems, a very low mineral density, or a recent fracture, then you should perform exercises only under the direct supervision of your physician, physiatrist, physical therapist, or other qualified health professional.

As we age flexibility exercises become increasingly important. I'm sure you can think of someone now who has lost mobility and in a sense "rusted up." If we aren't mobile, then our muscles and bones weaken. All too often there is rapid progressive deterioration in geriatric individuals once mobility is lost. Maintaining flexibility and maximum mobility is a prime consideration in the elderly and for treatment of osteoporosis.

A secondary benefit of maintaining flexibility, mobility and muscle strength is that it improves balance and thereby helps to prevent falls. Falls are the major traumatic etiology of osteoporotic fractures in the elderly. Among elderly women, 90 percent of all hip and spine fractures are attributed to osteoporosis. One of the most important goals in the treatment of everyone with osteoporosis must be to prevent falls.

Preventing falls is the goal of an exercise program that is aimed at improving your posture and balance, as well as muscle and bone strength.

In my experience I have found most individuals 60 years and older do not like and will not perform exercises requiring them to get down on the floor. Many of the elderly, even if they would get down on the floor, do not have the strength, due to years of muscle wasting, to get themselves up.

Scott Fisher RPT (Registered Physical Therapist) from Gary Grays Irish Hills Physical Therapy. Individuals with servere osteoporosis may want to begin exercising under the supervision of a physical therapist.

However older frail individuals with muscle wasting need to exercise the most. There are many exercises which can be done in the sitting position and are easy to perform for the elderly. Consult with your personal physician, physical therapist or qualified health professional to see which exercises are right for you.

I am extremely cautious with back extension exercises. The reason for this is that many (if not most, it seems sometimes) of the elderly I see have moderate or severe degenerative disc disease in their low back at L5S1 (between the fifth lumbar vertebrae and the sacrum) and sometimes L4-5 (between the fourth and fifth lumbar vertebrae.) Exercises which increase the arch of the low back such as floor leg extensions or standing low back extension bends often and in my experience usually, cause increasing low back pain and/or sciatica. There's nothing more destructive to someone beginning an exercise program than to have them hurt their back the very first day they start an exercise program. These low back exercises are beneficial for many individuals, however. An excellent low back exercise which flattens and strengthens the low back is the abdominal isometric exericse done with knees flexed. I highly recommend this exercise however, if you are able to get down and get up from a mat on the floor. Consult with your personal physician, physical therapist or qualified health professional to see if this and other low back extension exercises are right for you should you decide to do them.

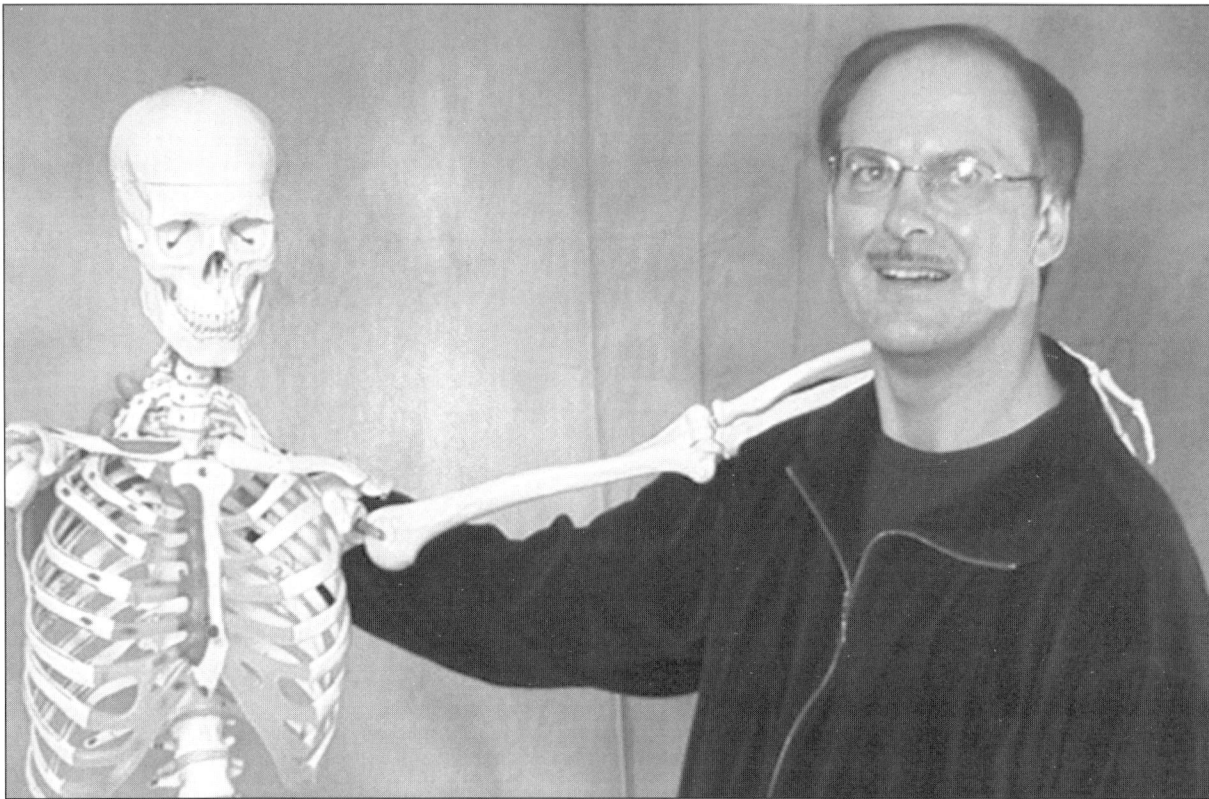

MINIMIZING THE RISK OF FALLS—
A SERIOUS PROBLEM FOR THE ELDERLY

Osteoporotic hip fractures kill 65,000 people a year. About 300,000 hip fractures occur annually in the U.S. and 95 percent are the result of falls. Twenty-four per cent of hip fracture victims die within one year, usually from complications such as pneumonia or blood clots in the lung related to either the fracture or the emergency surgery. One-half will be incapacitated, many permanently. Around 20 to 25 percent will require long-term nursing home care. Only one in three fully recover.

Bones break when the forces applied to them exceed their strength. Vertebral compression fractures can occur with very minimal force if your bone mineral density is low and your vertebrae subsequently weak. However, wrist fractures frequently occur when a person falls on an outstretched arm trying to prevent him or herself from landing hard on the floor; and most all of the more serious hip fractures occur from falling as well.

Numerous studies have found that of the elderly living at home or in communities, approximately 25 percent over the age of 65 fall each year, 33 percent over the age of 70 fall each year and 50 percent over the age of 80 fall each year. Accidental deaths are the sixth leading cause of deaths in the elderly in the U.S. and most of these are caused by falls. Falls increase with advancing age. Due to age-related bone loss most women and many men in their 70s are at risk for fractures from falls. The fear of falling experienced by many of the elderly is certainly a real and significant threat.

Often a hip or painful spine fracture causes a decrease in activities of daily living, social withdrawal, depression, loss of self-esteem and subsequent further loss in muscle strength and mobility from decreased physical activity. It sometimes sends some individuals into a downhill slide of further muscle wasting and weakness, overall deterioration of health and eventual death.

Take care of your bones by preventing falls. The strategy to prevent falling is two-fold:
1) eliminate possible causative factors
2) improve balance mechanisms by increasing muscular strength in the lower extremity legs and upper extremity arms.

To eliminate possible causative factors, identify your potential risk factors for falling and address each one as best you can. For more detailed methods to do so, see pages 69-79 in my book "Osteoporosis: Unmasking A Silent Thief" ISBN# 0-917073-03-7 Minimizing the risks of falls for the elderly. If you need help, call your local health department or center for aging and request it. I work with several home health agencies and frequently I'll call for elderly individuals and ask for a supervisor to go into the home and assess the patient and his/her environment and make recommendations for fall prevention.

Often a physical therapist is required to go into the home and work with a frail osteoporotic individual to strengthen leg and arm muscles so the person can get stronger and remain mobile. Many individual over age 65 want to begin an exercise program yet are in frail health and afraid of getting

TAKE CARE OF YOUR BONES AND THEY'LL TAKE CARE OF YOU!

hurt. If you have medicare and are in frail health with disabling medical conditions such as: weakness, poor balance, disuse muscle atrophy, muscle wasting and osteoporosis then see your physician and have him/her write a prescription to have physical therapy begun under the auspices of a certified physical therapist. You'll become stronger, develop better balance, better bones, feel great, live longer and healthier, and sleep well at night knowing you have professional supervision to help you start your exercise program.

Weakness of the leg muscles from stroke, inactivity, neurologic diseases or muscle wasting in a frail individual makes it difficult to get up and the individual can fall to the ground getting out of a chair and fracture a hip. Osteoarthritis of the hip or knee or a knee "giving out" frequently also leads to a fall. Upper-extremity musculoskeletal weakness or impaired mobility/range of motion of the arms increases one's risk of falling. Weakness of the arms makes it difficult for elderly often osteoporotic individuals to pull themselves up.

INCREASE YOUR WATER INTAKE WHEN EXERCISING

The average person should take in about 96 ounces (three quarts) of fluids (water) a day.

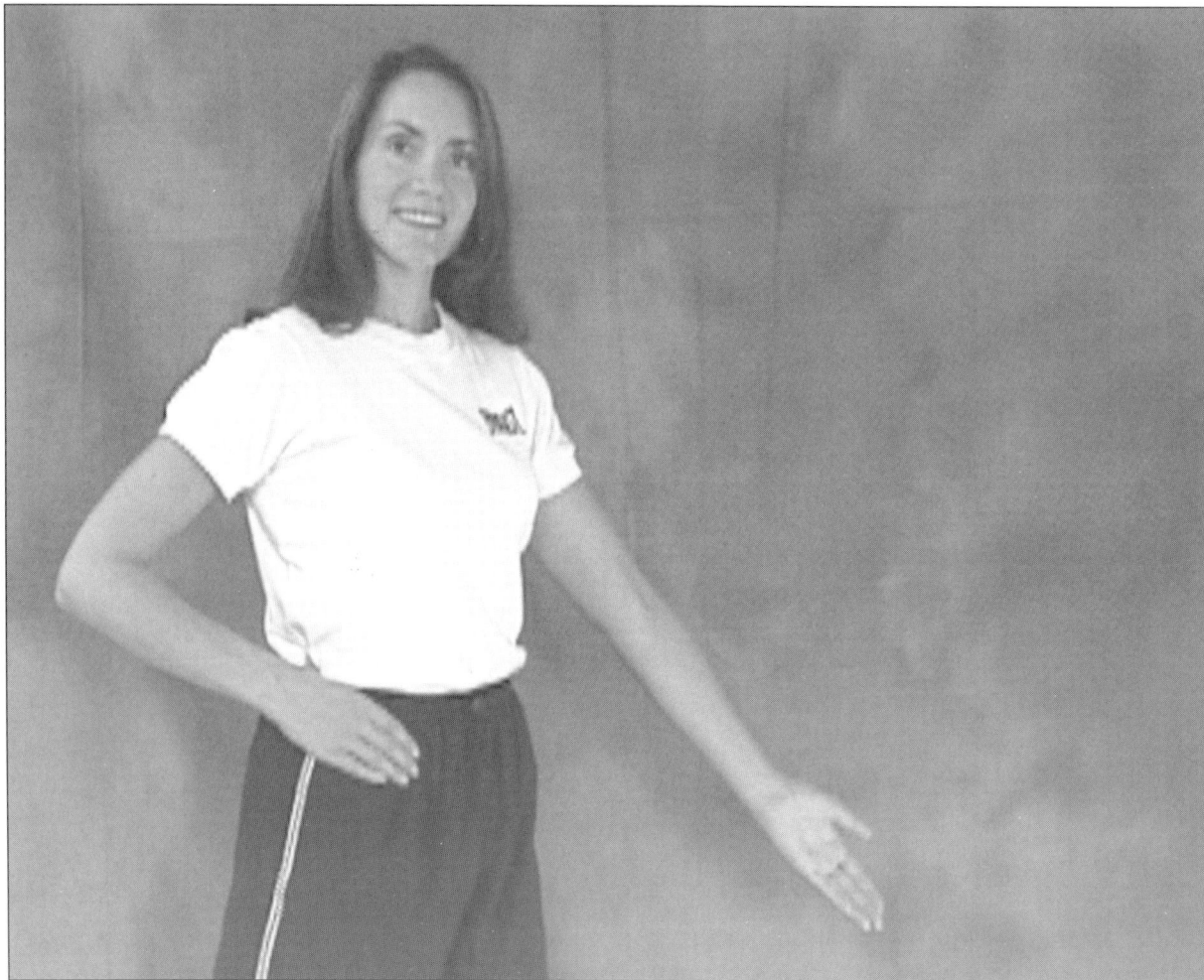

As a general rule, increase your water intake by one cup (eight ounces) for every 30 minutes of intense exercise.

Older individuals need to pay particular attention to fluid intake. Should too much fluid be lost you may feel faint, or dizzy, or become dehydrated. Some medications such as diuretics for high blood pressure or edema can cause increasing water loss. Some drinks with caffeine (ie. coffee, tea, caffeinated sodas) or alcohol are mild diuretics. Fluids can be replaced through water, milk, juice, "watery" fruits and vegetables such as apples, applesauce, oranges, grapefruit, grapes, melons, berries, greens, spinach, peppers, pears, cucumbers, celery, tomatoes, squash, etc.

"I concentrate on aerobics and resistance lifting. I like tennis also. If I miss a week of lifting I've found I lose strength. I take in relatively large amounts of water and keep my diet relatively fat free!"

Roy Lamberson – Age 42

EAT·RIGHT

for a healthier you

Weight Loss and Fitness

Chapter 32

% BODY FAT & BODY MASS INDEX:
Ideal Weight In Proportion To Height For Minimum Mortality

Exercise burns up calories and reduces our body fat by promoting the breakdown of storage fat. **Healthy body fat ranges for women over 30 years is 20 to 27 percent and for men over 30 years is 17 to 23 percent**. You are considered obese for women above 32 percent body fat and for men above 25 percent body fat. Body fat percentage is thought to be a better indicator of health than total weight. A total body bone mineral density analysis such as we perform upon request at the Osteoporosis Testing Center of Michigan gives body fat analysis not only for the total body, but percent body fat for each leg, arm and the abdomen.

Osteoporosis Testing Center
107 West Chicago Street
Brooklyn, MI 49230

Patient:	COLE, RAYMOND	**Attendant:**		
Birth Date:	10/29/1948 52.9 years	**Physician:**		
Height / Weight:	72.0 in. 180.0 lbs.	**Measured:**	10/10/2001	12:43:51 PM (3.50)
Sex / Ethnic:	Male White	**Analyzed:**	10/10/2001	12:45:43 PM (3.50)

Total Body Tissue Quantitation

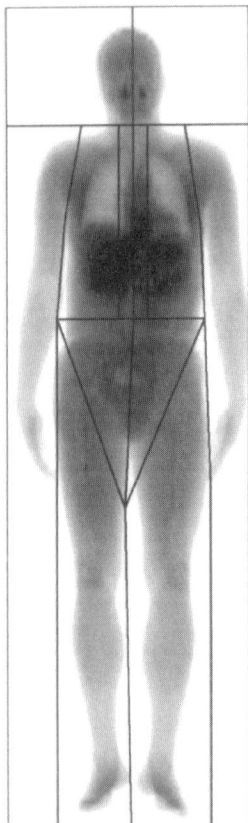

Composition Reference: Total

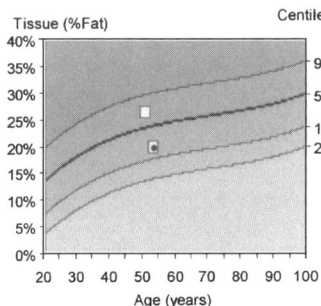

Trend Weight: Total

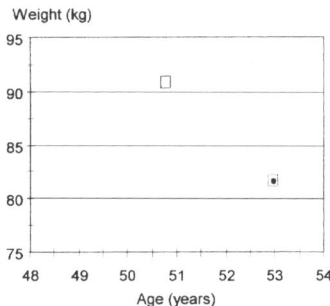

Region	Tissue (%Fat)	Centile [2,3]	T.Mass (kg)	Fat (g)	Lean (g)	BMC (g)
Legs	16.4	-	-	4,092	20,920	1,367
Trunk	23.9	-	-	9,608	30,536	1,021
Total	19.9	22	83.2	15,917	63,924	3,355

Trend: Total

Measured Date	Age (years)	Tissue (%Fat)	Centile [2,3]	T.Mass (kg)	Fat (g)	Lean (g)
10/10/2001	52.9	19.9	22	83.2	15,917	63,924
08/05/1999	50.7	26.4	-	90.0	22,847	63,731

COMMENTS:

Image not for diagnosis

76:0.15:153.85:31.2 0.00:-1.00 4.80x13.00 12.0:%Fat=19.9%
0.00:0.00 0.00:0.00
Printed: 10/10/2001 12:45:58 PM (3.50)
Filename: coler_gl00w97vx.dfb

2 - USA, Total Body Reference Population
3 - Matched for Age, Weight (males 25-100 kg), Ethnic

BODY COMPOSITION

Region	Tissue (%Fat)	Region (%Fat)	Tissue (g)	Fat (g)	Lean (g)	BMC (g)	Total Mass (kg)
Left Arm	16.9	16.0	5,163	871	4,292	274	-
Left Leg	16.4	15.5	12,648	2,070	10,579	686	-
Left Trunk	23.9	23.4	20,168	4,829	15,338	496	-
Left Total	20.0	19.2	40,159	8,021	32,139	1,652	-
Right Arm	16.9	16.0	4,727	799	3,929	256	-
Right Leg	16.4	15.5	12,363	2,022	10,341	682	-
Right Trunk	23.9	23.3	19,977	4,779	15,198	525	-
Right Total	19.9	19.1	39,682	7,897	31,786	1,704	-
Arms	16.9	16.0	9,890	1,669	8,221	530	-
Legs	16.4	15.5	25,011	4,092	20,920	1,367	-
Trunk	23.9	23.3	40,144	9,608	30,536	1,021	-
Total	19.9	19.1	79,842	15,917	63,924	3,355	83.2

GE Medical Systems
LUNAR

Prodigy
10221

By decreasing our body fat, exercise creates increased muscle mass and improves our <u>Body Mass Index (BMI). BMI is a height and weight calculation that helps determine weight-related health risks</u>. (See chart page 133). If your BMI is high you are at increased weight-related health risk.

The BMI for minimal death rates can be calculated. One might consider this to be the ideal BMI for an optimal possibility of a long life. For white women it is 24.3 and for white men is 24.8.

BMI of Minimum Mortality

WHITE WOMEN	WHITE MEN	BLACK WOMEN	BLACK MEN
24.3	24.8	26.8	27.1

As lean body mass improves our health improves. An increase in muscle mass by strengthening exercise increases lean body mass. Although muscle weighs more than fat, it does not take up as much physical space. This is why individuals who exercise decrease their measurement sizes.

"I get up in the morning and walk on the treadmill...I can tell a big difference...when you start exercising then you walk a little way it's not a chore anymore...I eat too good but exercising keeps my weight down, I don't gain any weight and I don't lose any weight."

LeVaughn Summers – Age 72

Body Mass Index Chart

Height (in feet and inches)

Weight (in pounds)	5'	5'1"	5"2"	5'3"	5'4"	5'5"	5'6"	5'7"	5'8"	5'9"	5'10"	5'11"	6'	6'1"	6'2"
100	20	19	18	18	17	17	16	16	15	15	14	14	14	13	13
105	21	20	19	19	18	17	17	16	16	16	15	15	14	14	13
110	21	21	20	19	19	18	17	17	16	16	16	15	15	15	14
115	22	22	21	20	20	19	19	18	17	17	17	16	16	15	15
120	23	23	22	21	21	20	19	19	18	18	17	17	16	16	15
125	24	24	23	22	21	21	20	20	19	18	18	17	17	16	16
130	25	25	24	23	22	22	21	20	20	19	19	18	18	17	17
135	26	26	25	24	23	22	22	21	21	20	19	19	18	18	17
140	27	26	26	25	24	23	23	22	21	21	20	20	19	18	18
145	28	27	27	26	25	24	23	23	22	21	21	20	20	19	19
150	29	28	27	27	26	25	24	23	23	22	22	21	20	20	19
155	30	29	28	27	27	26	25	24	24	23	22	22	21	20	20
160	31	30	29	28	27	27	26	25	24	24	23	22	22	21	21
165	32	31	30	29	28	27	27	26	25	24	24	23	22	22	21
170	33	32	31	30	29	28	27	27	26	25	24	24	23	22	22
175	34	33	32	31	30	29	28	27	27	26	25	24	24	23	22
180	35	34	33	32	31	30	29	28	27	27	26	25	24	24	23
185	36	35	34	33	32	31	30	29	28	27	27	26	25	24	24
190	37	36	35	34	33	32	31	30	29	28	27	26	26	25	24
195	38	37	36	35	34	33	32	31	30	29	28	27	26	26	25
200	39	38	37	36	35	34	33	32	31	30	29	28	27	26	26
205	40	39	38	37	36	35	34	33	32	31	30	29	28	27	26
210	41	40	38	37	36	35	34	33	32	31	30	29	28	28	27
215	42	41	39	38	37	36	35	34	33	32	31	30	29	28	28
220	43	42	40	39	38	37	36	35	34	33	32	31	30	29	28
225	44	43	41	40	39	37	36	35	34	33	32	31	31	30	29
230	45	43	42	41	39	38	37	36	35	34	33	32	31	30	30
235	46	44	43	42	40	39	38	37	36	35	34	33	32	31	30

☐ **Less than 19: Underweight—at underweight health risk**

☐ **19–26: Satisfactory—normal healthy weight-to-height ratio**

☐ **27–30: Overweight—at increased health risk**

☐ **Greater than 30: Obese—at considerable health risk**

Chapter 33

WHY BE NORMAL WEIGHT?

WHY BE NORMAL WEIGHT? Picture yourself carrying a pair of 15-pound bowling balls. Just imagine how tired and exhausted you would be at the end of the day.

Can you see yourself carrying 30 pounds of weight ALL DAY?

But that's just part of the story. What about the enormous stress on you spine and knees? And if that's not enough, what if you were to carry around four 15-pound bowling balls all day? Sound dreadful? Many individuals are 60 pounds overweight and doing just that! But aghast. _What if you are 100 pounds overweight? Picture a 100-pound sack of cement strapped to your waist and you're walking around with it all day._ Yipes, is it no wonder you are fatigued and worn out!

But that's just part of the story! Why be normal weight? Ask the insurance companies. They have known for years that overweight people have a higher incidence of many serious, chronic, debilitating and fatal diseases than people who maintain their normal weight. Statistically, for every 10-pounds we are overweight, we decrease our life expectancy by about two years! Now if only the 62 percent of Americans who are overweight would take to heart the saying, "The longer the waistline, the shorter the lifeline."

OBESITY IS A HEALTH RISK FACTOR FOR MANY DISEASES

In our affluent society, obesity is recognized as the most common and the most dangerous nutritional disorder. Obesity plays an important role in increasing our risk of developing certain diseases; it puts a strain on the heart, the internal organs and the skeletal system, and it can lead to energy loss and depression, which in turn perpetuates the cycle of overeating. Consider the evidence:

a. Obesity is a high risk factor for coronary artery disease, the number one cause of death in the United States. If we are overweight we tend to have increased blood cholesterol, which predisposes us to atherosclerosis (clogging of our arteries). Obesity also tends to increase triglycerides (fats) which also increase our risk of coronary artery disease. When we are overweight, our heart must work harder to provide oxygen to all our body's tissues; For each pound of fat we are storing, there are millions of additional cells which must be nourished.

b. Obese individuals are more likely to have high blood pressure. Obesity is recognized as a major cause of essential hypertension. The first step in treating this disorder is to get down to and maintain normal weight. High blood pressure also increases our risk of heart attack and stroke.

c. Obesity is correlated with the onset of adult diabetes mellitus. Diabetes is four times as common among overweight people than among those of normal weight. It is a serious disease that not only affects blood sugar levels, but can also have detrimental effects on the heart, kidneys, nerves and eyesight. Weight control is an important first step in treating diabetes mellitus.

d. Overweight people tend to suffer from constipation. There are two reasons for the connection between obesity and constipation. First, overweight people generally tend not to get adequate exercise. As a result, the diaphragm does not get to expand fully. It is the downward expansion of the diaphragm which "massages" the intestines and promotes peristalsis, which moves food through the intestines. The shallow breathing which accompanies lack of exercise tends to slow digestion down.

Secondly, overweight people often tend to eat poor quality foods — junk foods, refined foods, sugars and other "empty calories." These refined foods tend to be low in fiber. We now know that adequate fiber (found in foods such as raw fruits, fresh vegetables, bran and whole grains) is extremely important for normal bowel movement and in preventing diseases related to constipation such as hemorrhoids, diverticulosis and intestinal cancer.

e. Obesity also predisposes us all to gallstones. In response to excess calories, the body secretes more cholesterol into the bile, which is stored in the gallbladder. This often leads to the formation of cholesterol gallstones. Gallstones, which are extremely painful and can lead to other digestive disorders, affect 20 percent of all people and 25 to 30 percent of women over 40.

f. Obesity tends to predispose us to certain types of cancer. Obese women, both pre- and postmenopausal, have been found to be more likely to develop breast cancer. Obese women also have a higher incidence of cancer of the gallbladder, uterus and kidneys.

g. Obesity can cause degenerative osteoarthritis of our weight-bearing joints. Excess weight means excessive wear and tear on the joints of our bodies, particularly the hips, knees, ankles and low back. Most overweight individuals have a tendency toward back pain and degenerative arthritis in one or more of their weight-bearing joints. Typically, every week an obese, middle-aged individual 210 pounds on a 5-foot 2-inch frame asks me, "Dr. Cole, why do my back and knees hurt?" If you are 50 pounds overweight you are carrying the equivalent of a 50-pound bag of concrete with you everywhere you go all day. No wonder overweight individuals are often tired, complain of "no energy" and tend to develop degenerative disc disorders with secondary lower back pain and/or sciatica (pinched nerve in lower back), degenerative knee cartilage and painful heel spurs. It took millions of years of evolution for our bodies to develop the musculoskeletal balance that enables us to walk upright; it takes only a couple of years of overeating to throw that entire system off balance!

h. Obesity is a contributing factor in many other physical disorders. Obesity increases our risk of developing blood clots in our legs, gout, irregular periods in women and complications following surgery, in pregnancy or if using birth control pills. Wounds in obese individuals do not heal as quickly as in the normal individual. Obesity also predisposes us to something obvious but often overlooked—accidents such as sprained ankles, twisted knees, falls and fractures. It is not surprising, to find obese individuals in and out of the hospital for a variety of medical reasons.

In the long run, overeating will cause many illnesses and make innumerable other conditions worse. Just as it costs money to store surplus produce, it "costs" us to store excess fat. Extra oxygen is needed to support the surplus baggage in the form of fat cells. Obesity robs our bodies—and ourselves—of energy, energy which we could devote to other areas of our lives. Excess fat is like a parasite that leeches off of us and benefits us in no way.

i. Obesity often produces adverse psychological effects. Besides the chronic feeling of fatigue and sluggishness which interfere with activities and enjoyment of life, obesity can contribute to depression, loneliness and a feeling of low self-esteem. Our body, mind, emotions and spirit are all closely interrelated and interdependent. The mind and emotional factors can contribute to obesity, be adversely affected by obesity and fortunately, can play an important role in treating obesity. For example, sometimes a woman will overeat and become overweight so that psychologically others will stay away from her and thus she won't be able to be hurt again in a love relationship. The fat padding pads her from injury.

And there's more! Why is maintaining normal weight important? Think of weight control as a kind of "health insurance" which requires no premium other than your own commitment and attention toward keeping your weight normal. One of the primary principles of exercising your power to be well is that each individual is ultimately in charge of his or her own health. Becoming conscious of and managing what you put into your system is an important first step toward what I call <u>EXERCISING YOUR WELLPOWER.</u> In other words, using your power to be well by making positive choices for healthy living.

Chapter 34

OVERWEIGHT CHILDREN AND OBESITY
Children and Obesity

Sometimes we see obese people with obese children and assume a hereditary connection. Actually, obesity from overeating is often a learned family habit. Children learn from their parents and what they all too often learn is their parents' poor eating habits, habits like overeating, eating on the run, eating too quickly and eating too many junk foods or sweets. Children are very impressionable and usually copy their parents' likes, dislikes and habits.

The problem of obesity in children and teenagers is compounded by young people's need to be accepted and liked by their peers. Obesity often results in poor body image which can lead to shyness and withdrawal. This withdrawal can often lead to even more overeating. Karen, a teenager, came to me because she was concerned that her back was beginning to "hunch" due to her excess weight. I put her on a balanced diet and she lost 80 pounds. I found out later it was not her back she was concerned with, but her appearance. She had met a guy whom she liked and decided to change her image. Incidently, she later married the fellow.

Beware, however, of any unsupervised dieting, particularly in teenage girls. Teenaged girls, even those who are not overweight, will often attribute their social difficulties to their weight. They may, in severe cases, alternatively binge and purge (vomit) or go on crash diets. The condition of anorexia nervosa, literally self-starvation, is becoming frighteningly more prevalent in this country, particularly in teenaged girls. Like obesity, it has emotional roots and is often a symptom of frustrated communication within the family. Anorexia is far more serious than a young girl's attempt to lose weight; the condition may continue for years causing malnutrition and malfunction of the internal organs. In 25 percent of severe cases, it is fatal. Remember Karen Carpenter of the singing group: The Carpenters? What a sad way to end a beautiful singing career that brought joy to the hearts of so many.

One practical way to prevent obesity in children is to teach healthy eating habits by example. As the cliché goes, **"Our children are far more likely to be influenced by what we do than by what we say."** If your child or children are overweight, ask yourself these questions: How might this be a reflection of my own eating habits? What emotional state or problem might this overweight condition represent? What can I do to improve the situation? Similarly, if your child shows symptoms of anorexia, beware of therapies which focus only on the eating problem or on the child's emotional state. Like the human body, the family is an organism and the child's eating disorder may be a symptom of a deeper problem within the family.

Chapter 35

ALL TOO OFTEN...
THE REAL CAUSE OF OBESITY!

No one will argue that in some cases (in 1.6 percent to be exact), obesity is caused by a thyroid or adrenal gland disorder; or that for some it is a secondary result of low socio-economic status and a diet consisting of poor quality food; or that some people have a hereditary predisposition to obesity; or that for some children (one in eight children in this country is obese) obesity may stem from a poor eating example their parents have set for them. But for many individuals who are overweight, their obesity stems from another cause, one that is much more within the realm of their personal control than glands, heredity, poverty or who their parents are.

Obesity itself is often not a disease, but a symptom. Just as people smoke cigarettes out of a nervous habit, so people often overeat out of anxiety, boredom, frustration or as an internalized substitute for aggression. Often overeating is a pattern developed as a result of feelings of being unloved or love needs which are not being satisfied. Again, our language is rich in expressions that have to do with eating and one's emotions: "eating your heart out," "swallow your pride," "eat your words." Doing any one of these could prove to be fattening! Often a cycle will develop where overeating can create the very feeling we are overeating to forget.

Overeating provides physiological satisfaction by stimulating the satiety center of the hypothalmus in our brain. When we are not getting satisfaction from the other areas in our lives, eating can serve as a substitute. But when we face the results of overeating (low energy, poor body image, guilt over self-indulgence), we feel bad and want to smother our sorrows in food. Truly, overeating feeds on itself.

How does one break this cycle? There are people who have lost and gained hundreds of pounds. Look on any drugstore bookstand and you will see dozens of diet books. Pick up a magazine and you are sure to see this or that "miracle diet." If it is a testimonial to our health-consciousness that so many people have lost so many pounds, surely the methods have been inadequate since so many people have gained the pounds back.

Focusing on the weight itself and not the hidden emotional, spiritual and psychological issues can be short-sighted and doomed to failure. Of course, the problem of excess weight needs to be counteracted by a balanced caloric nutritional program, but this only deals with the external symptom, obesity. The real problems – boredom with one's life, disappointment with work endeavors, frustration from staying home and feeling imprisoned by the four walls and crying kids, anger from a marriage which is not working, self-pity and anxiety over job loss are more difficult to eliminate and take more time. However, once they are corrected, an overeating problem will often correct itself. If these problems are not handled, they will find another "symptom" to use to get attention.

Before you embark on the latest diet you have heard about, stop and take a good, honest look at the reasons why you overeat. Are you generally satisfied with your life? Are you bored, depressed, frustrated with any aspect of your life? Do you feel lonely? Deprived? Are you having enough fun? How do the habits you have developed around eating reflect your mental state?

Often we eat out of habit. Munching provides a sense of security and exerts a calming effect if we feel nervous. Do you look at eating as the high point of your day? Do you eat for entertainment? Surveys show that a majority of Americans prefer food to sex. It is not uncommon for women (and men too) to gain weight when they want to keep members of the opposite sex at a distance. Not only does this extra "padding" make one less attractive, but it often insulates against potentially painful feelings and experiences. A person recently hurt in a relationship might gain weight as protection against vulnerability.

Look at your life and see if any of these factors "ring a bell" apply to you as reasons for your overeating. If they do, it may be wise to tackle these problems first, since overeating may be your primary stress release and a symptom of deeper problems. If this "safety valve" of overeating is removed, far greater problems may result. If the original stress is not dealt with, another release mechanism may be substituted in its place. The cure could be worse than the original disease.

Chapter 36

IS YOUR "MOTIVATOR" MOTIVATING YOU TO LOSE WEIGHT?

ARE YOU WILLING TO DO WHAT IT TAKES TO LOSE WEIGHT?

There is an old tale about the mice who called a meeting to decide what to do about the cat who had been terrorizing them. After much hand-wringing and animated discussion, the mice arrived at the perfect solution—they would put a bell on the cat so they could hear her coming. The mice cheered jubilantly until they realized that there was not one amongst them who was willing to put the bell on the cat.

Likewise, you have made the decision to lose weight and are excited and optimistic about that decision (you might even want to go out and celebrate with a hot fudge sundae!) However, it is now up to you to "put the bell on the cat." That is, take up the challenge for action, action which might at times be uncomfortable and downright unpleasant. No matter which diet or weight loss approach you choose, you will necessarily be changing long-standing habits. So be prepared to feel a bit uncomfortable. Be prepared for your mind to seduce you into having "just one piece of pie" or going off the diet "just this once." To withstand the force of habits and desires, you will need to have a strong sense of purpose.

One effective way to shed pounds is to "declare war" on excess body fat. Ask yourself, "Do I *really* want to lose weight?" If the answer is an honest and sincere "yes," you want to next ask yourself, "Am I *enthusiastic and passionate* about losing weight?" Unless you can honestly answer "yes" with your whole being, you might as well not even begin a diet.

The most crucial element in successful dieting is enthusiastic motivation. Some people need external motivation like the high price paid to a weight loss clinic, the structure of an organization like Weight Watchers, hypnosis, or diets which specify the exact amount of food to be consumed with each meal. While all of these are good motivators, the very best motivation to change your eating habits must come from within. You must be able to motivate yourself constantly through your own thoughts. You must be able to visualize yourself thin. You must be able to develop and believe this new image of yourself, or else the "new you" may become so threatening to the "old you" that your mind will do everything in its power to keep you from losing the weight. Never underestimate resistance to change! To truly motivate yourself, you must want the change and be able to accept the consequences with all of your being.

YOU MAY WANT TO TAKE THE "WHY" TEST

Psychologists sometimes use a very useful process for determining underlying causes and motivation, simply called the Why Test. In the Why Test every answer evokes a "why" until you reach the bottom line – the underlying cause or motivation. Thus, the Why Process for Weight Reduction might go something like this:

Q. Why am I overweight?
A. Because I eat too much between meals.

Q. Why?
A. Because I am nervous.

Q. Why?
A. Because I drink too much coffee.

Q. Why?
A. Because I need that lift in the morning.

Q. Why?
A. Because I do not like to face the new day.

Q. Why?
A. Because I hate my job.

Q. Why?
A. Because I am not utilizing my talents there. . .

And so on. As you can see, the Why Test can often uncover the invisible factors in being overweight which need to change if we are going to lose weight effectively. Likewise, the Why Test can help us focus our motivation: Why do I want to lose weight?

Do the Why Test now, first focusing on "Why am I overweight?" and then on "Why do I want to lose weight?" The answers will be revealing. In fact, you can use the Why Test to clarify any health problem or emotional situation.

BUT I CAN'T SEEM TO...

Why is it so many people fail in their efforts at dieting? Did you know that the failure rate for dieters is more than 70 percent. It is any wonder that diet books are among the hottest selling items on the newsstand?

We are all aware that excess weight is no good for us. We may even be aware that for every 10 pounds we are overweight, we reduce our life expectancy by two years. And we may even know the role obesity plays in any number of diseases. So why is it that diets fail? Shouldn't it be enough to know the dangers obesity poses to your health?

One answer is that our minds tend to play tricks on us through excuses and unsound reasoning. The most common form of excuse usually takes the form of "I can't _____ (fill in the blank.)" This attitude takes the power out of our

hands and puts it in the hands of some external force. For example, there are actually smokers who wish that cigarettes would be completely outlawed so that they would be forced to stop smoking. The truth is, we are in control of our own habits and it is our responsibility to change. Psychologists will often confront the "I can't" statement by asking the client to say "I will not control my overeating" or "I choose not to control my overeating"—which places responsibility and control in the client's lap.

Other people deceive themselves by saying, "Sure I know the facts, but it will not happen to me." How could something that feels as good as overeating be that bad for me, the reasoning goes. The immediate payoffs for obesity, the satiation of hunger and the temporary relief from frustration, anger, boredom or anxiety, "speak louder" than the long-term payoffs for dieting. Though we may know what is good for our health we don't always do what is good for our health. The prospect of dying a few years earlier seems somewhere off in the distant future. Meanwhile pass over another piece of pie. In order to stick to a diet, we must truly experience the payoffs of dieting as far greater than the payoffs of eating.

Unfortunately, this motivation most often comes only after one's well-being is threatened. Individuals who have had a heart attack—and thus a close brush with death—are more highly motivated to lose weight and begin assuming full responsibility for their health. The difference between the person who reads that obesity may cause a heart attack and one who has had one is tremendous. The heart attack survivor no longer believes "It can't happen to me." It has happened to him. The resulting charged feelings can be the most powerful motivation there is.

Similarly, the teenaged girl who is overweight may be "awakened" by the attractive young man in her math class with whom she has fallen in love. All of a sudden, her appearance is of utmost importance – the scale has been tipped, so to speak and now losing weight has a far more immediate payoff than overeating does. I have noticed similar motivation in women who want to fit into a sleek dress for a wedding, men who want to re-enlist in the Air Force or Navy Reserves and people who want to look good for their upcoming school reunions.

As you can see, certain emotions like love, joy, desire for success and wanting to please a spouse can generate tremendous enthusiasm in our lives. These strong emotions provide an immediate boost that abstract ideas (e.g., obesity can predispose me later in life to diabetes) cannot.

How then can you motivate yourself to lose weight and maintain your ideal weight over time? Search your life for concrete reasons for losing weight. Write these reasons on a sheet of paper. Be as specific as possible. For instance, instead of writing, "I want to lose weight because obesity adversely affects my health," say, "Excess weight is giving me high blood pressure, causing those arthritis pains in my back, knees and ankles, making me tired and embarrassing me in public. People think I have poor self-control or no pride in my appearance. Besides, I have a wedding to attend in three months." And so on. List the specific reasons why you want to lose weight now.

For you to really lose weight, you must be convinced that the lifestyle habit of overeating is harmful to you here and now. You must be truly convinced that the payoffs of being normal weight are more valuable to you than the temporary payoffs of overeating. Read your list of reasons daily to renew your commitment to losing weight and remind yourself of the concrete benefits you will derive out of being your normal weight. Write notes to yourself to stay on track and avoid unconscious and "nervous" eating. A note on the refrigerator, "What you are looking for is not in here" is a gentle but effective reminder.

One of the problems you will eventually face is that you perceive yourself to be hungry and your mind is insisting that "It's all right to go off the diet just this once." The problem with doing that is when perennial dieters go off their diets, they feel guilty for indulging themselves. They see this self-indulgence as "wrong" and when we do wrong, punishment is in order. Any how does the overweight person punish him or herself? By saying "What is the use?" and going on a full-scale eating binge!

To avoid this vicious cycle, I suggest you adopt the "**Stop, Look and Listen**" approach to eating. You feel "hungry?" Great. Stop and feel hungry. Actually experience the sensation of hunger. Look before you eat to see that your "hunger" is not merely boredom or anxiety or habit. Listen to what your body is really saying you need to do. Chances are, you do not need to eat. If you are absolutely convinced that your body cells are asking for nourishment, by all means eat, but eat slowly and lovingly. Savor each bite. Enjoy yourself.

But if it is some other kind of nourishment you need, see to it that you handle that need instead of smothering it with food. The Stop, Look and Listen approach is the most effective way of changing eating habits from inside that I know of. Master this approach and dieting will become unnecessary.

Chapter 37

COMMITMENT TO YOUR WEIGHT REDUCTION PROGRAM

Commitment to a regular weight loss program is much like commitment to a regular exercise program for terrific fitness, health and better bones. (See Chapter 4 - Commitment to your Fitness Program.) *How much do you really want it?*

Within days you could be living your dream and enjoying the benefits of weight loss. Feeling self-mastery, more confident, competent, a reborn energized you. Imagine yourself 30 days from now experiencing the benefits of living your dream…now look at the alternative…living as you are now.

It's simple…**commitment spells the difference between failure…and success**. The terrific body image and optimal physical well-being you've been wanting is just weeks or months away. **Don't let anything keep you from getting it**. Commitment…makes the difference…and gets results.

A SURE WINNER

"I exercise about 45 minutes a day with about 25 minutes on a Schwinn Air-Dyne bike and 20 minutes of light weight-lifting with 10-pound dumbbells. I began exercising about three months ago and since then have lost over 40 pounds. I'm also staying away from the breads, potatoes, sugars and cutting down on portions. I drink almost 4 quarts of water a day.

Since I've been exercising I don't get out of breath anymore and my energy has really increased...I don't doze off anymore on the couch in the evening like I used to. I began to exercise and lose weight because I found I was over 300 pounds and couldn't breathe when I bent over to tie my shoes. Now, I feel good... I can easily bend over to reach my shoes now... When I get up in the morning I feel a whole lot better!"

**Brad Blackwell
– Age 47**

That's the key in a nutshell. There's no use in beginning a weight loss program without complete and dedicated 110 percent commitment. Lifelong commitment! If you can't actively say out loud and put into writing your lifelong commitment of time and effort to a regular weight reduction program, then do not even begin. Without this firm dedication providing a firm foundation, you'll find 101 excuses when you're stressed or want to munch out of habit, or on and on... not to stick to your diet. How bad do you want it? Are you totally convinced of the benefits of weight loss and willing to put in the effort to realize your goal of a normal weight? How great is your desire? Your reason to lose weight sparks your motivation. Your passion to be a normal weight determines your future success sticking to your program.

How much do you value being normal weight? Be honest. Is it a priority in your life?

I sit down every New Years and write out my Values, Goals and Plan-of-Action. I write out and prioritize my values and then set goals for the long-term, year-end goals and short-term, six to one month goals in accordance with my priorities, and then write out a plan-of-action. If losing weight is not one of your top five values, you consequently will find lots of excuses not to stick to your weight loss program. To succeed in sticking to your weight loss program being normal weight must be one of those things you value and thereby are willing to commit to, even when times get rough, without question.

What are your top five values in life in priority of importance?

1) _____

2) _____

3) _____

4) _____

5) _____

So weight loss is one of your top five values? If it is then continue to read this chapter. If not then don't kid yourself or even begin a weight loss program. Here's why: If you really don't deeply and truly value being normal weight then you'll drift into self-defeating behavior. If you haven't made the firm decision to make weight reduction a priority in your life, you won't stick to a regular program. Without a firm commitment you'll find a host of ways to sabotage yourself and take the easy road rather than persevere and take the road less traveled. Long-term adherence to normal weight requires lifelong commitment. It requires strong motivation because you value it and have strong personal reasons for sticking to it.

No one starts out with intentions to take the easy way out and give in to excuses not to be normal weight. All individuals can probably say they would like to be normal weight. But hold on to your britches! A lot of people sprint out of the starting blocks dieting furiously and intensely…but never finish! But just like the sports axiom says " It's not important who starts the game…but who finishes the game." Being normal weight requires a lifelong commitment of effort. *Design your weight-reduction program to maintain normal weight that will last a lifetime!* Weight loss is not something you do as a short-term gain for the day, but rather maintaining normal weight is a long term investment in your health.

If maintaining normal weight is up there as one of your values, if you are passionate about changing your life forever and if you are willing to take the steps to make maintaining normal weight an indispensable part of your daily life like grooming, exercising and sleeping, then continue…:

You must first know what you want before you can bring it into your life and make it your reality. So…

What are the five reasons you want to change your life by losing weight?

1) _____

2) _____

3) _____

4) _____

5) _____

What are your five primary behavior patterns that prevent you from losing weight?
(In other words, what are the five major destructive eating habits you have that have caused you to be overweight?)

1) _____

2) _____

3) _____

4) _____

5) _____

How can you prevent the above five potential obstacles from blocking you and turn them into an opportunity you can easily hurdle over?
(In other words, what five good health habits can you do to reverse these destructive habits?)

1) _____

2) _____

3) _____

4) _____

5) _____

What are the actual specific weight loss goals you want to accomplish?

(You may want to list amount of weight loss in specific time frames, specific blouse or dress sizes, body fitness goals, etc.)

1) _____

2) _____

3) _____

4) _____

5) _____

Now that you know what you want to do, you need to find out how you are going to do it. so list…

How are you going to accomplish your specific weight loss goals?

1) _____

2) _____

3) _____

4) _____

5) _____

Are you willing to commit undauntedly to the behavior changes you'll need to take to create the *BEST BODY BEST BONES* you want? If you can answer "yes" with no reservation, then read on to find out how to begin to turn your life around now…

• •
• •
• •

Focus inward and picture yourself at your endpoint, having accomplished and achieved your goals, having changed your life. Picture yourself feeling the change that has occurred. See yourself as that normal weight person, feel yourself energized and in total mastery and control of your physical body. Let there be *no doubt* in your mind you're there. Be 110 percent sure and totally confident. Experience reaping the benefits of being normal weight as a daily part of your life. (You will find it helpful in the beginning to cultivate and reinforce your desire by putting your goals and and how you are going to accomplish your weight loss goals up on your refrigerator or at your bedside or framed on a plaque on your desk or wall. This reinforces your inner, goal-directed bio-computer to bring these into your life. Review or preferably read them out loud each morning and evening.)

Now, you're ready to begin! List your Start Date and Time:

Day_____ Date_____ Time_____

Congratulations!
Just think about what you have to look forward to!

Chapter 38

CALORIC CONTROL

ALL diets come down to caloric consciousness. Many are masked by this or that fad, or this or that gimmick, but inherently worked into their program is caloric control in one way or another. *You must burn up more calories than you take in.* The "flab" will start to go away only when calories consumed are less than those needed by the body. The body then mobilizes the body fat and burns the "flab" for energy. Most fad or "gimmicky" diets will not hurt an individual in the short run, but if on them for a long time, may be seriously detrimental to an individual's health.

To gain one pound of fat only requires an extra 3,500 calories. If you consume only 200 calories more a day than your body needs, you will gain approximately 200 calories X 365 days = 20.86 pounds or approximately 20 pounds of stored fat per year.

Just think of it, 200 calories per day is less than a small candy bar. Wow! And a weight gain of 20 pounds a year. Now, think about it more in this light. Do you really need that candy bar? After the age of 30 the average American gains approximately 2 to 3 pounds per year. Just a little you say. That may seem like a small amount and nothing to take serious notice of, but just think in ten years at the age of 50 , this is up to an extra 60 pounds overweight. Now that is something to sit up and take notice of! That little bit of flab each year can go a long way.

Most clinically obese persons underestimate the amount of calories they consume in a day by almost 50 percent. In other words, if they think they are taking in 1000 calories a day they are actually taking in 1500 calories a day.

CALORIE CARELESSNESS

Consider what happens over a period of time when you take in unneeded calories through carelessness or excess. If you are now 20 years old and through "calorie carelessness" you gain just two pounds a year, by the time you are 50 you will be 60 pounds overweight! There is a mistaken belief that we "naturally" fill out and become heavier as we get older. Not true! People tend to put on weight as they get older because they tend to be less active and their metabolism slows at about one percent per year after the age of thirty. However, they continue to eat the way they have always eaten. The result, an expanded waistline.

How easy is it to gain eight pounds in six months? As easy as having an extra glass of cola each day. An 8 ounce glass of cola contains 165 calories. Multiply that by seven and you have 1155 calories a week. Multiply that by 26 and in six months you have taken in 30,000 extra calories. Divide 30,000 by 3,500 (the number of calories in a pound) and you have gained a little over eight pounds, just by having one extra glass of cola a day. The chart below indicates how other foods can put on between five and 25 pounds over six months time.

POUNDS GAINED IN SIX MONTHS

2 12 oz. cans of beer = 350 calories/day **18.20**
2 oz. potato chips = 322 calories/day **16.74**
1 donut (honey-dipped) = 260 calories/day **13.52**
1 piece apple pie = 345 calories/day..**17.94**
1 slice American cheddar cheese = 105 calories/day...................**5.46**
4 oz. ice cream = 150 calories/day...**7.80**
1-1/2 chocolate bar = 218 calories/day.......................................**11.33**
1 white icing cupcake = 230 calories/day...................................**11.96**
8 oz. chocolate malted milk = 500 calories/day **26.00**
1 peanut butter/jelly sandwich = 275 calories/day....................**14.30**
1 toast and peanut butter = 170 calories/day...............................**8.84**
2 teaspoons sugar = 92 calories/day...**4.78**
1 tablespoon butter = 100 calories/day **5.20**
1 order French fries = 220 calories/day.......................................**11.44**
1 cheeseburger = 220 calories/day **16.01**
1 scoop chocolate fudge = 229 calories/day...............................**11.90**
1 hot dog = 265 calories/day **13.78**

On the other side of the ledger, brisk walking at 4.5 miles an hour burns up seven calories a minute. Walking one-half hour at 4.5 miles per hour burns up 210 calories. If we do this five days a week, we can burn up 1,050 calories per week, multiplied by 26 equals 27,300 calories in six months. Divide that by 3500 calories/pound and you get 7-3/4 pounds. So, by walking briskly for 30 minutes a day, five days a week for six months, you can burn up and lose eight pounds.

This may seem like an effortless weight loss program, which it is, but it might be more useful to look at it as a weight maintenance program, as insurance that your weight will not accidentally creep up. Or, to look at it another way, not walking briskly 30 minutes a day, five days a week for six months will cause you to gain eight pounds. It is all a matter of perspective. At any rate, if you take 30 minutes out of your lunch hour each day to take a brisk walk, the benefits will be two-fold. First, you may not end up eating as much and second, you will be burning up the equivalent of an 8-ounce glass of cola.

Chapter 39

THE ROLE OF EXERCISE IN WEIGHT LOSS

A good weight loss program includes a moderate caloric reduction below maintenance calories needed by the body (i.e. 20 percent less or 500 calories below caloric maintenance.) and a moderate exercise regime. Most individuals think the main role of exercise in a weight loss program is to burn up calories when performing the exercise activity. However, this is not so. The primary goal of aerobic exercise in weight loss is to increase resting metabolism by up to 15 percent to burn up more calories at rest. The primary goal of muscle-strengthening (weights) exercise is to alter the body composition so there is increased lean muscle mass and decreased fat. Muscle burns up calories at a higher rate than fat thereby also increasing our basal metabolic rate. Both help in a weight loss program.

I sometimes see individuals who begin an exercise program to lose weight and think that because they exercise they can eat whatever they want. They think they can lose 50 pounds by increasing their activity level alone and continuing to eat exactly as they always had when they were gradually gaining weight. Studies have shown that individuals who walk about 16 miles a week tend to stay at their weight despite what they eat. That's great for maintenance of desired weight once you are at your goal weight, but to lose weight requires a reduction of caloric intake.

One of the more difficult things most people have to do in their life…is lose weight. Good weight loss programs recommend a combination of dietary calorie intake control…and exercise. Exercising for fitness alone will not cause tremendous weight loss, but it is extremely valuable in maintaining a normal weight once normal weight is attained. In analogy, it takes a lot of effort to push a 4,000 pound car from rest and get it moving to 10 mph. However, once it is going at 10 mph it doesn't take much energy to keep it going at that speed. As a general rule, "you won't walk your self thin, but walking will keep yourself thin!"

Individuals will often diet and exercise for two or three weeks and when they don't lose as significant an amount of weight as they want, they become frustrated and upset. They may say "what's the use" and use this as an excuse to take the easy way out and quit.

Also I've heard it a thousand times…"I diet for a while and then I can't take it anymore…I blow it and then can't stop eating." Rather than focusing on the strict weight reduction or a fad diet I'd rather see an individual focus on moderate restriction of caloric intake and increasing activity level through moderate intensity exercise. The result? The weight will gradually take care of itself in due time with this approach and the individual will feel much better as well.

If greater than 30 pounds overweight, walk or ride an exercise bike for your aerobic exercise, but do not run. Running puts too much stress on your knees and feet and the continuous bouncing contributes to wear and tear degenerative disc disease of the low back. When walking, walk on a flat surface not an incline. If you have degenerative disc disease in your low back, exercises which tend to flatten the low back help but exercises which increase the lordosis (arch in the low back) aggravate degenerative disc disease. An incline, forces you to increase the arch in your low back to walk and this causes low back strain and pain. Individuals with chronic low back pain will find that walking moderately is OK for them, but walking fast and thus creating a sort of bouncing motion of the low back will aggravate their low back condition.

"I exercise about an hour a day pretty near every day. I like to walk around the block!"

**Leslie Jackson
– Age 86**

The truth is, being overweight and being physically fit are two entirely different things. Each is totally independent of the other. **Overweight individuals can be very physically fit**. As you exercise, your fat problem and lean body weight will automatically improve as well. Well-toned muscular persons according to standard weight tables may be "overweight." They may have thin waist or dress sizes but muscle takes up less space and weighs more than fat. So ordinary normal weight tables do not necessarily apply to a well-fit individual. Body composition is a better indicator of good physical condition than actual weight. As a general rule, individuals who want to lose weight do more cardio work (i.e. exercise bike or walking) whereas individuals who want to define their muscles do more muscle-strengthening. But both help in a weight loss program.

Chapter 40

NUTRITION INFORMATION YOU'LL FIND INCREDIBLY IMPORTANT AND BE GLAD YOU KNOW

PROTEIN

Protein is the primary raw building material for all our body's tissues whether it be muscles and tendons, bones, red blood cells, antibodies, connective tissues, liver, heart, brain, kidneys, enzymes, etc. Protein derived from animal sources such as chicken, turkey, beef, fish, eggs, milk etc. contains all 22 essential amino acids required by the body and are therefore known as complete proteins. Protein from plant sources such as fruits, grains, vegetables, etc. lack some of the essential amino acids required by the body and are therefore known as incomplete proteins. Various arrangements of these twenty-two amino acids are used to synthesize our body's tissues.

Protein has the distinction from fat and carbohydrate in that it can be utilized for both building our body's tissues and broken down for energy. As an energy source protein provides four calories per gram. Excess protein can be converted to fats and stored in the liver, muscle and other tissues. Under duress such as a very high protein diet when the body needs glucose, it will use protein for energy before it will use it to build body tissues. Under extreme duress it will burn tissue proteins for energy first from the liver and then from the muscles and therefore may cause muscle wasting. The body is not able to store protein like it does carbohydrate and fat. When protein is used for energy or when there is excess protein, the protein is deaminated (nitrogen molecule removed) and removed via the kidneys as urea. An acidic residue remains and must be buffered in the blood. This is done by the removal of calcium from the bones to buffer the residue. As a result, a chronic high protein intake may lead to a loss of calcium in the bone and eventually osteoporosis.

Proteins are broken down into amino acids in our intestines by enzymes and absorbed into our blood stream. Our blood carries protein to wherever cells may need it for building structures.

The *Recommended Daily Allowance (RDA):* In 1941 the Food and Nutrition Board of the National Academy of Sciences established the Recommended Daily Allowance (RDA) as "The levels of intake of essential nutrients that, on the basis of scientific knowledge, are judged to be adequate to meet the known nutrient needs of practically all healthy persons." The RDA of protein for the average 154 pound male is 60 grams per day. This is based on an RDA of 0.8 gm/kg./day. Athletes require more protein, with an active recreational athlete requiring 1 to 1.2 gm./kg./day and an endurance athlete requiring 1.4 to 1.6 gm.kg.day.

For daily maintenance as a percentage of Total Caloric Intake (TCI) protein should not be less than 15 percent nor more than 30 percent.

CARBOHYDRATES ▄▄▄▄▄▄▄▄▄▄▄▄▄▄▄▄

<u>Carbohydrates</u> are our body's primary energy source. All complex carbohydrates must be eventually converted into the simple sugar called glucose before they can be used for energy. Some of the glucose is converted into glycogen in the storage cells of our liver and muscles and stored. Excess glucose is converted to fat and stored in our body tissues. Yep! Those love handles around your waist and other fat stores! This is not to insinuate that carbs make you fat… not true… eating above maintenance calories makes you fat!

Complex carbohydrates such as vegetables and whole grains are absorbed from our intestines slowly and require more steps for conversion to glucose. They therefore maintain a more constant blood sugar level as opposed to the rapid absorption of simple sugars. Simple sugars cause wide fluctuations in our blood glucose with the pancreas secreting insulin to remove the glucose by moving into our body's cells. Overweight individuals in later life who generally have high fat diets frequently tend to develop insulin resistance and subsequent hyperinsulinemia which often leads to Diabetes Mellitus of adult onset. Insulin resistance also leads to complications such as hyperlipidemia, coronary artery disease and atherosclerosis.

The American media abounds with controversy over whether or not our sweet tooth is insidiously destroying us. One thing for sure, we seem to have an addiction for sweets. On Valentine's Day we associate sweetness with the symbol of kindness and goodness. We describe someone nice and kind as sweet. We also think of it as an immediate energy source. But, does our propensity for sweet-tasting items possibly lead us down the path of ill health? You say: How can that be possible because whenever manufacturing companies want to sell an item they add sugar to it to make it sweet? It sells products, therefore it must be good for us! Or is it really?

When you think about it, our ancestors did not have a sweet tooth. Hundreds of years ago they did not even know what refined sugar was. Their diet consisted of fresh vegetables, whole grains, some fruits and some meat and fish. Today in America we grow up with large amounts of refined sugar in most of the modern foods we eat so we accept it as natural and the normal standard of things. However, is it really that good for us?

Our body's natural metabolic engines were not designed and built to run on refined sugar. Refined sugar is a product of our modern industrial society reflecting a marked shift in

dietary patterns from the agricultural society of years ago. We Americans consume approximately 128 pounds of sugar per person per year. That is almost one-third pound, per person, per day which equals 600 calories per day. This represents 24 percent of the daily calories consumed by the average person. Why do we take in so much sugar if it is our western society's most common addiction and considered to be the most common, as well as most dangerous food additive? Probably the answer is ignorance and misinformation.

STARCH (COMPLEX CARBOHYDRATES)
Versus
SUGAR (SIMPLE CARBOHYDRATES)

Carbohydrates come in two forms:

1. *Complex carbohydrates - (polysaccharides) called starches*
   i.e.: whole grain breads, cereals, vegetables, fruits, juices, etc.

2. *Simple carbohydrates - refined sugar foods*
   i.e.: table sugar, cola, candy, many processed and sweetened foods, etc.

STARCH – COMPLEX CARBOHYDRATES

Complex carbohydrates (starches) are slowly broken down in the intestines by enzymes into glucose, our body's metabolic fuel. This breakdown occurs gradually, smoothly and constantly over a prolonged period of time resulting in a regular, constant flow of glucose into our blood stream. Most starches also contain vitamins, minerals and most importantly, fiber. Fiber is an important ingredient for the normal propulsion of nutrients through our intestines. Fiber maintains a balance of absorption of nutrients and removal of waste products and the promotion of health in many other ways as well. Starches do not cause rapid increases or decreases in blood glucose levels. Because they release glucose more slowly and evenly into the blood stream, they postpone hunger for long periods of time. This is why many nutritionists recommend raw vegetables, for example, carrots as a snack.

Foods high in complex carbohydrates include:

Whole grain or unrefined foods such as whole grain cereals, wholegrain breads, pasta, rice, bagels, banana nut bread, biscuits, bulgur, cheese pizza, cream of wheat, English muffins, French bread, graham crackers, pancakes, pita bread, raisin bread pudding, saltine crackers, wheat cereal, wheat tortilla, white or whole wheat bread, etc.

Fruits, particularly those with skins such as apples, pears, plums, cherries, peaches, etc.

Vegetables: all root as well as leafy vegetables such as potatoes, peas, beans, corn, etc.

Starches are only found in plant life. Plants take in carbon dioxide and water and combine them to form the simple sugar glucose by a process known as photosynthesis. Photosynthesis requires ultraviolet light as a catalyst (form of energy) for this conversion and plants frequently add chlorophyll as a green coloring to the leafy plants. Thousands of small glucose molecules are combined to form larger molecules of starches. The reason plants do this is that starches are stored in their seeds (endosperm) to serve as foods for new young sprouting plants. Take for example a kernel of corn; that kernel must have all of the energy requirements, vitamins, minerals and nutrients to sustain the growth of a new corn plant.

Breads, cereals, flours, etc., are derived from wheat. A grain of wheat contains three parts :

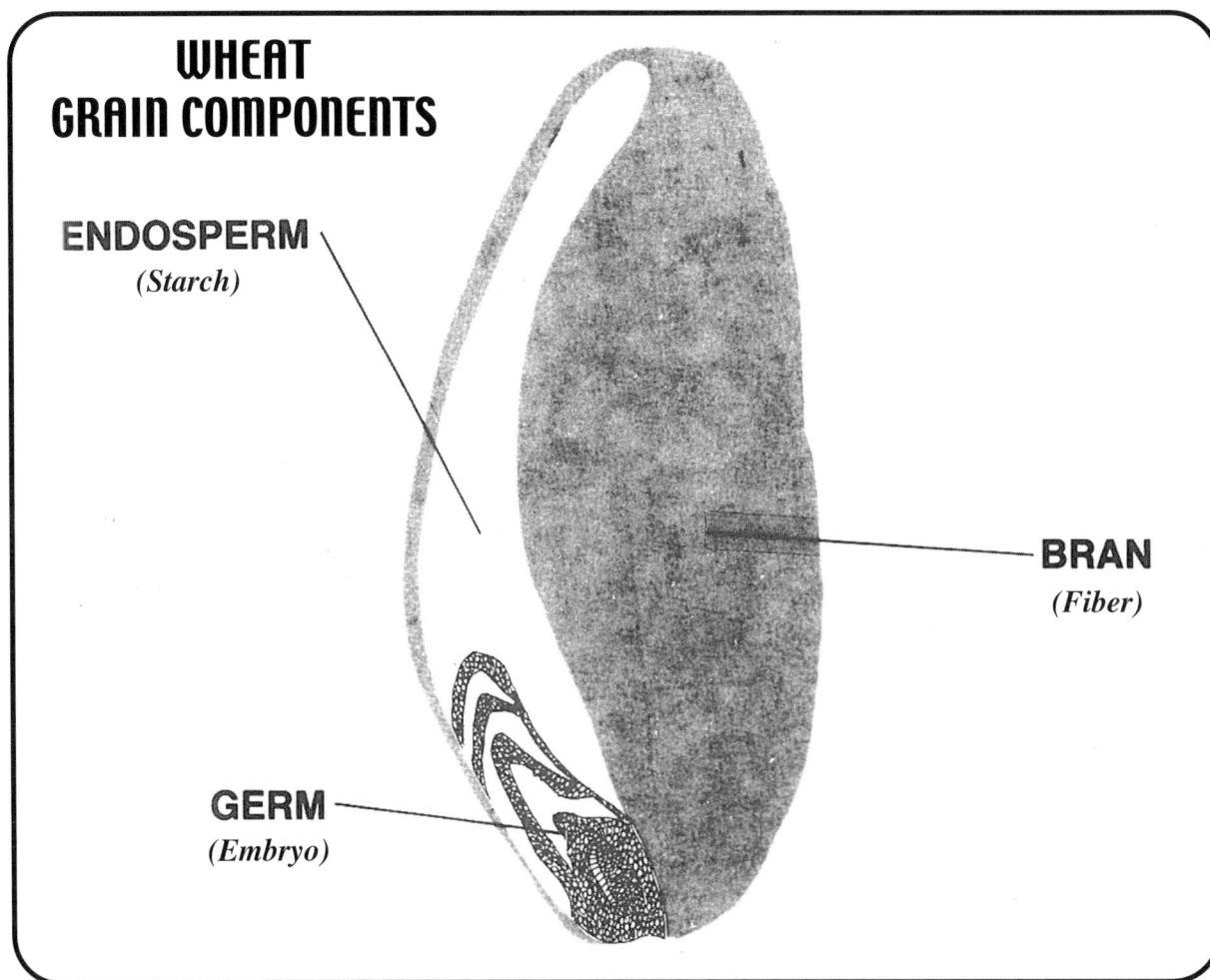

WHEAT GRAIN COMPONENTS

ENDOSPERM
(Starch)

BRAN
(Fiber)

GERM
(Embryo)

1. The germ which contains the new wheat embryo.
2. An outermost covering called bran which is fiber and some vitamins (it is interesting to note that when grain is refined this fiber part is removed).
3. An endosperm containing starch which serves as a nutrient energy supply for the newly sprouting plant.

White bread is made from white flour. Refined white flour contains the endosperm only and does not contain the bran or germ. Vitamins, minerals and nutrients which were originally in the whole wheat are missing in refined flour as they are contained in the removed bran and germ. This applies to refined cereals as well. To obtain all of the vitamins and essential nutrients originally in the wheat grain, we must eat whole grain bread, whole grain cereals and whole grain foods.

The same is true for whole grain brown rice and refined polished white rice. Refined white rice is missing fiber and many vitamins and minerals. Kernels of corn, beans, peas, potatoes, apples, oranges, pears, etc., are all essentially seeds for sprouting new plants and as such if not refined are good sources of complex starch carbohydrates as well as vitamins and minerals. Refining, canning, processing and boiling them in water causes the loss of many vitamins and minerals.

Fresh fruits and vegetables retain their nutrients. Frozen fresh fruits and vegetables retain considerable nutrients as well. However, boiling them in water causes many of the vitamins and minerals to seep out into the water and go down the drain instead of down the digestive tube of our bodies.

Complex starch carbohydrates are converted in our intestines into simple sugars, primarily glucose, which is actively transported through the stomach and intestinal wall into our blood stream. From the blood stream it is carried into the liver where it is converted into glycogen (animal starch). From there it is stored in our bodies. Animal starch or glycogen is broken down when the need arises into carbon dioxide and water by a metabolic process called oxidation. Oxidation releases energy to our bodies in the form of ATP (adenosine triphosphate). <u>As an energy source carbohydrates provide four calories per gram</u>.

SUGARS—SIMPLE CARBOHYDRATES

Sugars are sweet, crystalline soluble carbohydrates which in our diet are usually of two forms: The monosaccharides and the disaccharides.

1. Monosaccharides
2. Disaccharides

<u>Monosaccharides</u> are one molecule of sugar and consist of simple sugars like glucose, fructose and galactose. (Note: All sugars end in the suffix "ose.") Glucose is the most abundant simple sugar. This molecule is combined to form many disaccharides and is organized into much larger molecules of starch. Glucose, also called dextrose, is what we call blood sugar. Fructose is found primarily in fruit. It is also called levulose. Galactose is a simple sugar which combines with glucose to form milk sugar (lactose).

<u>Disaccharides</u> consist of two monosaccharide molecules combined together. The three most common ones are:

Sucrose

Lactose

Maltose

Sucrose is a disaccharide which is a combination of a fructose and glucose molecule. Sucrose comes from sugar cane and beets and is what we know as white, refined table sugar. Lactose consists of a molecule of glucose and galactose. This forms the major disaccharide in milk and is known as milk sugar. Maltose consists of two glucose units combined together. It is what we call malt sugar.

We tend to think of sweetness in terms of table sugar (sucrose). However, there are many different types of sugars and table sugar is just one of them. Other sugars are sweeter than table sugar and some not as sweet. For example, fructose or fruit sugar is 70 percent sweeter than table sugar. Lactose or milk sugar is only 14 percent as sweet as table sugar.

The problem with the simple sugars is that they are broken down rapidly in the stomach and intestines. Since they are not complex molecules they require little digestion. They quickly pass into the blood stream and then blood glucose levels can be quite erratic.

"Carbohydrate bombs" or excess simple sugars makes us fatigued. Have you ever noted how tired you become after a large carbohydrate meal or after eating that piece of cake or pie?

Not all sugar absorbed is glucose. For example, when table sugar (a disaccharide) is digested in the intestines, it is broken down into a molecule of fructose and glucose. Fructose is used biologically by our body also, but glucose plays the most important role in meeting the energy demands of our biological processes. Fructose does not affect insulin levels, but is taken by our blood stream to our liver and muscle cells and converted into complex animal starch (glycogen) for future use as energy. (Note: Large amounts of fructose can cause abdominal pain and cramping and diarrhea.)

Our body's metabolic engine, so to speak, runs on glucose but when too many simple sugars are absorbed, excessively large amounts of glucose are dumped into our system. As if when it rains, it pours! The complex carbohydrates and starches on the other hand, sort of sprinkle a little bit of glucose here and there in a consistent level into our blood stream. Now what does all this mean to our body?

HOW EXCESSIVE REFINED SUGAR AFFECTS OUR HEALTH

Physiologic Changes: Carbohydrates are the major fuel which our body uses for energy. As already mentioned, carbohydrates come in complex forms (starches) and simple forms (like refined sugar). The starches release energy in a constant, continuous flow rate, but the simple sugars cause erratic fluctuations in blood sugar levels and in our body's overall energy levels. This erratic fluctuation can affect us adversely physically, psychologically and emotionally.

You might visualize complex starches as providing metabolic fuel to run the engine of a car at a constant speed. Whereas, if you feed the car's engine the simple sugar glucose instead of starch, energy may be released all at one time and/or in erratic fashions. Our body's accelerator might be pressed, released and pressed again. Then, maybe as the accelerator is released, the body's metabolic engine may stall out, giving hypoglycemia (low blood sugar from too much sudden insulin produced by our pancreas to lower the high blood sugar) symptoms of light-headedness, dizziness, weakness, fatigue, etc. For smooth running of our body's engines we need a constant delivery of fuel.

Weight: Our intake of simple carbohydrates in the United States is out of hand and so is obesity. Simple carbohydrates are fattening "empty calories" as they usually consist of refined sugar elements alone and do not contain other protein, vitamins, minerals or fiber of good nutritional value. Our American sweet tooth and love for refined carbohydrates, despite making us apparently robust, often leads to vitamin and mineral deficiencies. In other areas of the world where complex carbohydrates form the bulk of the diet, adequate vitamins, minerals and other nutrients are a natural part of their life. In the last 50 years Americans have seen a marked decrease in the consumption of complex carbohydrates and an increase in simple sugar consumption. This is grossly evident as sucrose is hidden in refined cereals, coke, candy, etc.

Sixty-two percent of Americans are overweight. This parallels the increase in dietary simple carbohydrates. cola, candy, sugar, syrups, etc. these are essentially 100 percent simple sugars and thus concentrated in "empty" calories which often end up being converted into fats and stored around the waistline. Simple carbohydrates do not produce a feeling of fullness as the complex carbohydrates do. Remember, complex carbohydrates are part of foods which are high in fiber like fruit, leafy vegetables, bran, etc. Fiber produces a feeling of fullness. Sugar-sweetened foods or drinks like cola, candy, etc., do not produce as much of a feeling of satisfaction because they are usually lacking fiber. They are of no good nutrient value and seem to produce a sort of addiction in which the more sweet tasting things we eat, the more we desire. As a result of this habitual intake of excessive empty calories, one's weight increases. Why? Because excess calories are stored in the body's warehouse by converting the sugar into fat storage depots.

Diabetes: People who are diabetic should avoid refined, simple sugars. The reason for this is that high intake of refined sugars places a tremendous demand on their bodies for the production of insulin to reduce the sugar level. Their blood sugar levels can also fluctuate very radically. Diabetics should maintain more of their intake in starches which can just as easily be converted into energy by the body but at a much more constant level. There is also evidence to indicate that high intake of refined sugar promotes the onset of adult-onset diabetes in many hereditarily susceptible individuals.

Hypoglycemia (Low blood sugar): There is no telling exactly how many, but many Americans suffer from hypoglycemia. In very over-simplistic terms, for these individuals, in response to a diet high in sugar, their pancreas overproduces insulin which lowers the blood sugar too much. Symptoms vary from person to person, but may include fatigue, headaches, anxiety, depression, blues, nervousness, schizophrenia, nausea, weakness, faintness, shakiness, apathy, light-headed-ness, sweats and palpitations. Many symptomatic individuals may not necessarily have six-hour glucose tolerance tests compatible with classic low blood sugar, but rather demonstrate a flat glucose tolerance curve (blood glucose does not raise and fall normally, but stays at low levels for the whole test). This is more often associated with those exhibiting symptoms of fatigue.

Dental Cavities: Bacteria have a life of "heaven on earth" when we ingest simple sugar because they grow rapidly in its presence. They digest sugar while on our teeth surfaces, producing an acid which erodes the tooth enamel, causing tooth decay and encouraging an environment for periodontal disease. Sticky, chewy or hard candies that we suck on are the worst because they place a highly concentrated dose of sugar on tooth enamel. Sugar-sweetened drinks and such things as ice cream, are not quite as conducive to the formation of tooth decay. Tooth decay is more closely related to the times sugar sticks on our teeth rather than on the total amount of sugar ingested. For this reason, dentists recommend that we brush our teeth after eating sweet foods. Tooth decay is also related to the frequency of sugar consumption rather than the total amount of sugar consumed. For this reason, dentists recommend that we avoid sweets in-between meals and at bedtime.

Blood Pressure: Recent studies in animals indicate that a high sugar diet coupled with a high salt intake gives a combined synergistic effect to elevate our blood pressure. The testing was performed on rats and monkeys, but researchers feel that the results will some day be proven valid for human beings as well.

Fats: Individuals with high simple sugar intakes tend to have higher levels of blood fats than other individuals. This is related to hyperinsulinemia. Excessive fats predispose us to atherosclerosis and its complications (i.e.: coronary artery disease).

Physiological Effects: Increased simple carbohydrates in our diet produce a sudden surge of energy due to an increase in blood glucose. However, it is very temporary and lasts only a couple of minutes. After this we are left right back where we started or with an even lower blood sugar level (as in the hypoglycemic). Possibly these fluctuations in blood sugars from sweetened foods can account for erratic behavior such that an individual may be emotionally high or hyperactive one moment and a short time later depressed. In other words, psychologically excited and then let down again.

People who consume high intakes of refined carbohydrates tend to be more "hyper" and "on the go." There might be a relationship between this and personality types. Someday nutritionists may prove a direct relationship in many cases between high refined sugar intake and anxiety (or nerves). Individuals who consume the bulk of their calories in starches and protein and avoid refined sugars with their sudden surges and erratic fluctuations of blood sugar levels, are more even-tempered, and easygoing. This is important information to consider if you have children or find yourself anxious, "hyper" or irritable a lot. The psychobiological effects of refined sugar as well as many other nutrients are just beginning to be better understood.

Biologically we do not need refined sugar, but physiologically most of our Western society is addicted to it. Good taste and nutrition, however, do not necessarily go hand-in-hand. We think of refined sugar as a source of quick energy, a "pick-me-up." We think of it as something to make us feel better or a mid-afternoon snack to curb hunger. The problem is there are "catches" to this reasoning. The feeling of increased energy, satisfaction and euphoria is present for only a few minutes before our body converts the simple sugar into glycogen and stores it in our muscles and liver. Also as previously mentioned have you ever noticed the "Carbohydrate bombed out feeling" you have after a large refined carbohydrate meal or after cake or high carbohydrate dessert?

Physical Effects: We have been ingrained with the idea that refined sweets before an athletic event give us energy. Refined sugar actually weakens our muscles and drains our energy. In most individuals refined sugar weakens muscular strength rather than strengthens it. Many of the foods (i.e.: cereals with sugar added) may be draining our life energy rather than replenishing it.

During vigorous exercise the energy utilized is derived from glycogen storage of high energy phosphate bonds in adenosine triphosphate (ATP). During strenuous exercise the muscles draw on this store of energy. Well-trained athletes also derive some muscle energy from the breakdown of fatty acids. Although research studies are inconclusive, thus far they seem to indicate that refined sugar just before or prior to an athletic event, for one reason or another, decreases the immediate strength of our muscles. However, it may be of help in endurance events lasting longer than one hour. In these events glucose is carried to the glycogen depleted muscles, converted into glycogen, metabolized via the Kreb's cycle and high-energy ATP phosphate bonds are released.

Heart Disease: Some researchers theorize that the incidence of coronary artery disease is increased by the action of refined sugars. Data is insufficient on this, but simple carbohydrates are converted to fats and these individuals develop high levels in their blood of fats and/or cholesterol which may increase atherosclerosis. The mechanism for this probably involves the hyperinsulinemia response to elevated glucose.

Diabetics apparently develop a much higher incidence of cardiovascular disease than does the normal population. Too much insulin or hyperinsulinemia can promote deleterious changes in the cardiovascular system. It is well-known that most insulin-using diabetics eventually develop cardiovascular complications such as atherosclerosis. Research indicates it is insulin that is primarily responsible for these changes. Insulin can cause lipids to be deposited in arterial walls. It also increases fat storage in adipose (fatty tissues) by stimulating the synthesis of lipids and prohibiting their breakdown.

BEATING YOUR "SUGAR ADDICTION"

Individuals with "sugar addiction" would be best off to increase their intake of complex carbohydrates (starches) and decrease their intake of simple carbohydrates (sugars). Complex carbohydrates have the best octane rating as metabolic fuel.

When looking at all of the adverse effects of increased sugar in our diet, one thing becomes crystal clear. Whatever the biochemical mechanisms are, excessive sugar stresses our whole person. In the long run, excess may not only affect our quality of life, but may decrease our quality of life as well.

Increased eating of sweetened foods is a habit we Americans have incorporated slowly into our lifestyles. The food industry all too well realizes that a hot selling dietary product can best appeal to a large number of people if it is sweetened with sugar. Just like most car and liquor commercials insidiously arouse your attention by sex appeal, the food industry grabs your attention by a sweet appeal. Our society has become accustomed to this.

Our society tolerates the sweetness addiction. Just eliminating sugar from the table is not the answer. Seventy percent of refined sugar is hidden in processed foods. It is camouflaged in soft drinks, baked goods, desserts, salad dressings, catsups, many canned vegetables, canned fruits, cereals, candy, etc.

The first thing to do is to stop your sweet habit. In the beginning you will have an intense craving for sweets. Do not give in. This craving is a psychological addiction and will go away in approximately one week. See yourself as being able to enjoy a sweetened food in small quantities if you wish, but no longer caring for or even able to take in large quantities of sweets.

HELPFUL TIPS FOR "PULLING THAT SWEET TOOTH"

Read the label carefully on foods before you buy them.

Avoid pre-packaged and refined foods if possible.

Keep in mind that foods ending in "ose" are disguised forms of sugars.

Do not buy foods in syrup as syrups usually contain a high concentration of sugar.

Avoid sugar-containing soft drinks.

Avoid refined desserts like pies, cookies, cakes.

Do not use candy as a reward to children for being good.

Decrease or eliminate sugar from your table.

Keep low-calorie, complex carbohydrate snacks in the house like fresh fruit or vegetables or low-fat yogurt.

Buy a vegetable shredder and make multi-vegetable salads and soups.

FATS

<u>Fats</u> are absolutely essential for life functioning. They are important building blocks for our body as well as an important source of energy. Fats are necessary to maintain our body's temperature, build cell membranes, make hormones like the prostaglandins, form blood clotting elements, transport fat soluble vitamins in our blood and regulate many our body's cellular processes. Some vitamins are called fat-soluble vitamins (Vitamins A, D, E and K) and fats are needed to transport these through the intestines and into our body. Fats are also our body's highest source of energy, giving <u>nine calories of energy per gram</u> as opposed to four calories per gram for carbohydrates and protein.

Most fat is consumed in the form of *triglycerides* which are three fatty acids connected to a glycerol molecule. **Desirable triglycerides levels are less than 150 by the National Cholesterol Education Program (NCEP) guideline.** Unsaturated fats are of two types separated chemically by double bonds in the molecule: Unsaturated fats are considered better for us than saturated fats.

SATURATED FATS

Saturated fats are of animal origin and harden at room temperature. These animal fats are found in eggs, milk products, meat, shortenings, lard, all dairy products, coconut and palm oils, butter, bacon drippings, etc. Saturated fats tend to raise our blood cholesterol levels. As a general rule no more than 10 percent of our total caloric intake of fats should be from saturated fatty acids. Saturated fats have carbon atoms that are saturated with hydrogen atoms. Interestingly, saturated fats are not a necessary bodily dietary requirement.

UNSATURATED FATS

Unsaturated fats are of three types:
1. **Polyunsaturated** (primarily vegetable origin)
2. **Monounsaturated** (primarily vegetable origin)
3. **Trans-Fats or Hydrogenated** (artificially made)

1) *Polyunsaturated*

Polyunsaturated fats have carbon atoms which can accept more hydrogen atoms. They are predominantly of vegetable origin, liquid at room temperature and are found in corn oil, sunflower seeds and oil, safflower seeds and oil, cotton seed oil, sesame oil, soybean oil, fish, fowl (turkey and chicken, etc.). Studies have found by substituting polyunsaturated fats for saturated fats in many individuals, the blood cholesterol level is lowered and the risk of developing heart disease and other complications is decreased.

2) *Monounsaturated*

The primary sources of monounsaturated fats are olive oil, peanut oil and polyunsaturated, ie. fish, fowl (turkey & chicken) and vegetable oils such as corn oil, safflower oil, soybean oil. Monounsaturated fats can take two or more hydrogen atoms. These are considered neutral as far as heart disease is concerned and do not affect serum cholesterol one way or the other. Fish, however, contains omega-3 fatty acids which protects us from coronary artery disease.

3) *Trans-fats or Hydrogenated fats*

Trans-fats, also known as hydrogenated fats, ie. margarine, are semi solid and are artificially made so they are not found in nature. Hydrogenated fats do not occur naturally but are man-made when polyunsaturated fatty acids are partially hydrogenated. In other words, they are processed with hydrogen to make them hard at room temperature and give longer shelf life. It is thought by some that hydrogenated fatty acids may alter cell membranes, allowing possible carcinogens to more easily pass through and cause cancer. For this reason, excessive partially hydrogenated fats (i.e. margarine) may best be limited in our diet.

FATS, ATHEROSCLEROSIS & CORONARY ARTERY DISEASE ▬▬

Excessive fats can be harmful as they can deposit in the walls of our arteries causing atherosclerosis, which narrows these arteries predisposing us to coronary artery disease, stroke, decreased circulation and a host of other problems. Atherosclerosis can cause premature aging, forgetfulness, confusion, decrease in peripheral circulation, coldness feeling, cramping, blockage of the arteries to the eyes and ears, aortic aneurysms, fatty deposits in the skin particularly under the eyes and complicate diseases such as diabetes, kidney disease, gallstones and obesity. As of yet there are no magical pills or elixirs the equivalent of Draino® or Liquid Plumber® to remove atherosclerotic plaques from our arteries, so the best treatment is prevention.

By an indirect method, a high intake of refined sugar predisposes us to atherosclerosis. If sugar is not burned for energy, then our body converts it into saturated fats, which promotes atherosclerosis. Excessive alcohol consumption promotes astherosclerosis also because excess carbohydrates from the alcohol are converted into saturated fats.

Some theorists also feel that a high level of saturated fats makes the red blood cells of our bodies stick together more easily which may further increase the risk for coronary artery disease. Lowering saturated fats and increasing polyunsaturated fats seems to reduce this tendency to form blood clots.

Of interest is that people who eat a lot of fish and fish oils (such as Eskimos) have a very low incidence of atherosclerosis, stroke and heart disease. Fish oils and fish fats are different in that they contain high amounts Omega-3 fatty acids. These Omega-3 fatty acids prevent atherosclerosis and blood cell clotting. Omega-3 fatty acids are not found in any food but fish and fish oils. They are abundant in cod liver oil and fish oil supplements, as well as perch, mackerel, tuna, cod, trout, salmon, etc.

Fats are subject to free radical oxidative attack which produces potential carcinogenic (cancer producing) agents. Individuals on high fat diets should consider increasing intacks of antioxidants (i.e. Vitamins A, E, C, copper, manganese, selenium and zinc) to help prevent the formation of potential carcinogens.

FATS AND OUR AMERICAN DIET

As mentioned previously, the average American obtains 42 percent of their calories from fats. However, optimally we should obtain less than 20 percent. Total caloric intake from fat should never fall below 10 percent because the body needs fats for essential life processes. Fat consumption greater than 30 percent leads to slower metabolic rates and obesity. Interestingly, I've heard it said that my home state of Michigan has the greatest percentage of overweight individuals in the U.S.

If the fat content of our diet is decreased, it will help to prevent heart disease, bowel cancer, breast cancer, atherosclerosis, hypertension, gallbladder disease, liver disease, diabetes and obesity. Decreasing fat intake in our diet helps maintain normal weight because as mentioned before, there are *nine calories per gram of fat as opposed to only four for carbohydrates and protein.* As a rule of thumb, when losing weight most men will consume 40 to 60 grams of fat per day, which is 360 to 540 calories, and women 25 to 40 grams of fat per day, which is 225 to 360 calories.

One of the major benefits of eating fat is that it produces a feeling of satiety and fullness in our stomachs. Fats slow our stomach's production of hydrochloric acid (HCl) which slows absorption and creates a feeling of stomach fullness. Ever notice how hungry you are after you eat a piece of fruit or candy but not after you eat something fatty ie. meat.

In case you didn't sit up and take notice! *The average percent of fat in total caloric intake in the U.S. is currently 42 percent. The goal should be to make it less than 20 percent.*

CHOLESTEROL

Cholesterol is not truly a fat although when most people think of fats, they think also of cholesterol. The reason for this is that true fats and cholesterol are closely related, both in our diet and body. *Cholesterol is a fat-like substance that can be obtained only from foods of animal origin.* In general, many foods high in saturated fats are also high in cholesterol. Our body can make cholesterol in the liver so we actually need none in the diet. When we discuss atherosclerosis it is really the cholesterol deposits which primarily cause the astherosclerosis.

SOURCES

Cholesterol is found in meat, whole milk, butter, cheese, cream, egg yolks (one large yolk contains 225-275 mg cholesterol), shrimp, etc. Animal fat contains cholesterol, but vegetable oils do not, as foods of plant origin do not contain it. Foods which contain saturated fats often contain cholesterol, and it has been established that most saturated fats raise our blood cholesterol, particularly the type of cholesterol (carried by low density lipoproteins, LDLs) that promotes coronary artery disease and atherosclerosis. Cholesterol oral intake of less than 300 mg per day is recommended.

The average American's cholesterol level is 225 mg whereas the desired optimal level is less than 200 mg. by the National Cholesterol Education Program (NCEP) guidelines.

THE TWO FACES OF CHOLESTEROL & ATHEROSCLEROSIS:

Is there good cholesterol and bad cholesterol? Why is it that some people with a high dietary intake of cholesterol or high blood levels do not develop atherosclerosis and heart disease whereas others with a low dietary intake and normal or low blood levels do? The answer is not that there are two different types of cholesterol, but that different people, for reasons unknown, handle cholesterol differently. In the body, fats, (lipids) and proteins combine to form what is called lipoproteins. Two are of particular importance as they transport cholesterol through our bloodstream.

High density lipoproteins, HDLs (or Happy cholesterol) have been found to be of benefit in prevention of heart disease by removing cholesterol from our arterial walls. Some people have high amounts of HDLs and therefore do not seem to develop atherosclerosis as much as others. Of note is that exercise increases HDLs. **Optional HDLs would be above 60 and satisfactory HDLs would be above 45.**

Low density lipoproteins, LDLs (or Lousy cholesterol) have been found to increase the risk of coronary heart disease because they deposit cholesterol in the arterial walls. In other words, HDLs carry cholesterol away from the arterial wall cells and LDLs carry cholesterol to the arterial wall cells. Some people have low HDLs and high LDLs which promotes atherosclerosis. Studies indicate that lowering saturated fats helps prevent atherosclerosis and coronary heart disease. When atherosclerosis forms in arterial walls, cholesterol is often high and the LDLs are high. **Optimal LDL levels are less than 130 for apparently healthy individuals and less than 100 for individuals with risk factors for Coronary Heart Disease (CHD) or who have Coronary Heart Disease.**

Antioxidants help prevent the release of free radicals in our tissues which may predispose us to premature aging and such things as atherosclerotic heart disease. Vitamins A,E,C, zinc, selenium, copper and manganese are thought to have anti-oxidant effects. The antioxidant vitamin E also has been found to elevate blood lecithin and decrease our blood cholesterol at levels of 600 mg or more a day. The antioxidant vitamin C daily decreases the serum cholesterol also. The usual minimum antioxidant daily vitamin C intake is at least 500 mg per day. Excessive amounts such as 4 to 7 grams per day can cause GI upset and increase the possibility of kidney stones. Vitamin A seems to increase lecithin and decrease cholesterol levels as well.

Niacin reduces serum cholesterol and is available in a slow release form. It frequently causes facial flushing so must be started low and increased slowly incrementally up to 2 to 3 grams if possible. It has histaminic effects, so it can cause itching as well.

Some studies seem to indicate that atherosclerosis can be prevented by a diet high in lecithin. Our body produces lecithin in response to a meal high in fat or high in calories. After being made in our liver, it is secreted into gallbladder bile, excreted into the intestine and absorbed into our bloodstream. It helps to remove fats and cholesterol from our blood. It also serves as a structural component for all of our cells. In patients with extreme atherosclerosis it has been found that in response to fats in the bloodstream, the blood lecithin level stays abnormally low. If lecithin is increased in the bloodstream, however, atherosclerosis may be prevented. Blood cholesterol levels have dropped and fat levels remain normal with one to two tablespoons of lecithin daily. Wheat germ and yeast are high in lecithin.

Maintenance of normal weight tends to reduce the cholesterol and fat levels in our body. Increasing certain types of fiber in the diet, particularly pectins found in many fresh fruits, also reduces our blood cholesterol levels. Research is underway studying fats, cholesterol, atherosclerosis and elevated homocysteine, and low folic acid, size and density of HDL and LDL particles, apolipoproteins A and B, VLDL's, etc.

THE BOTTOM LINE REGARDING FATS AND CHOLESTEROL IS... our average American diet is much too high in fat (particularly saturated fats) and cholesterol. This predisposes us to atherosclerosis with its myriad complications and increases our risk of cancer.

Our first goal must be to decrease all dietary fats (saturated, polyunsaturated and hydrogenated) whenever possible. We must decrease our intake of all fats from 42 percent to 10 to 20 percent of the calories in our diet. We must decrease particularly our intake of saturated fats. Of the 20 percent maximum dietary fats, most of it should be in the unsaturated form. We should increase in our diet those factors mentioned above which tend to lower cholesterol and fat levels in our body.

Our second goal is to decrease dietary cholesterol whenever possible. By decreasing dietary cholesterol we help to prevent heart attacks, hypertension, gallstones, gallbladder disease, liver disease, premature atherosclerosis as well as other complications too numerous to mention.

HOW TO DECREASE FATS AND CHOLESTEROL

Decrease the amount of red meat in our diet. Red meat includes beef, veal, lamb, etc.

Meticulously trim the fat off our meats (but this alone is not enough as this accounts for only 40 percent of the fat; 60 percent is still in the meat).

Increase the amount of vegetables, whole grains and fruits (particularly fresh fruits) in our diet as these tend to contain more unsaturated fats and promote the production of lecithin which lowers the blood cholesterol. They also tend to be higher in fiber which helps to lower fats and cholesterol and speed intestinal transit time.

Use low-fat dairy products (for example skim or low-fat milk, low-fat yogurt) whenever possible.

Avoid the trap of fast food restaurants as they usually contain a high amount of fat in each meal.

Substitute fowl, fish, dry beans and peas as a protein source for red meats. When eating fowl (i.e. chicken, duck, turkey) remove the fatty skin.

Avoid high cholesterol organ meats like brains, heart, liver or kidneys. Avoid too much shrimp also as it is high in cholesterol.

Avoid processed foods which may contain hydrogenated fats.

Butter is mostly fat, so avoid it if possible.

Avoid sour cream and be careful of the hidden fats in fried foods, french fries, cream sauces, soups, gravies, salads and dairy products.

Broil, bake or grill meats rather than fry them. Many saturated fats are discarded in the drippings this way.

Use vegetable oil (i.e., corn oil, safflower oil) instead of animal shortenings (i.e., lard).

Buy lean meats and avoid meats with a high fat content (i.e., bacon, sausage, regular hamburger).

Our liver makes cholesterol at night when we sleep. In fact, if we never took in any cholesterol we could still live. This is because over 90 percent of the cholesterol in our body is the result of our liver manufacturing it during our sleep. So despite an almost vegetarian diet some individuals may still have a high cholesterol. Some medications (i.e., "statins") are available from your physician which lower cholesterol by blocking the liver's ability to make cholesterol. See your doctor to determine whether this may be beneficial for you. Some medications (i.e. "fibrates") are also available from your physician which lower triglycerides (fats). (They apparently do so by inhibiting the formation of triglycerides causing the breakdown of the triglyceride-rich lipoproten VLDL.)

Your physician may consider a non-systemic agent that binds bile acids in the intestine forming a complex that is excreted in the feces. Cholesterol is the major precursor component of bile acids so cholesterol is lowered.

FIBER

What is FIBER? Dietary fiber is that part of our diet which passes through our intestine undigested as roughage, sometimes called residue. Dietary *fiber is found only in plants* as it gives plants structural stability. Roughage in moderate amounts is necessary in our human digestive system to help preserve and promote our health.

TYPES OF FIBER

Different types of plants contain different types of fiber. There are approximately one dozen types with each having its own protective role in the digestive processes of our body. Fiber is grouped into two general types: 1) insoluble and 2) soluble.

INSOLUBLE FIBERS

Insoluble fibers absorb water like a sponge. In fact, they can absorb several times their weight in water. For example, 100 grams of bran holds 400 to 500 grams of water. This increases our stool's bulk, keeping it semi-soft and easily passable. Insoluble fibers are found primarily in whole grains. These include wholegrain breads and cereals (which include the bran and germ or the "innards" of the grain), unpeeled apples and pears, fresh peas and carrots, beets, radishes, eggplants, potatoes and most leafy vegetables.

Insoluble fibers

Type	High Amounts Found In
Cellulose	Bran (90 percent cellulose), unpeeled apples and pears
	Peas, carrots.
Hemicellulose	Bran, whole grain breads, beets, radishes, eggplant.
Lignin	Pears, fried or brown potatoes

Insoluble fibers relieve constipation and in fact, some bulk laxatives contain large amounts of insoluble fibers.

SOLUBLE FIBERS

Soluble fibers are of two major types: The pectins and the gums. Some soluble fibers dissolve in water to form a kind of jelly or gel-like substance which is called pectin. Apples, grapes and other fresh fruits fall into this category. Other soluble fibers dissolve in water to form gums. These are the fibers found in beans, corn, oats, seeds, etc.

Soluble fibers

Type	High Amounts Found In
Pectins	Fresh fruits, apples, grapes, bananas, oranges,
	Carrots, potatoes, cabbage
Gums	Beans, corn, oats, seeds

Nutritionists have realized for years that water soluble fibers (as well as water soluble vitamins and minerals) may remain in cooking water and thus be lost.

HEALTH BENEFITS OF FIBER

Fiber is of benefit in:

        Preventing and relieving constipation.
        Preventing and relieving diverticulosis.
        Preventing and relieving spastic colon.
        Preventing and relieving colitis.
        Preventing and relieving Crohn disease (regional enteritis or ileitis).
        Preventing and relieving gallstones.
        Preventing and relieving obesity.
        Preventing and relieving hemorrhoids.
        Preventing colorectal cancer.
        Helping to control diabetes.
        Hypertension.
        Hyperlipidemias (increased fats and/or cholesterol).
        Heart disease (coronary artery disease).
        Others (to be discovered yet).

By increasing the bulk and consistency of our stool (giving it a semi-soft consistency and thus easier elimination), insoluble fibers maintain a more rapid transit time of digestive products through our intestines. This helps to prevent bowel cancers. If feces stagnates in the bowel too long the intestinal bacteria act upon undigested fats and produce carcinogens (cancer-causing substances).

From a bodily-aging perspective, one of the most valuable benefits of fiber is to prevent diverticulosis of the bowel, which afflicts approximately 40 percent of middle-age Americans. Diverticuli are weakenings of the bowel wall giving small, grape-like outpockets or sacs. They most commonly occur in people who experience chronic constipation or straining at stool and are prevalent in our Western society due to the fact that the average American "He-Man" diet of "meat and potatoes" is deficient in insoluble fiber. Symptoms of diverticulosis or diverticulitis (inflamed diverticuli) can be very discomforting consisting of constipation, occasional bowel spasm, gas, nausea, abdominal discomfort and "bloating of the abdomen." In problem cases of diverticuli, some studies indicate an asymptomatic rate of almost 90 percent by adding bran (insoluble fiber) to the diet each day.

Hemorrhoids are dilated veins in the rectum (similar to dilated varicose veins in the legs) affecting at some time or another more than 50 percent of American adults. They are usually caused by increased pressure in the rectal veins from chronic, hard stools, straining to have a stool, sluggish bowels and constipation. By making stool passage easier, fiber decreases pressure in the veins thereby preventing hemorrhoids from developing.

Irritable bowel and spastic colon are likewise helped by the addition of fiber to the diet. Fiber helps produce normal peristalsis of the bowels and relieves spasm and irritability which may be present. In my own practice I have had innumerable cases of persons having symptoms of diverticulosis and irritable bowel with no relief. After I placing them on high-fiber diets, within several months these individuals are free from their symptoms and living normal lives again.

An acquaintance had been in and out of the hospital several times for episodes of irritable bowel. At times she would develop excruciating abdominal pain and constipation. She also had painful surgery for hemorrhoids. When she discussed her problems with me, I suggested she increase the insoluble natural fiber in her diet or possibly add a fiber supplement. She began doing so by eating All-Bran cereal every morning and several months later called to let me know she was asymptomatic. It has been five years and she still has not had to seek help for this condition, nor has she experienced these symptoms since. None of her doctors had recommended that she increase fiber in her diet as a means of treating her irritable bowel. She had instead been treated with a variety of medicines, but to no avail. All the while, a natural remedy was there. All she needed was to become aware of it.

High fiber foods also help to control weight by swelling the gut, thereby producing a feeling of fullness. So if you eat high fiber food, you tend to feel less hungry. It is a low calorie way to feel full.

The soluble fibers (pectins and gums) have been found to be extremely effective in reducing the amount of cholesterol and triglycerides in our blood. In cases of hyperlipidemia (increased cholesterol and/or triglycerides) researchers have found that cholesterol and triglycerides can be lowered by a combination of high fiber, low fat, low cholesterol diet, particularly a diet rich in soluble fibers.

Studies also indicate that for normal persons a low fat, low cholesterol, high complex carbohydrate, high soluble fiber diet remarkably lowers the cholesterol and triglycerides in the blood stream. Researchers have found it is particularly the soluble pectin fibers which help lower cholesterol the most. High fiber diets have been found to increase the amount of HDL (High Density Lipoproteins). High lipoproteins prevent atherosclerosis and heart disease, so a high HDL/LDL ratio helps to protect us from having a heart attack.

Some studies indicate that if dietary fiber is increased our blood pressure tends to decrease. The reason for this is unclear but it follows that a high fiber diet along with decreased salt (sodium, Na) intake may help to control hypertension.

A diet high in fiber has been found to help many diabetics. Soluble fibers (pectin and gums) effect the blood sugar the most and the insoluble fibers effect the blood sugar the least. The pectin forms a jelly or gel which binds sugar in the stomach and the bowels. This decreases the sudden glut of sugar into the bloodstream and slows the conversion of starches into simple sugar. These fiber benefits are found only if the fiber is included as part of a meal, not as an in-between meal snack. One of the first methods of control of blood sugar in the obese adult onset diabetic is weight loss. A high fiber diet does double duty in that it helps to both control blood sugar levels and promote weight loss.

High fat diets, particularly of saturated fats, predispose us to the formation of colon carcinogens. In response to diets high in saturated fats our liver produces large amounts of bile acids. They are then stored in the gallbladder and as needed, secreted into the intestine. A high concentration of bile acids in the intestine predisposes us to the formation of carcinogens and consequently the development of colon cancer. Fiber dilutes the bile acids, absorbs them with its sponge-like capabilities and decreases the carcinogenic effects on our bodies. The potentially carcinogenic bowel acids, as well as fats and cholesterols, are removed by the fiber as feces and flushed down the toilet.

PROBLEMS WITH FIBER?

As Aristotle said, "Moderation in all things," and concerning fiber this is a key concept to keep in mind. High fiber diets tend to cause an increase in intestinal gas production and therefore you may find yourself passing more gas. Too much fiber and you may leave yourself open to a deficiency of some nutrients, particularly iron and zinc. Fiber clutches on to some nutrients and impairs their absorption. You "end up" passing them out into your feces instead. But, among normal, healthy individuals obtaining fiber from foods in a normal well-balanced diet, vitamin and mineral deficiency has not been found to be a problem. In rare cases a high fiber diet may aggravate rather than help ulcerative colitis or regional ileitis and very large amounts of fiber occasionally may cause a twisting of the sigmoid colon or blockage of the gastrointestinal tract.

HOW MUCH FIBER?

We should include 25 to 60 grams of fiber a day in our diets. Ideally these fibers should include insoluble as well as soluble fibers since each offers different health benefits. For example, insoluble fibers like bran and whole-wheat products relieve constipation, prevent hemorrhoids, maintain normal intestinal peristalsis and prevent diverticular disease. Soluble fibers (pectins and gums), including fresh fruits and vegetables like apples, grapes, carrots, beans, peas and leafy vegetables have other benefits. For example, they lower blood cholesterol and fat levels, slow the conversion of starches to sugars, etc.

It is a wonder to me that it took us so long to realize the effect fiber has on us! Have we not noticed how our diet—on the whole—has changed over the last 100 years? From a time when most food was consumed in its freshest form, our ancestors were not afflicted with many of these preventable diseases we have today. We are programmed by TV advertisements to buy "convenience" and "fast foods" which are loaded with fat and preservatives and low in fiber. *The average American diet contains only 19.9 grams of fiber, far short of the 25 to 60 grams recommended per day.*

Unfortunately food processing often removes fiber from the foods we eat. For example, a baked potato has three times more fiber than its equivalent in canned potatoes, brown cooked rice contains 6 grams of fiber per 1/3 cup whereas white cooked rice has only 0.5 grams. One slice of whole wheat bread contains 2.4 grams of fiber whereas one slice of white bread has 0.77 grams of fiber.

Wheat in one form or another is one of the staples of our American diet. It is used in bread, flour, crackers, cereals and hundreds of foods we consume. However, in refining it for its taste and looks, as the food industry has done over the years, fiber and essential nutrients have been lost. A whole wheat grain consists of three ingredients:

1.   Bran (outermost part of protective covering) - fiber
2.   Germ (seed)
3.   Endosperm (nutrients for the developing seed).

Whole wheat flour contains all three ingredients. Refined white flour contains only endosperm. The fiber and wheat seed have been removed.

Remember, fiber comes **only from plants**. It is only present in grainy foods, fruits, rice and all vegetables. It does not exist in animals and therefore is not present in meat, fish, milk, eggs, soft drinks, candy, etc.

GOOD SOURCES OF FIBER ARE:

FRUITS
Apples with skin
Pears with skin
Bananas
Oranges
Dried Figs
Prunes
Strawberries

VEGETABLES
Asparagus
Broccoli
Brussels Sprouts
Carrots
Celery
Spinach

STARCHY VEGETABLES
Acorn squash
Baked potato
Yam with skin
Corn
Green peas
Lima beans

LEGUMES
Navy, black and kidney beans
Chickpeas
Lentils
Split peas

BREADS
Bagels
Corn tortilla
Rye crackers
Whole wheat
Rye
Pumpernickel bread

CEREALS
Bran cereals
Oatmeal
Puffed wheat
Shredded wheat
Wheat germ
Oat bran

GRAINS
Barley
Brown rice
Bulgur wheat
Kasha
Millet

NUTS & SEEDS
Almonds
Dry-roasted peanuts
Peanut butter
Sunflower seeds
Sesame seeds
Walnuts

The "Nutrition Facts" label on canned, packaged and frozen food tells you how many grams(g) of fiber are in one serving.

THE BOTTOM LINE . . .OR. . .WHAT DOES IT ALL MEAN TO US? ▬

So next time you go to buy bread, consider buying whole wheat instead of white bread.

Consider adding two tablespoons of bran cereal to your diet each day.

Instead of a candy snack consider having a fresh fruit such as an apple, banana, cantaloupe, grapefruit, orange, peach, or pear.

Instead of eating pie for dessert consider adding to your meal one-half cup of beans, peas, beets, corn, lentils, celery, carrots, cabbage, broccoli, potatoes, spinach, squash, turnips, cauliflower or other vegetables.

Increasing fiber in our diet is not a magical elixir, but adequate amounts of both soluble and insoluble fiber are absolutely essential for optimal health.

FOOD PYRAMID ▬

The Departments of Health and Human Services (HHS) and Agriculture (USDA) have established a simplified nutrition graphic based on food groups.

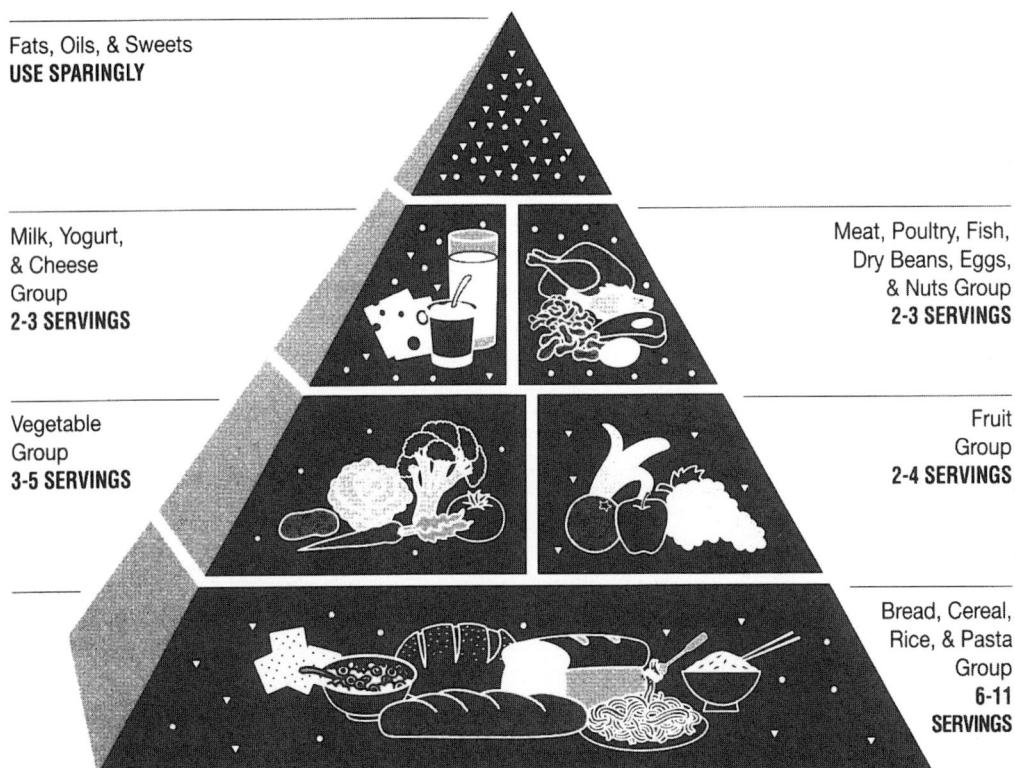

Fats, Oils, & Sweets
USE SPARINGLY

Milk, Yogurt, & Cheese Group
2-3 SERVINGS

Meat, Poultry, Fish, Dry Beans, Eggs, & Nuts Group
2-3 SERVINGS

Vegetable Group
3-5 SERVINGS

Fruit Group
2-4 SERVINGS

Bread, Cereal, Rice, & Pasta Group
6-11 SERVINGS

SOURCE: U.S. Department of Agriculture/U.S. Department of Health and Human Services

FOOD PYRAMID

These guidelines serve as a <u>basic guide</u> but need to be adapted to your specific nutritional needs and of course, are maintenance needs guidelines and not necessarily for the individual who is on a weight reduction diet. For many on a reducing diet, it is bottom heavy in grains (ie., bread, cereal, rice, pasta etc.)

NUTRITION FACTS

Since 1994 all packaged foods must have a food label indicating their "Nutrition Facts". Nutrition fact labels must contain, for average serving sizes, the total calories, calories from fat, saturated fat and cholesterol.

They also must contain percent Daily Value. Most give this based upon a 2,000 calorie per day diet. Nutrition facts that are listed based upon the 2,000 calorie per day intake are: Total Carbohydrate, Dietary Fiber, amount of Sugars that are in the total carbohydrate, Protein, Vitamins A and C, Calcium and Iron. Other vitamin and mineral amounts may be listed. Often the percent Daily Values for both the 2,000 and 2,500 calories per day diet are given if space permits.

When eating out, be aware that restaurants are required to provide nutritional information for meals labeled as Heart Smart or Heart Healthy and for those labeled as Low Fat.

Nutrition Facts

Serving Size   8 fl. oz.   (240 mL)
Servings per container   about 4

Amount per serving

Calories 130   Calories from Fat 35

	% Daily Value*
Total Fat 4g	6%
Saturated Fat 0.5g	2%
Cholesterol 0mg	0%
Sodium 105mg	4%
Potassium 440mg	15%
Total Carbohydrate 13g	4%
Sugars 7g	
Protein 10g	20%

Vitamin A 30%	•	Calcium 20%

Iron 10% • Vit D 10% • Vit E 25%
Thiamin (B1) 10% • Riboflavin (B2) 4%
Niacin (B3) 4% • Pantothenic Acid (B5) 6%
Pyridoxine Hydrochloride (B6)   8%
Folate (B9) 10% • Vitamin B12 50%
Biotin (Vit H) 4% • Phosphorus 15%
Magnesium 15%   •   Zinc 6%

Not a significant source of dietary fiber, Vitamin C.
* % Daily Values are based on a 2,000 calorie per day diet. Your needs may be higher or lower depending on your calorie needs:

	Calories	2,000	2,500
Total Fat	Less than	65g	80g
Sat Fat	Less than	20g	25g
Cholesterol	Less than	300mg	300mg
Sodium	Less than	2,400mg	2,400mg
Potassium		3,500mg	3,500mg
Total Carbohydrate		300g	375g
Dietary Fiber		25g	30g
Protein		50g	65g

Chapter 41

DESIGNING A WEIGHT REDUCTION PROGRAM THAT WILL WORK FOR YOU

THE **KEY** TO WEIGHT CONTROL AND DIETING

There is no unsolved mystery to weight loss. Quite simply what goes in must be counterbalanced by what gets burned up. Our human body is a highly efficient mechanism which does not believe in waste. Excess calories are stored as fat. To diet is to eat fewer calories than our bodies need to perform daily functions. When we diet, the body must use up some of the stored fat as nourishment. Thus we lose weight.

THERE IS A DIFFERENCE BETWEEN DIET AND DIETING. Intestinal bypass operations aside, there is no way around the mathematical fact, calories taken in minus calories burned up equal weight gained or lost. The reason why many diets ultimately fail is that "dieting" is often mistaken for "diet." "Dieting" is the process of losing weight; "diet" is what we consume on a day-to-day basis. Thus, people go on a diet, lose the desired weight, but gain it back because they return to their old eating patterns, the ones which made them fat in the first place. To make dieting results stick, we must change our diet—what and how we eat—permanently.

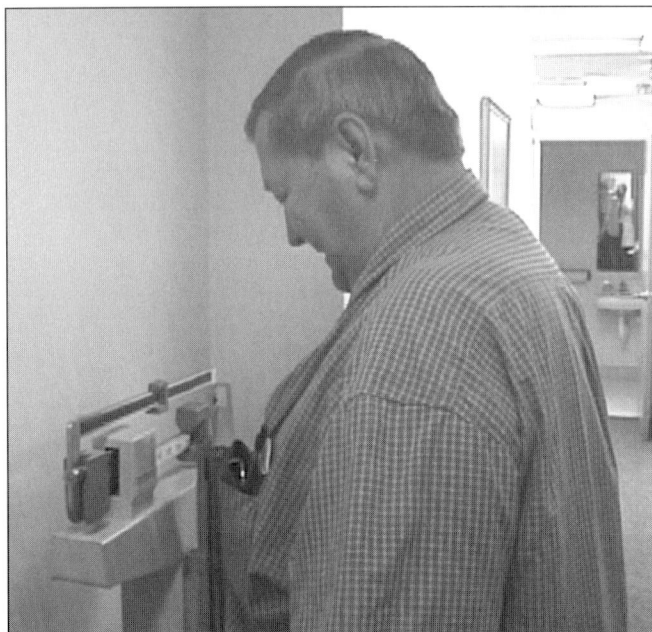

DESIGNING THE REDUCING DIET THAT WORKS FOR YOU

All diets limit caloric intake and most do so by recommending an exact amount of food (or type of food) you can eat on any particular day. Usually, caloric intake is restricted to 1,000 - 1,200 calories a day for a moderately active woman, 1,500 - 1,800 calories for a moderately active man. Variations depend upon such factors as, the size of the person, lean body mass, activity and starting weight.

There are many popular reducing diets such as Weight Watchers, Atkins, Scarsdale, Gourmet, Beverly Hills and literally hundreds of others. What most diets have in common is a restriction of high calorie foods such as bread, pastries, pies, cakes, cookies, sugar, milk products, fats, ice cream, soft drinks, jams and jellies, syrups, alcohol, beer, wine, honey, fried or creamed foods and snacks such as potato chips. These foods are usually replaced with fresh vegetables, low fat dairy products, fresh fruits, and whole grains foods which provide more nutrition per calorie.

High protein formula diets are often popular because they are easy to follow and offer rapid weight loss. They are effective for many people because they take the decision-making out of dieting and are best suited to a quick but substantial weight loss for a period of up to eight weeks. Keep in mind, however, that these diets do not provide sound, everyday eating habits. This you must provide for yourself once you have reached your ideal weight. Otherwise you will find yourself on a constant roller coaster of rapid weight loss and just as rapid weight gain. These diets also often lead to muscle and calcium loss. Before you embark upon a diet, once again, consider what is right for you. While the basic principles of nutritious, low-calorie dieting are the same for everyone, the way you choose to employ these principles may differ depending on your condition and goals. Mary, who is 5 feet 2 inches, 120 pounds, may feel a bit sluggish and chubby at that weight, so she decides to "crash diet" and lose 10 pounds in three weeks so she can look nice as a bridesmaid at a friend's wedding. Barbara, 5 feet 2 inches and 190 pounds however, has an entirely different problem and will need a long-term diet suited to her lifestyle habits, work, psychological and emotional needs.

Do not lose too much weight too quickly! Crash dieting can lead to weakness, dizziness and fatigue. Most nutritionists say the healthiest rate of weight loss is about eight pounds per month, even though most dieters want to lose more quickly. Certainly, do not lose more than 3 1/2 pounds per week for any long period of time. Under no circumstances attempt a severe crash diet (where more than five pounds a week are lost) for more than a few weeks without being closely supervised by a physician or other dietary expert.

(NOTE: Food for thought! I see many elderly sedentary individuals in the office in anguish over their weight. They mentally punish themselves because they're considerably overweight. All right, I'll say it… because they're obese. Don't beat yourself up over your weight. I'm totally against a 70 to 85 year old, 75- to 100-pound overweight man or woman going on any of the strict "quick-fix" fad diets on the market. At that age why are you gambling with your life to lose a few pounds? At that age why punish yourself with attempts at a strict rapid weight loss diet? Eat sensibly and follow basic and sound nutrition guidelines!

IMPORTANT DIETING INFORMATION YOU MUST KNOW

Good nutrition is really nothing but choosing good fuel for your body, just like you choose good fuel for your car.

Eat five to six small meals spaced every 2 1/2 to 3 hours rather than three large meals a day. This prevents the large fluctuations or ups and downs of blood sugar which can cause alterations in body functioning, mood changes, hunger and other body functions.

A simple 1,000-calorie weight reduction diet for a five-foot-two inch 50-year-old, 150 pound woman may look something like:

25 percent Protein   62 grams @ 4 calories per gram 250 Calories
Increased lean meat, fish 2 to 3 times a week, breast of chicken and turkey;

55 percent Carbohydrate 138 grams @ 4 calories per gram 550 Calories
Decreased pasta, potatoes, breads, sweets, candy, cakes, pies, colas and other refined sugar containing drinks, alcohol, etc. Considerable increase in vegetables and some increase in fruit.

20 percent Fat   22 grams @ 9 calories per gram 200 Calories
Decreased animal fats, butter, oils, etc.

The average diet of most individuals today approaches 11 percent protein, 47 percent carbohydrates and 42 percent fat.

Many reducing diets increase protein up to 20 to 30 percent of total calorie intake as this maintains blood sugar at a more constant level. The result is better appetite control and fewer hunger sensations. Most are usually safe for up to six months as long as you have no kidney damage (i.e., renal insufficiency) because protein digestion by-products (i.e. urea nitrogen) need to be removed via the kidneys. ***An idividual with renal insufficiency should not go on an increased protein weight loss diet.*** Such a diet also stresses the liver and causes increased calcium loss in the urine. Of note is that if you go off of an increased protein diet and have something sweet, your body craves the quick fix of the sugar and you'll experience an almost uncontrollable craving for more sweets. Diets with greater than 30 percent protein should probably only be undertaken under close supervision. These types of diets also have the potential for considerable muscle wasting and subsequent loss of muscle mass. The reason for this is the body's metabolic engines need glucose as its gasoline, if it doesn't get enough glucose in the diet it'll burn storage fat but also take some protein from muscle and convert it into glucose as well.

As discussed in Chapter 40, carbohydrates come in two forms: starches, or complex carbohydrates (for example, bread, pastry, flour, cereals, most vegetables, etc.) and sugars, or simple carbohydrates (for example, refined cane sugar, beet, maple and malt sugar). Most of our carbohydrate intake should consist of starch and sugars should be minimized.

    Protein   = 4 calories per gram
    Carbohydrates = 4 calories per gram and
    Fats   = 9 calories per gram.

Additionally, 3,500 calories equal one pound of fat. This means that if you take in 3,500 more calories than your body needs, you will gain one pound. Conversely, if you take in 3,500 calories less than your body needs or burn up 3,500 calories, you will lose one pound. Dieting is really simple arithmetic.

To compute your _approximate_ Daily Caloric Maintenance (the number of calories you need to consume in order to keep your weight the same), multiply your ideal weight by 15 calories. This amount applies to the moderately active person. Thus, the moderately active man who normally weighs 172 pounds requires 2,580 calories to maintain that weight. The moderately active woman whose ideal weight is 110 pounds has a 1,650 calorie/day requirement. If she takes in only 1,000 calories per day she will burn up 650 calories per day in stored fat (1,650 minus 1,000 equals 650). If she continued this diet for two weeks she would burn up 650 calories per day for 16 days or, 10,400 calories. Since 3,500 calories are equal to one pound, she would lose approximately three pounds. NOTE: These values are for moderately active people. Most people who are over-weight, however, tend to be sedentary. It seems obesity and inactivity go hand-in-hand. So, if you seem to require fewer than the "normal"' amount of calories, it may be because you are less active than you think. There are other variables to consider as well, such as lean body mass.

One of the realities of dieting is that most people do not sit down and count every calorie or meticulously analyze each meal to determine if it is nutritionally balanced. If you do not want to spend a lot of time figuring out if your diet has the right amount of carbohydrates, proteins and fats, then the following diet utilizing the KISS method (Keep It Simple Sweetie) should work for you.

SIMPLE SAMPLE DIET USING THE KISS (KEEP IT SIMPLE SWEETIE) METHOD

As a rule of thumb, a well-balanced, low-calorie, nutritious meal consists of a moderate serving of lean meat or fish, 1/2 cup of fresh vegetables or fresh fruit, water or a diet drink. To visualize the portion size, turn your palms up. The palm of your hand represents approximately a moderate serving of fish or meat, so you can eat as much as you can fit into the palm of your hand. Your cupped fingers represent approximately 1/2 cup of fresh fruit or vegetables, so you can eat as much fruit or vegetables as you can put in the palm of your hand. Place a glass of water or a diet drink in the other hand and you have literally placed your diet in your hands. This represents one meal. Three such meals a day and a possible light vegetable or fruit snack in the mid-morning, mid-afternoon and possibly early evening will give you the intake of about 1,000 to 1,200 calories for a woman. A man tends to have a larger hand, so he would consume a slightly larger serving of lean meat and 3/4 cup of fresh vegetables, for a total of 1,500 to 1,800 calories per day. Eight ounces of low-fat milk may be substituted in place of the meat allotment. Be sure to include with your diet a multiple vitamin with iron and minerals each day.

SAMPLE MENU (KISS METHOD FOR A WOMAN) FOR WEIGHT LOSS

BREAKFAST 7:30 a.m.
> One boiled egg or carton of Eggbeaters®, 1/2 small grapefruit or oatmeal
>
> Decaffeinated coffee or tea unlimited no sugar or cream
> Artificial sweetener is OK

SNACK 10:30 a.m.
> 10 small pretzel twists (5.2 calories each)

LUNCH noon
> One moderate serving of lean meat, breast of chicken or turkey, or fish (i.e., can of tuna in water); or can of Healthy Choice® chicken with rice or Progresso® soup
>
> One-half cup of vegetables (i.e., beets, carrots, beans, brussels sprouts, cabbage, tomatoes, cauliflower, lettuce, mushrooms, okra, radishes) or fresh fruit (i.e., apple, applesauce, banana, apricots, cantalope, grapefruit, grapes, tangerine, figs)
>
> Water or diet drink

SNACK 3:30 p.m.
> 10 small pretzel twists (5.2 calories each)

DINNER
> One moderate serving of lean meat or fish.
>
> One-half cup of vegetables (i.e., peas, onions, celery, asparagus, broccoli, spinach, peppers, turnips, squash, cucumbers, frozen, mixed vegetables) or fresh fruit (i.e., orange, nectarine, peach, pineapple, plums, raisins, prunes, watermelon, pear, honeydew melon)
>
> Water or diet drink

EARLY EVENING SNACK (if desired)
> Diet drink
>
> One to two medium carrot sticks or celery stalks or small serving of plain lettuce or 1/2 cup of vegetable or a fresh fruit.

Pay attention to the quantity of your food intake. **As a general rule of thumb, decrease your quantity of food intake by 20 to 25 percent to lose weight.**

Chapter 42

HOW I LOST 55 POUNDS IN SIX MONTHS

You know the clichés: **People aren't as interested in what you say as in what you do**, lead by example, the proof is in the pudding, actions speak louder than words. Patients who knew me when I was much heavier years ago are always asking, "How did you lose your weight?" Well…

I became motivated to lose weight while standing naked in front of the mirror and looking at myself one day. I was aghast in horror…the pot belly, middle-age spread, love handles, puffy face, the fatigue, shortness of breath, so on and so on.

I really believe in being able to look in the mirror and in all honesty to assess whether you are being the best person you can be. While psychologically, emotionally and spiritually I could say I was fairly satisfied, my body had "gone to flab." While I was an active person, I wasn't physically fit. When my teenagers were home it was easy to maintain fitness keeping up with and exercising with them, but now that the empty nest syndrome had crept up on me, I had let myself slip into a more sedentary lifestyle and the middle-age sedentary weight gain syndrome. I vowed with everything in me to take action immediately to remedy this situation and to <u>never</u> let it happen again.

I lost 55 pounds in six months using the diet below and became a proponent of physical fitness using the fitness program in this book.

BREAKFAST 6:30 a.m.
- One carton of Eggbeaters® {120 calories, 24 grams protein, 0 grams fat, 0 grams carbohydrate}, 3 Bob Evans Country Lite® sausage links {120 calories, 14 grams protein, 8 grams fat, 0 grams carbohydrate}
- One packet of instant oatmeal {160 calories, 4 grams protein, 0 grams fat, 32 grams carbohydrate}
- coffee, no sugar or cream

SNACK 10:00 a.m.
- 24 mini pretzel twists – {Approximately 5.2 calories per small pretzel for 65 calories, 1.5 grams protein, 0 grams fat, 14 grams carbohydrate}
- Water

LUNCH noon

- Can of tuna (albacore), salmon, or breast of chicken in water, or can of soup such as Healthy Choice® chicken with rice or Progresso® beef & mushroom soup {200 calories, 16 grams protein, 4 grams fat, 26 grams carbohydrate}
- Apple or one cup of steamed vegetables (i.e., Carrots, broccoli, peas, corn) {120 calories, 2 grams protein, 0 grams fat, 20 grams carbohydrate},
- Diet drink

SNACK 3:30 p.m.

- 24 mini pretzel twists – {Approximately 5.2 calories per small pretzel for 65 calories, 1.5 grams protein, 0 grams fat, 14 grams carbohydrate}
- Water

DINNER

- One moderate serving (8 ounces) of lean meat, breast of chicken, turkey or pork, or fish {260 calories, 46 grams protein, 7 grams fat, 3 grams carbohydrate}
- One cup of steamed vegetables (i.e., Carrots, broccoli, peas, corn) {120 calories, 2 grams protein, 0 grams fat, 20 grams carbohydrate}
- Lowfat pudding {90 calories, 0 grams protein, 0 grams fat, 22 grams carbohydrate}
- Diet drink

EARLY EVENING SNACK

- Sometimes one to two medium carrot sticks or baby carrots {40 calories, 0 grams protein, 0 grams fat, 8 grams carbohydrate}
- Water

(Note: I really make four low-fat Bob Evans Country Lite® sausage links each morning but only manage to eat three. Three are for me and one for our African Gray bird Isaiah who is "glued to my arm" each morning as we eat breakfast watching the other birds at the bird feeder on our patio.)

I try to have fish such as salmon or cod for dinner at least two times per week for its cardio-protective effects.

My favorite steamed vegetable combination is…place carrots in the steaming pot for about ten minutes and then add broccoli and steam them together for another 9-10 minutes.

Sample of MY AVERAGE TOTAL DAILY NUTRITION
was approximately

BREAKFAST
4 Eggwhite Eggbeaters® {120 calories, 24 grams protein, 0 grams fat, 0 grams carbohydrate}
3 Lowfat sausages {120 calories, 14 grams protein, 8 grams fat, 0 grams carbohydrate}
1 Packet instant oatmeal {160 calories, 4 grams protein, 0 grams fat, 32 grams carbohydrate}

SNACK
24 Small pretzels {130 calories, 2 grams protein, 1 grams fat, 28 grams carbohydrate}

LUNCH
Healthy Choice® soup{200 calories, 14 grams protein, 4 grams fat, 29 grams carbohydrate}
Apple {120 calories, 3 grams protein, 0 grams fat, 20 grams carbohydrate}

SNACK
24 Small pretzels {130 calories, 2 grams protein, 1 grams fat, 28 grams carbohydrate}
• Water

DINNER
8 oz. Fish {230 calories, 46 grams protein, 8 grams fat, 3 grams carbohydrate},
1 Cup steamed broccoli & carrots {120 calories, 3 grams protein, 0 grams fat, 20 grams carbohydrate}
Low fat pudding {90 calories, 0 grams protein, 0 grams fat, 22 grams carbohydrate}

EARLY EVENING SNACK
{40 calories, 0 grams protein, 0 grams fat, 8 grams carbohydrate}

TOTAL DAILY NUTRITION:
{1,500 calories, 1112 grams protein, 22 grams fat, 190 grams carbohydrate}

Approximately   30 percent protein   15 percent fat   55 percent carbohydrate
As a general rule for safe **weight loss,** most nutritionists recommend calorie percentages from protein should not exceed 30 percent, fat not to exceed 25 percent and complex carbohydrates should make up at least 50 but no more than 60 percent of caloric intake.

Most nutritionists recommend preferred **daily maintenance** nutrition ranges for maintaining normal weight to be:

	Acceptable	Best
Protein	15-30 percent Total Caloric Intake	15-20 percent Total Caloric Intake
Carbohydrate	40-60 percent Total Caloric Intake	55-60 percent Total Caloric Intake
Fats	10-30 percent Total Caloric Intake	20-25 percent Total Caloric Intake

Chapter 43

TWELVE DIETING MYTHS YOU MUST BE AWARE OF

MISCONCEPTIONS ABOUT DIETING

Myth #1

Diet pills burn up calories. Diet pills do not in themselves burn up calories or cause weight loss. They help by suppressing appetite. More important than diet pills is good motivation.

Avoid "quick fix" weight loss pills you see on TV infomercials, send away for in suspect magazines, or even hear about from unknowing radio commentators. Many "miracle pills" have hidden or possibly unknown or untested for long-term dangers and are not a substitute for sensible, every day, lifelong eating habits. Most of the quick fix pills of course tell you not to eat after supper or within four hours of going to bed. Anyone on a sensible diet will lose weight if they follow that piece of advice. Avoid "quick fix" fad diets.

If you feel it necessary, see your physician for an FDA-approved appetite suppressant or an intestinal fat blocker (note: may cause vitamin deficiency, gas and oily bowel leakage or "accidents").

Myth #2

Retaining water accounts for much of your weight problem. Excess water usually accounts for only a few pounds. Many seriously overweight individuals feel bloated not because of water retention, but due to excess fat cells and the fat deposits in their fingers, legs, etc.

Myth #3

We naturally get heavier as we get older. This is absolutely false. Extra weight often creeps into the abdomen and thighs of men and women over 25, but this has nothing to do with aging. True, the average person gains about 2 to 3 pounds per year after the age of 30, but it's not because we naturally get heavier. It's due to an increasingly sedentary (inactive) lifestyle and the fact that even though our metabolism's caloric needs decrease by about 1 percent each year after the age of 30, we continue to eat just as many calories as we did at 18.

Myth #4

Vitamins increase your appetite. This is often used as a rationalization by individuals who have not adhered to their diet. A multivitamin supplement with iron is an excellent way to insure adequate nutrition while dieting and in no way increases the appetite.

Myth #5

Overweight people are happier people. Although we often conjure up the stereotyped, robust Santa Claus image of jolliness and good cheer, psychologists have found that overweight people often tend to use this front to hide their real unhappiness with themselves. They often substitute oral gratification as a means of relieving stress or depression and the satiety feeling from food becomes a "Linus blanket."

Do not allow yourself to slip into the habit of eating for solace. As soon as you become aware of your low mood, substitute an enjoyable activity instead or if necessary, seek help.

Myth #6

I can drink light beer or low calorie beer daily and lose weight. In general, this is false. I can honestly say I have never seen anyone continue to drink any type of beer on a regular basis and lose weight. And, if your calories are being taken in by beer, you are not receiving many other essential nutrients (i.e., proteins, vitamins, other trace elements) which are found more abundantly in other foods.

Myth #7

Exercise increases my appetite. Actually moderate exercise three to five times a week decreases the appetite and provides an important emotional and psychological "boost" that makes you feel healthier, more active and more dynamic.

Exercise burns up calories and keeps you toned and fit. It helps you feel better and feel better about your body. Many overweight people suffer from lack of exercise. They are too tired to exercise and as a result sit around eating, getting more obese and getting more tired.

Myth #8

Drinking water causes bloating. No, it does not. In fact, water in-between and just before meals provides a feeling of fullness and decreases appetite. Water is essential for cleansing of body tissues and for normal elimination, particularly during dieting. Any excess water is passed during urination. It is not absorbed into your tissue, so it will not bloat you up.

Myth #9

Salt has calories in it. Salt does not contain calories. However, you should decrease your intake of salt because excess salt causes fluid retention which may cause bloating. Do not salt your food and avoid highly salted foods. In fact, keep the salt shaker off of your table entirely.

"I've been exercising 3 days a week Monday, Wednesday, Friday for the last 15 years. It all started when my oldest son got me a membership to the Y after my wife died. I've been going to the Y regularly ever since!

I walk 2 miles and use all the Cybex machines there. It really makes me feel great and with the Lord's help I've met a lot of really great people there. With me staying in shape exercising, I'm staying in pretty good shape for an old duffer!"

Raymond Kraft
– Age 68

Myth #10

Skipping breakfast or any meal helps you lose weight. Actually, skipping meals often leads to snacking or overeating at the next meal. It can also result in wide fluctuations in blood sugar levels, which can in turn affect your mood, your metabolism and your overall well-being. It is a much better idea to eat three equally spaced, low-calorie meals a day.

Myth #11

You can eat regularly at fast food places and still lose weight. Usually not. There are many hidden calories in fast foods. For example, a Big Mac contains about 557 calories, french fries 215 calories, medium-sized cola 220 calories, for a total of 992 calories. That is nearly 1,000 calories a meal. If you are on an 1,200 calorie a day diet, you have already eaten most of your day's calories. A Whopper at Burger King contains 630 calories. A Colonel Sanders crispy Kentucky Fried Chicken dinner contains 950 calories. With cola, that puts you at nearly 1,200. A large dip Dairy Queen cone contains 450 calories, a large malt 830 calories and one plain donut at Dunkin' Donuts 260 calories. As you see, it is very difficult to eats at fast food places and expect to lose weight. Fast foods put on weight fast!

Myth #12

I follow my diet, and still I gain weight; everything I eat turns to fat. Many times I have heard people say…

"I eat like a bird and still gain weight."

Not all the time but more often than not when individuals <u>carefully</u> examine their eating habits however, they see the bird they eat like is actually a scavenger vulture. Check your food list to make sure there are no hidden calories such as filler, fats, grease, breading, etc.

Weight is not something that just attaches itself to us. Weight comes from calories and calories simply do not come out of thin air. The only way to bring calories into our body is by ingesting them through food and drink. Be calorie conscious. Excess calories make you fat! Excess calories make you fat! Excess calories make you fat! That's it in a nutshell. Just like when buying a house consider – Location! Location! Location! The undisputed key to weight loss is to consider – Calories! Calories! Calories! Look carefully and honestly at the quality (type) and quantity of food you eat and oh…did I forget to mention consider… Calories! Calories! Calories!

Chapter 44

THE FIFTY TIPS "YOU MUST KNOW" TO LOSE WEIGHT

THE 50 INDISPENSABLE TIPS I USED TO LOSE WEIGHT

Tip #1

Set realistic short-term goals! We need immediate, positive feedback and gratification when we are dieting. To do so, it is important to set realistic short-term goals. If you are 5 feet 5 inches and weigh 239 pounds, do not just say you are going to get down to 130 pounds and begin dieting. This is too distant a goal. Instead, set a realistic goal of reducing to 234 pounds in two weeks, 232 pounds in three weeks, 225 pounds after another two weeks and so on. By all means, decide on an ideal weight to achieve ultimately, but set short-term goals <u>in writing</u> so you have a step-by-step plan. Diet one day at a time and one week at a time. If you can succeed in achieving your short-term goals, you will certainly succeed in achieving your long-term one as well.

Tip #2

Do not snack or eat before going to bed. If during the 7 to 8 hours of sleep at night your body's metabolic engine can't get the glucose fuel it needs to run from digested food in the stomach, it will burn up stored fat to obtain it. Preferably, do not eat a meal within four hours of going to bed for the same reasons. If you must eat, I have found it helpful to eat a protein like albacore tuna in water or the no-drain packages. The body doesn't tend to break down the protein for fuel so you will still lose weight by the morning by burning stored fat.

Tip #3

Analyze your eating habits. You may be shocked at the results. Do you tend to munch absent-mindedly during the day? Do you eat for hunger, for enjoyment or out of habit? Do you eat junk foods? Do you drink a lot of calories in the form of milk, beer, etc.? Do you constantly taste food while you are cooking? Do you nibble here and there? Do you "eat up a storm" at one meal, taking as many as 2,000 or 4,000 calories? Are you conscious of the types of food you are eating as you are eating? Do you eat sensible portions? Are you really taking in only 1,200 calories? Has eating at fast food places become such a habit or psychological addiction that you often have "Big Mac" attacks, visit the "Colonel," visit "The Home of the Whopper," or need a taco?

Closely examine your eating habits and vow to change them. Decide to decrease the quantity of the food you eat and increase the quality. Substitute low-calorie, nutritious foods in place of the "empty calories" you have learned to eat out of habit. Remind yourself that you are in control of your eating habits, not the other way around. With each bit ask yourself, "Do I really need this? Am I just eating out of habit, or as a substitute for other things that are lacking in my life?" Listen to the answers to those questions and use them to direct you toward change in your life. If necessary, see your physician, a dietition, personal trainer or other nutrition expert for help.

Tip #4
Give yourself a daily pep talk: "I am Healthy & Happy, Slim & Strong, Confident & Competent!"

Each day when you awaken, tell yourself "I am slimmer today. I desire and eat only healthy foods which promote weight loss so as to achieve my ideal weight." Become a champion for healthy living and weight loss for yourself...and an example for others. The best way to lead is by example and the best way to lead our children into what it takes for healthy living is to be a living example for them to follow.

Look at yourself in the mirror and as you notice yourself getting slimmer, smile (this physically reinforces the image) and say out loud, "I'm doing a great job." Acknowledge and pat yourself on the back as you do well. Be you own best cheerleader!

Tip #5

Drink a glass of water before each meal. This will give you a sense of being full and will reduce your appetite.

Tip #6

Exercise 30 minutes before eating. Moderate activity tends to decrease your appetite. You may consider exercising about 7:30 in the evening and then not eat afterwards before going to bed. Your body needs to replenish its glucose so it'll burn up fat from your fat stores.

Tip #7

Diet with someone else. Dieting with a "buddy" means you can lift each other's spirits and share low-calorie meals. Food is a form of communication and when shared with another person is more satisfying and even tastes better. Diet with a spouse, family members, your roommate or a friend. You might want to challenge each other.

Tip #8

Savor every bite you eat. Obese people tend to eat quickly, sometimes out of guilt they want to cover up the fact that they are eating so much. So slow down. Feel each bite in your mouth, taste it, smell it and chew it slowly. You might even want to chew each mouthful ten times.

Slow your eating pace by cutting portions into small pieces. This will prolong your enjoyment of the amount of food you have and it will also allow your system to tell you when you are full. It takes nearly 20 minutes for the food entering your system to signal your satiety center that you have eaten enough, so take at least 20 minutes for each meal. Laying your eating utensils down between each mouthful will also help slow your eating pace.

Tip #9

Do not eat in front of the TV. This promotes unconscious eating and is conducive to overeating, habit eating and snacking. Instead, whenever you eat a meal or snack, sit at the table and use a full place setting. Doing so will insure that you eat more consciously - and enjoy what you eat more.

Tip #10

Do not nibble during the day or in the evening. Do not snack in between meals. Eat only at meal times, preferably five to six small meals spaced every 2 1/2 to 3 hours. Avoid all snack foods such as potato chips, candy, etc. Set regimented meals, eating only at these meal times and not when you tell yourself you are hungry.

Tip #11

Do your grocery shopping after a full meal. When you shop for food while hungry you will buy more junk food, more things that you do not really need. You can discourage impulse food buying by making a shopping list and sticking to it.

Tip #12

Broil, bake, roast, steam or boil your meat rather than frying it. Also, meticulously trim away all the fat before cooking and take the skin off chicken. This will reduce the calories.

Tip #13

Avoid fast food. Eat at home more, at restaurants less. At home you are more likely to know exactly what you are eating. Restaurants, particularly fast food places, tend to have a lot of hidden calories in their foods.

Tip #14

Eat a lot more vegetables and a moderate amount of fresh fruits. They contain well-balanced nutrients, tend to be lower in calories and contain pectin, an enzyme believed to inhibit the absorption of fats.

Tip #15

Exercise. Combine aerobic and light weight-training exercise - such as the **BEST BODY BEST BONES FIT FOR LIFE PROGRAGM** at least three days a week with your dieting. The best weight loss programs combine dieting with exercise.

"I'm 85 years old and I exercise for about a half hour three days a week with five-pound weights. I also walk 2 miles a day first thing in the morning most days. I began exercising regularly when I was in my 50s. When I go to Florida I do aquasize about 3 days a week. Exercising makes me feel energetic. I like to walk outside first thing in the morning. To keep feeling young you must keep at it. You've got to exercise regularly. I do it every morning, otherwise I may sometimes not do it. It's easy to get out of the habit but if you keep doing it you really feel great!"

Bettie Iott
– Age 85

Substitute the exercise habit for the eating habit. It is easier to lose weight if you feel well and exercise helps you feel better.

Tip #16

Substitute water primarily or a one calorie diet drink for soft drinks. Many drinks have hidden calories, too. Diet drinks will help you avoid excess sugar as well.

Tip #17

Do not salt your foods. Salt increases fluid retention and is a primary culprit in high blood pressure. Instead, use a salt substitute.

Tip #18

Avoid refined sugar and foods containing large amounts of sugar. They are high in calories. Despite a temporary lift, they ultimately may cause rebound low blood sugar and a feeling of fatigue and hunger. You don't want or need these "Empty Calories."

Tip #19

Include at least 25 grams of fiber in your diet daily. Fiber ensures movement of food through the bowel, thereby preventing stagnation and absorption of unnecessary calories. High fiber foods tend to be low in calories yet more filling, so you feel hungry less. It reduces one's cravings for high fat high sugar foods by controlling intestinal absorption thereby exerting regulatory effects on maintaining stable glucose levels. Whole grains, bran, oatmeal, fresh fruits and vegetables are excellent sources of fiber. If you have difficulty in this area or have bowel disease such as diverticulosis, then you may want to strongly consider a fiber supplement such as Metamucil®, Citrucel®, or Fiber Con®.

" I like to dance maybe two times a week in Adrian or Tecumseh. Of course, the ladies I dance with are a lot younger than I am. I like to jitterbug."

Wayne Weatherwax
– Age 97

Tip #20

Be calorie conscious. Excess calories make you fat! **Calories! Calories! Calories!** That's it in a nutshell. Just like when buying a house consider – Location! Location! Location! The undisputed key to weight loss is to consider – Calories! Calories! Calories! Look carefully and honestly at the types of food you eat. Check your food list to make sure there are no hidden calories such as filler, fats, grease, breading, etc.

Tip #21

Change your lifestyle to help you lose weight. If you have a predominantly sedentary lifestyle, become more active. Make time to do more activities you enjoy.

Are you eating for entertainment? Place food in its proper perspective rather than having it be a primary form of entertainment. Do not set yourself up for occasions when you may desire to overeat or eat rich foods.

Tip #22

Do not keep high calorie, prepared snacks or junk food in your home. This includes candy, pastries, chips, soft drinks, etc. Substitute low-calorie drinks, some fresh fruit and preferably vegetable snacks. A carrot, a stalk of celery or apple can be just as satisfying (more so even) once you wean yourself away from snack food. Most fruits are high in disaccharide sugars but lack bulk so they don't contribute to satiety. Do not test yourself by having this unnecessary temptation.

Tip #23

Enlist the moral support of family and friends. Ask them to give you constructive comments when appropriate, to encourage you and help you, but let them know there is a difference between moral support and nagging! Make sure you spend time with people who really are willing for you to change. Avoid people who want you to overeat so that they will have company in indulging themselves!

Tip #24

Eat five to six small meals spaced every 2 1/2 to 3 hours rather than three large meals a day. This prevents the large fluctuations or ups and downs of blood sugar which can cause alterations in body functioning, mood changes, hunger and other body functions.

Tip #25

Pay attention to the QUALITY of your food choices. Most safe successful weight loss diets are MODERATE PROTEIN, LOW FAT, LOW/MODERATE CARBOHYDRATE. For most individuals this would mean a moderate increase in their intake of protein, a severe decrease in their intake of fat and a moderate decrease in thier carbohydrates to lose weight. This means…

DECREASE: Bread, bakery, colas, cake, candy, pasta, pies, sweets and starches such as potatoes and rice.

INCREASE: Lean meat, fish, breast of chicken or turkey, vegetables and fruits.

INCREASE: Water and change to diet drinks.

A 1,000 calorie weight reduction diet for a five-foot two-inch 50-year old, 150-pound woman may look something like:

25 percent Protein   62 grams   @ 4 calories per gram   250 Calories
Increased lean meat, fish 2-3 times a week, breast of chicken and turkey etc.

55 percent Carbohydrate   138 grams   @ 4 calories per gram   550 Calories
Decreased pasta, potatoes, breads, sweets, cakes, pies, colas, alcohol, etc.

20 percent Fat   22 grams   @ 9 calories per gram   200 Calories
Decreased animal fats, butter, oils, etc.

The average diet of most individuals today approaches 11 percent protein, 47 percent carbohydrates and 42 percent fat.

Tip #26
Pay attention to the QUANTITY of your food intake. Decrease your quantity of food intake by 20 to 25 percent.

Tip #27
Be happy. Always carry happiness with you or you can search the world and you will never find it. I've seen many individuals who think when they retire they will then begin to be happy. You guessed it. They are more miserable than ever because now they have a lifetime to ruminate on their unhappiness. Material things, retirement, etc., only make you more comfortable but will never make you happy or fulfilled. Create happiness and a fulfilling life now. It is impossible to lose weight if you are unhappy with your life. Be genuinely grateful for what you have. Forgive those you need to forgive. Be the person you want to be. Your new attitude will affect everyone around you. And, you will no longer need to bury your sorrows in food.

Use dieting as an opportunity to do something you really enjoy doing. Do you enjoy tennis? Dancing? Have you always wanted to take a ceramics or drawing class? Substitute the gratification you get from these new activities for the gratification you get from food. Keep active. It is very difficult to lose weight when you are bored.

Tip #28
As you lose weight, encourage others to do the same. Just as a smile is highly contagious, your example can be contagious as well. By encouraging others you will be creating more support for yourself.

Tip #29

Check and re-check your eating behavior patterns. Chances are you have been overeating out of a long-standing pattern. Become aware of these patterns and modify them to accommodate your new low-calorie lifestyle and you will never have to "diet" again.

Tip #30

If you are overeating as a result of emotional stress or other psychological issues, begin now to attempt to work out solutions to these problems. It's no secret that food satisfies your need for pleasure. For example, if things in your life aren't working out quite the way you want them to, food provides instantaneous oral comfort and satisfaction. And when the fleeting moment of that comfort and satisfaction is gone…you just reach for some more. To control calorie intake your desire to lose weight must be greater than your desire for temporary oral pleasure from food.

The hunger center of the brain and the anger center of the brain are next to each other. Notice that when you are hungry it's easier to get angry. When you are sad, eating provides pleasure. The satiety center and the pleasure center of the brain are also next to one another. By satisfying your hunger food you stimulate your pleasure center and you feel good. That is until the alkaline tide sets in and makes you tired if you eat sweets or a lot of carbohydrates. Siesta time. That's why many Europeans take a long lunch with nap from 2 to 4 p.m. in the afternoon.

Do not hesitate to seek professional help and possible anti-anxiety or antidepressant medication if you may benefit from it.

Tip #31

Commit yourself to achieving your ideal weight. If you feel you just want to "lose a few pounds" you probably will not succeed unless you have a very definite goal. Losing weight requires total commitment on your part and total conviction. You must convince yourself that you must lose weight. Attempt to find a significant, concrete motivation for you to lose weight. This might be a once-a-year family reunion, a wedding, a public appearance, to fit into your new size 7 sexy swim suit by July 4, or whatever works for you. If your obesity is aggravating an already-existing condition such as diabetes, hypertension, degenerative osteoarthritis of your knees, ankles or back, or if you have a heart condition, this should be all the motivation you need to commit yourself to lose excess pounds now.

Tip #32

Do not dwell on failure. If you slip up and overindulge, do not dwell on guilt and scold yourself. There is a strong tendency to want to give up at this point, resulting in an even more damaging binge. Instead of focusing on what you have done wrong, envision yourself doing it correctly from now on. Forgive yourself and look at your temporary slip-up as an opportunity to renew your commitment.

Tip #33

Do not attempt to follow a strict diet on holidays. Holidays like Thanksgiving or Christmas, for example, are days of celebration and enjoyment. There is no need to stuff yourself or splurge on pastries, but do allow yourself to enjoy a satisfying meal with your family or relatives. The benefits of fully enjoying such an occasion far outweigh any weight that might be lost on those special days.

Tip #34

Make breakfast your largest meal. Go lighter on supper or your evening meal. We are not necessarily what we eat, but what we eat, digest, absorb and incorporate into our system. If 500 calories are eaten in the morning, fewer of those calories will be absorbed into our system as fat than if we ate those 500 calories in the evening. This is probably true because of autonomic nervous system activity. After you eat breakfast and go off to an active day, your digestive system is not as active. In the evening however, we tend to lounge around and then go to bed. The only activity going on is digestion, which means that fewer calories are burned and more are converted to fat for storage for some future time. For this reason, it is a good idea not to eat calorie-containing foods or drinks after 6 p.m. In particular, do not eat a snack such as cola or potato chips before going to bed.

Tip #35

Stop eating before you feel full. It takes time for the food you have eaten to send a message to your brain that you are full. Slight feelings of hunger will disappear within 30 minutes of when you eat.

Tip #36

Do not skip meals. When people skip a meal, the tendency is to snack or overeat at the next meal. The key words for successful dieting are "regularity" and "moderation."

Tip #37

Do not cheat on your diet. Making exceptions here and there will only decrease your motivation and sincerity to achieve normal weight. If you are losing weight and have a good thing going, keep it going. Do not stray off track. Remind yourself constantly of how good you feel about sticking to a diet.

Tip #38

Do not substitute oral gratification as a means of relieving stress. Beware of the depression trap. If you should find yourself depressed about something, do not allow yourself to slip into the habit of eating for solace. As soon as you become aware of your low mood, substitute an enjoyable activity instead.

Tip #39

Avoid seconds when you eat. This can best be achieved by eating slowly and consciously, by savoring each mouthful. When we take more food than we need, it is usually because we are eating so quickly that our "fullness" has not registered yet. So slow down. You will be surprised to find you do not want seconds.

Tip #40

Leave the table when you have finished eating. Clear the table immediately and go to another activity. If there are any leftovers on your plate, throw them away immediately (or if you have chickens, feed them to the chickens.) Do not feel obligated to finish food left on your children's plates. It will not do starving children in Biafra any good, in spite of what your parents may have told you. That food you eat because you do not want it to go to "waste" will go to "waist" instead. So if food cannot be saved for another meal, throw it away.

Tip #41

Keep food out of sight. Out of sight is out of mind. Dieting is in a way psychological warfare and you must use every and any weapon at your disposal to combat old habits. Keep food in hard to reach cabinets, in plain brown bags or other containers that do not reveal contents. You can even keep the refrigerator bulb off to draw attention away from the goodies in the fridge. Have you ever noticed that when food is just lying around, it tends to disappear into your mouth? Avoid this temptation. Put food away.

Tip #42

Do not drink excess calories. I have heard some people complain they are not losing weight and swear they are not eating many calories. In analyzing their meal plan, I often note that they are drinking a quart of milk a day. That is 664 calories right there. Beer drinking falls into the same category, only worse since beer is high in calories yet low in nutritional value. At least milk offers balanced nutrition (except for iron). Colas are flavored water with lots of "empty sugar calories."

Tip #43

Avoid "quick fix" fad diets and "quick fix" weight loss pills. Many "miracle diets" have hidden dangers and do not promote sensible, everyday, lifelong eating habits. Most of the quick fix pills, of course, tell you not to eat after supper or within four hours of going to bed. Anyone on a sensible diet will lose weight if they follow that piece of advice. Fruitarian diets are suspect as they are sometimes low in protein and lacking certain vitamins.

If you feel it necessary, see your physician for an FDA-approved appetite suppressant or an intestinal fat blocker (note: may cause vitamin deficiency, gas and oily bowel leakage or "accidents.")

Tip #44

Have a maximum allowable weight. Once you have reached your ideal weight, continue balanced, sensible eating habits, but have a maximum weight which triggers an alarm in your mind. Continue to weigh yourself regularly and if you have reached that maximum, put the brakes on and re-commit yourself to caloric dieting. Maintaining ideal weight is a lifelong commitment. It can be handled effortlessly provided your weight gain does not get too far out of hand.

Tip #45

Stand naked in front of a mirror and take a good look at yourself. Are you satisfied with the body you see? If you are not happy with your weight, decide now to do something about it. To further motivate yourself, take a photograph of yourself in a swimming suit before you begin to diet. After you have lost a considerable amount of weight, again photograph yourself and do so again when you have achieved your ideal weight. You should hold on to the original "before" photograph as a reminder that you never want to be overweight again. You might even tape it to the refrigerator.

Tip #46

Each morning and evening utilize visualization for 10 or 15 minutes and see yourself as you ultimately want to look. To visualize, close your eyes, take a few slow, deep, relaxed abdominal breaths and progressively relax each muscle group, beginning with your toes and moving up to your head. In this relaxed, meditative state of mind, see yourself at the weight you want to be.

Visualize yourself touching your stomach, your arms, your legs, etc. and notice they are thin. See yourself fitting into slim clothes, looking fit and trim in whatever size clothes you want to wear. See yourself throwing out all of the oversized "fat" clothes, although you might want to hang onto one pair of enormous slacks just as a reminder.

Hear other people telling you how happy they are to see you have lost weight, what a success you are, what an example you are to them, how proud they are of you and how attractive you look. See them look admiringly at you.

See yourself with an abundance of newfound energy, as the excess weight no longer drains you of it. See yourself feeling happy and feeling great. Visualize yourself exercising (walking or jogging regularly, walking more and riding less, taking the stairs instead of an elevator.) Feel the wonderful euphoria that comes with regular, moderate exercise. See yourself exercising regularly and loving it, burning up calories and firming up your muscles for a fantastically toned figure. Feel yourself enjoying the taste of low-calorie foods and actually developing an aversion to high-calorie foods. See yourself with a change in attitude – you now want to taste and smell only foods which are low in calories and health-producing. If you have trouble actually visualizing, you might try imagining a movie screen in front of you and watching it as if you were watching a movie.

Before visualizing, set a short-term goal for yourself to be a certain weight and put it in writing. Also, write down how you expect to achieve it. For example: "I plan to lose 8 pounds in 30 days by eating 1,200 calories a day." Not only will this enable you to identify a specific goal, but you will have concrete actions to take to accomplish them. Actually see yourself at the desired goal when you visualize. Periodically cue yourself during the day to go into this meditative state for short periods of time (one to five minutes). You can do this by telling yourself that you will be in a relaxed, meditative, visualizing state after three deep abdominal breaths. Then repeat your previous visualizing experiences.

If during the day you find yourself feeling hungry and wanting to eat something not on your reducing diet, then take three slow, deep, relaxed breaths, recall your previous pleasant visualizing experiences and see your hunger desire melting away as you focus on your goal. Reinforce yourself with visualization during thee day as often as necessary, but be sure to begin each day of your diet with a minimum of ten minutes of visualization.

Tip #47

Keep a daily diary of everything you eat. During your early stages of dieting, keep a listing of the amount of food you eat each day, the calories, the time you eat and how you feel at the time you are eating and what else you are doing at the time. Keep track of every calorie you consume. Some people like to be really exact and weigh their food in strict proportions. Others on a daily basis subtract their intake of calories from their daily maintenance calories to determine their daily calorie loss. While this is an excellent tool for the beginning dieter to use to analyze his or her eating habits, it need not be carried on for a long period of time. For example, my automobile has a gauge on it to let me know if I am using excess gas. After having used it for five or six days, I no longer have to look at it to know that when I press down on the accelerator, I am going to get a specific decrease in mileage. I have learned through experience. Likewise, once you have kept track of your diet for a period of time, you will develop a natural ability to gauge how many calories you are consuming or whether you are eating out of compulsion or emotional distress.

Tip #48

Use small plates and take only small portions of food. You might also want to prepare your plate at the stove rather than the table and wait one full minute before digging in

Tip #49

Accentuate the positive. For example, some people find it helpful to place a sign on their refrigerator which says, "I only eat what turns to health and beauty." Instead of focusing on not eating the wrong foods, concentrate on eating the right ones. Try not to think about monkeys and you will think about nothing but monkeys. Similarly, do not occupy your mind with what you do not want. Fill your mind with thoughts and pictures of what you do want. Do not punish yourself for desiring high calorie foods. Allow these desires to be and then actively visualize yourself desiring, eating and enjoying only the right foods.

Tip #50

If you weigh yourself daily then do so at the same time every day and weigh yourself just once a day. Weight tends to vary depending on the time of the day. To avoid unnecessary disappointment or confusion, it is best to weigh yourself the same time each day, preferably unclothed, in the morning.

THE 4 KEYS TO WEIGHT CONTROL

To summarize, the ideal diet for permanent weight reduction and maintenance of proper body weight consists of:

1. *Serious, enthusiastic commitment!*

2. *Nutritional awareness!*

3. *Caloric intake restriction!*

4. *Moderate exercise!*

Fit For Life

Insert

Your Portrait

Here

Chapter 45

IT'S NOT WHO STARTS THE GAME BUT WHO FINISHES

It's not important if you exercise for two, three or four years but whether you're exercising in 20, 30 or 40 years. ***Short-term gains are not that important, but rather fitness needs to be a solid, long-term investment!*** Fitness needs to be a part of your life…Forever!

You must come to terms with yourself about your commitment to a lifetime of moderate, health-enhancing exercise. If your exercise program is dependent upon the encouragement and admiration of others as can sometimes occur in health clubs, then you'll only achieve short term success.

When you first begin to exercise, it may take extra effort to get self-motivated so that it is a natural habit like brushing your teeth. But eventually as time progresses and you become more proficient at it, it'll become a natural part of you. Once your long-term motivation is as natural to you as brushing your teeth, then you have mastered this health-enhancing tool.

100 Years Old and Going Strong!

Elvert: "I turned 100 years old in December, 2001. We still are quite active, take care of ourselves and live in our own home although we can't drive anymore. I like to work in the garden. The one thing I won't do anymore is get down and scrub the floors!"

Gatha: "We can't keep track of how many great and great great grandchildren we have anymore. I once started counting how many we had and when I got to 84 I quit counting!

I bowled until I was about 89 and Elvert stopped bowling when he was 96. Not because we had to stop but because we couldn't drive to the lanes and had to depend on others to take us. The last day I went I had one game of 173. I had a good hook. I had bowled regularly ever since I was young!"

Elvert-Age 100   and   Gatha-Age 91   Young

Chapter 46

HERE'S WHAT THE BEST BODY BEST BONES FITNESS PROGRAM CAN DO FOR YOU!!!

The Incredible Benefits of Exercise

Could you feel better, look better and do you want to live a long life? Then what an opportunity! The most dramatic effect of exercise on your health and well-being comes about if you have led a sedentary lifestyle and are one of these who are inactive prior to your beginning an exercise program.

Exercise will help relieve depression, anxiety, stress, tension, fatigue, insomnia, hypertension, diabetes, heart disease and constipation. It raises HDL (good) cholesterol and lowers LDL(bad) cholesterol. It decreases pains from osteoarthritis (wear and tear arthritis) and helps with a host of other illnesses. And this is just the beginning!

Exercise reduces the appetite and appreciably increases our metabolism which burns more calories at rest so we stay thinner. After age 20 our basal metabolism decreases approximately 2 percent every 10 years. This is why as we get older it's easier to gain weight and harder to lose it. Exercise increases muscle mass and muscle burns more calories per day than fat. Women tend to slowly gain weight after menopause. Most gain six to seven pounds one to two years after their monthly periods stop. The reason for this is that the monthly menstrual period blood loss burns up calories. After menopause this calorie burner is no longer present.

In addition to the beneficial effects of exercise on bone formation and our musculo-skeleton, there are other substantial *halo* benefits.Whenever we exercise moderately, our body manufactures endorphins and enkephalins which improve your energy level, emotional well-being and immune system—creating what has sometimes been called the "runner's high." These *feel good* drugs are more powerful than morphine. If we are physically fit we tend more of these present in our system. Exercise improves our self-image, self-esteem, self-confidence and enables most individuals to experience a greater feeling of mastery over their life.

Physically fit individuals tend to produce fewer catecholamines. These are hormones our body produces in response to stressful situations which tend to produce anxiety, depression and even illness. Physically fit people are better able to handle stress without adverse effects such as hostility, frustration and anxiety. A regular exercise program is usually far more effective in the long run in dealing with "nerves" than a tranquilizer. Tranquilizers temporarily cover up the problem, but exercise is a positive energy outlet for dealing with and dissipating the energy put into the problem. Popping pills is passive, but exercise is active involvement in improving our life and well-being. Of course, a short term tranquilizer may be the best way to handle an acute problem, but in the long run exercise will be far more effective as a way to gain real control and mastery over our life.

Regular exercise not only tunes up our body, but tunes up our mind as well. Regular conditioning improves oxygenation of your brain, improving logical thinking abilities, memory, reaction time, coordination, intuition and creativity. Although all these incredible benefits are experienced by exercise…

the number one reason individuals exercise is that they feel better.

Take advantage now of the tremendous health benefits of lifelong moderate exercise with the **BEST BODY BEST BONES FITNESS PROGRAM! You** may never have an opportunity to turn back the hands of time like this again. <u>You'll feel good</u>, <u>look good and live longer</u>! Don't pass up this opportunity for the best investment of your life, to invest in your life!

You've thought about it…now do it! You'll be glad you did!

Fitness Wisdom

Chapter 47

FINAL WORDS OF WISDOM REGARDING BEING A WALKING & WEIGHT FITNESS INSPIRATIONAL ROLE MODEL FOR OTHERS

Once you begin to look and feel great other people will look at you as an inspirational role model for them and want to know what you have done to transform your life and if it is possible for them to do the same. You will know and sense intuitively when the time has come that you are no longer just the student but have become the teacher as well. **<u>Be there for them.</u>** By bringing out the finest in others, we bring out the finest in ourselves.

"I've been a teacher for 36 years and am retiring in six days. I've taught over 4,000 students and it's great to see so many of them so successful. I walk away my stresses three to four days a week, outside if possible or if inclement weather I walk on a treadmill watching the national news for a half hour. Exercise makes me feel better, sleep better, lose a little weight and gives me more energy! I often use light dumbbell weights and do flexibility exercises regularly. Since I've been exercising regularly I have a lot less low back pain which has plagued me the greater part of my life. I'm going to continue to walk throughout my retirement. _If I could give advice to my students about exercise it would be to start now and don't stop._ Work exercise into your regular program for the day just like eating and sleeping."

Dale Cryderman – Age 58

the end

Other Information

spotlight on health

Other Information

Glossary of Terms

ABSORPTIOMETER
A medical testing machine to measure bone density.

ADENOSINE TRIPHOSOHATE (ATP)
High energy compound formed from oxidation of carbohydrate or fat, energy supply of muscle and other body tissues.

ADIPOSE TISSUE
Body tissue in which fat is stored, sometimes called fatty tissue.

AEROBIC EXERCISE
Utilizes our body's maximum ability to take oxygen in through the lungs, transport it to our muscles and utilize it for work output. Typically, a steady, rhythmic exercise that utilizes oxygen for energy in our body's large muscle groups for a prolonged period of time i.e. brisk walking, running, bicycling. Commonly thought of as causing one's heart rate (measured by one's pulse) to reach 60 to 85 percent of maximum heart rate for twenty minutes or longer. Very healthy for our cardiovascular and pulmonary systems. In terms of fitness, the term aerobic exercise is used interchangeably with cardiovascular exercise.

AGILITY
Ability to move quickly and easily while maintaining skillful control of our body.

ALVEOLI
Small air sacs in our lungs where oxygen and carbon dioxide exchange places.

AMENORRHEA
Lack of or abnormal cessation of menstrual periods.

ANDROGENS
Male sex hormones, hormones which produce male characteristics, i.e., testosterone androsterone, dehydroepiandrosterone (DHEA).

ANAEROBIC EXERCISE
Exercise that primarily burns energy from sources other than oxygen because the intense exercise is too strenuous for the normal flow of oxygen from the lungs. Absence of oxygen, nonoxidation metabolism. Short bursts of intense exercise utilizing the body's stores of fat and carbohydrate for energy with a by-product of lactic acid build-up in the muscles and blood. For example, moderate walking is aerobic, and the oxygen supply from the lungs can keep up with the demand in the muscles and tissues, however, if the intensity is increased to very strenuous, prolonged running where the supply of oxygen from the lungs cannot keep up with the demand of the muscles and tissues, the exercise would become anaerobic with associated shortness of breath (from carbon dioxide build up in the lungs) and fatigue and sore muscles from lactic acid build-up in the muscles.

ANOREXIA NERVOSA
An eating disorder characterized by an inappropriate body image that one is fat and subsequent excessive dieting, loss of appetite, refusal to eat and severe weight loss. Primarily found in teenage girls and young women and may cause amenorrhea and subsequent osteoporosis.

ARTERIOSCLEROSIS/ ATHEROSCLEROSIS
Narrowing and hardening of the arteries by lipid deposits. Usually present in some degree in the elderly.

ARTHRITIS
Inflammation, pain and swelling of the joints.

ATROPHIC
Wasting away.

BALANCE
Capacity to maintain one's equilibrium while moving. Involves visual input, input from the semicircular canals in our middle ears and input from receptors in our muscles.

BILATERAL SALPINGIO-OOPHORECTOMY
Surgical removal of both of the ovaries and fallopian tubes.

BODY COMPOSITION
Relative amount of fat and lean tissue. A ratio of fat to lean mass (muscle, tissue, bone, organs). As one becomes more physically fit generally body fat decreases and lean muscle mass increases. An optimal ratio of fat to lean (muscle) mass is a method often used as one of the indicators of good fitness.

BONE DENSITOMETRY
A medical test that measures the bone density.

BONE MINERAL DENSITY
The ratio of bone mass to volume, indicating bone compactness. Bone density increases rapidly through adolescence, more slowly until about age 35 and then plateaus and declines. Bone density is measured most frequently in the spine, hip, wrist, forearm and/or heel for the detection and diagnosis of osteoporosis.

BONE FORMATION
That part of a bone-remodeling cycle in which osteoblasts synthesize a protein matrix of fibers upon which crystals of calcium and phosphorus are embedded during mineralization to provide strength and rigidity.

BONE MASS
Amount of mineral measured in the bone.

BONE MATRIX
Meshwork of protein upon which bone minerals are deposited.

BONE REMODELING
A continuous process in which small amounts of bone are removed and replaced by new tissue. During the resorption phase, old bone is dissolved and eliminated by osteoclasts. This is followed by the formation phase, in which protein fibers and calcium are deposited by the bone-forming osteoblasts.

BONE RESORPTION
The breakdown part of bone's life cycle, during which the old and damaged bone tissue is resorbed. Osteoporosis occurs when resorption is greater than formation.

BRONCHIOLE
Medium size airways. Undergoes spasm sometimes making breathing difficult, as in exercise-induced asthma.

CAFFEINE
An alkaloid drug with a stimulating action, found in coffee, tea and cola-type soft drinks. Consuming excessive caffeine is a risk factor for osteoporosis, because of its diuretic properties increasing the urinary loss of calcium.

CALCIFEDIOL
25 hydroxy-vitamin D_3, a form of Vitamin D produced in the liver.

CALCITONIN
A naturally-occurring hormone secreted by the thyroid gland which inhibits bone resorption. Salmon-calcitonin, a synthetic formation, is used to slow the bone resorption rate in osteoporotic patients.

CALCIUM
A metallic element needed for normal development and function of the body and used in bone structure (85 percent of bone's strength)

CALORIE
Amount of heat required to raise 1 kilogram of water 1 degree Celsius. An energy measurement.

CAPILLARIES
Smallest blood vessels (between arterioles and venules) where oxygen, nutrients and hormones are transported into our tissues and carbon dioxide and wastes are removed from our tissues.

CARBOHYDRATE
A basic source of energy derived from green plants (simple and complex). Carbohydrates are stored as glycogen primarily in the liver and muscle. Carbohydrate excesses are stored as fat.

CARDIAC
Heart

CARDIAC OUTPUT
Volume of blood pumped by the heart each minute.

CARDIORESPIRATORY ENDURANCE
Aerobic fitness or maximal oxygen intake.

CARDIOVASCULAR
Heart and blood vessels. In terms of fitness, cardiovascular exercise is used synonymously with aerobic exercise.

CERVICAL SPINE
Neck. The first seven bones (vertebrae) at the top of the spinal column.

CHANGE OF LIFE
Menopause. Average age for a woman is 50.

CHOLESTEROL
A type of fatty substance found in the body. In increased amounts in the bloodstream it has been shown to cause atherosclerosis and increase the risk of heart disease. It can be made in the liver and is a common cause of gallstones and is a precursor of many steroid hormones.

CLIMACTERIC
Menopausal symptoms.

COLLAGEN
An insoluble protein found in connective tissue including skin, bone, ligaments and cartilage. Collagen represents about 30 percent of total body protein.

COMPOSITION
Often called body composition. A ratio of fat to lean mass (muscle, bone, tissue, organs). As one becomes more physically fit generally body fat decreases and lean muscle mass increases. An optimal ratio of fat to lean (muscle) mass is a method often used as one of the indicators of good fitness.

COMPRESSION FRACTURE
Fracture of a vertebrae in the spine in which the bone collapses or is crushed.

CONTRACTION
Tension of a muscle.

COOL DOWN
At end of exercising, consists of low-level exercise and stretching used to disperse heat, attain good circulation and allow the heart, lungs and muscles recovery time.

COORDINATION
Harmonious flow of muscle groups working together in the performance of an undertaking for smooth motion.

CORTICAL BONE
Also known as compact bone because it has a densely packed, hard, solid matrix structure. Cortical bone is very solid and strong, usually found toward the surface of all bones and gives long bones like the leg, hip and arm their strength. Cortical bone makes up approximately 80 percent of the skeleton. Cortical bone has a slower metabolic rate than trabecular bone so it is remodeled at a much slower rate than trabecular bone.

CORTICOSTEROIDS
Refers to steroid type substances produced in the adrenal gland and/or medications that have a steroid-type response.

DENSITOMETRY
Test used to measure the bone mass or density.

DORSAL SPINE
Thoracic spine.

ELECTROCARDIOGRAM (ECG, EKG)
A graphic recording of the electrical activity of the heart. A sort of electrical "picture" of the heart.

ENDORPHINS
Chemical substances produced mostly in the brain that may have pain lessening properties similar to those of opiates.

ENDURANCE
The ability to keep going or to resist fatigue. Cardiorespiratory endurance is the ability to deliver oxygen and nutrients to our tissues and remove waste products over a sustained period of time. Muscular endurance is the ability of our muscles to sustain repeated contractions over a period of time.

ENZYME
A protein secreted by cells, inducing chemical changes in other substances.

ERT
The abbreviation for estrogen replacement therapy. The replacement of estrogen after menopause.

ESTRADIOL-E$_2$
The major estrogenic hormone secreted by the human ovary in the premonopausal woman. Generally considered to be the most potent form of the three major female estrogens at the receptor level.

ESTRIOL-E$_3$
An estrogen found in women. Is thought to be the least potent of the three major estrogens in a woman's body.

ESTROGEN
A female sex hormone produced mainly by the ovaries which influences bone density by slowing the rate of bone resorption, improving retention of calcium by the kidneys and improving the absorption of dietary calcium by the intestine.

ESTROGEN RELACEMENT THERAPY (ERT)
A therapy that restores estrogen lost when natural estrogen production in the ovaries is dramatically reduced due to the onset of natural or surgically-induced menopause.

ESTRONE-E$_1$
An estrogen found in women. Less active than estradiol. Estrone can be manufactured in body fat. After menopause is the most common form of estrogen found in the bloodstream in women.

EXTENSION
Brings the limbs into a straightened condition. Movement of a joint causes the limbs above and below it to move away from one another. The opposite of flexion. Extension of the spine means the spine is arched backward during this type of exercise.

FAT
Stored energy source; stored in adipose tissue for future use when extra calories are ingested. Oxidized with the release of energy.

FATIGUE
A condition of tiredness usually brought on by over activity.

FITNESS
Combination of aerobic capacity, muscular strength, good balance and good posture that enhances health.

FLEXIBILITY
The ability of the body to move joints and muscles through their full range of motion.

FLEXION
Bending. Movement of a joint causes the limbs above and below it to come together. Flexion of the spine means the spine bends forward from the waist and is rounded during this type of exercise.

FRACTURE
Broken bone.

FREQUENCY
Number of times per day or week.

FDA
The abbreviation for the Food and Drug Administration.

GLUCOSE
A sugar, the most important carbohydrate in the body metabolism. The main fuel which the body uses for energy.

GLYCOGEN
The form in which carbohydrates are stored in the liver and muscles for future use, to be converted to glucose.

GROWTH HORMONE (GH)
A hormone produced in the anterior pituitary gland that may indirectly stimulate bone formation and subsequently has a positive effect on the treatment of osteoporosis.

HEART ATTACK
Myocardial infarction. Death of heart muscle.

HEART RATE
Frequency of heart contraction.

HIGH-DENSITY LIPOPROTEIN (HDL) CHOLESTEROL
A carrier molecule that takes cholesterol to the liver for removal; commonly known as good ("**H**appy" is an easy pneumonic to remember it) cholesterol.

HIP FRACTURE
Fracture of the upper femur at the hip.

HORMONE
A substance produced in one organ that controls or affects the functions of other organs in the body, like estrogen.

HOT FLASHES (flushes)
An intense warmth from within which can develop suddenly, often awakening a menopausal woman at night. Estrogen deficiency is usually the cause. This may be one of the first signs of menopause.

HRT
Hormone replacement therapy. Use of both estrogen and progesterone in the postmenopausal woman.

HYDROXYAPATITE
Hard crystalline mineral salts in bone,

HYPERTENSION
High blood pressure.

HYSTERECTOMY
Surgical removal of the uterus.

IDIOPATHIC
A disease in which the cause is not known.

IMPACT EXERCISE
Exercise that causes an impact or jolt in the bones like jogging and jumping rope.

INTENSITY
Degree of difficulty. With increasing intensity the speed, rate or level of activity is increased.

ISOMETRIC
Contraction against an immovable object so that the muscle is tensed but does not actually shorten but maintains a constant length. Pushing against a wall or immovable object would be an isometric exercise.

ISOTONIC
Contraction against a constant resistance. The muscle shortens and lengthens during this type of exercise. Lifting free weights such as barbells or dumbbells would be an isotonic exercise.

LACTIC ACID
A metabolic by-product of anaerobic (non-oxygen) exercise, with intense or vigorous exercise. It is an anaerobic by-product of glycogen metabolism and accumulates in the muscles and inhibits their enzymatic activity causing fatigue and soreness.

LEAN BODY WEIGHT
Total body weight minus fat weight.

LDL
The abbreviation for low-density lipoprotein. This is a type of cholesterol that may cause arterioscerosis. This has earned the title bad ("**L**ousy" is an easy pneumonic for remembering it) cholesterol .

LH
The abbreviation for luteinizing hormone, a hormone produced in the pituitary gland, that signals the ovary to release the egg.

MAGNESIUM
A metallic element necessary for healthy growth and development of the skeleton, muscle and nervous tissue. Required to convert the inactive form of vitamin D to the active form vitamin D3. Deficiency is common in the elderly.

MAMMOGRAM
An x-ray procedure used to detect breast abnormalities and cancer.

MEDROXYPROGESTERONE ACETATE
Abbreviated MPA. Synthetic progesterone used in hormone replacement for postmenopausal women. Also used as a contraceptive and to control abnormal menstrual bleeding.

MENARCHE
Beginning of the first menstrual period in a young girl.

MENOPAUSE
The time of a woman's last menstrual period, marking the end of her reproductive years. Levels of estrogen fall at this time as the ovaries have ceased their reproductive function.

MUSCULAR FITNESS
Healthy strength, muscular endurance and flexibility.

NUTRITION
The utilization of food, this includes ingestion, absorption and metabolism. To provide the body with adequate energy (calories) as well as needed minerals, fluids and nutrients. Some nutrients are stored in the body and can be drawn upon when intake is not sufficient.

OBESITY
Usually pertains to excessive body fat (more than 20 percent of total body weight for men and more than 30 percent for women.)

OOPHORECTOMY
The surgical removal of the ovaries.

ORAL CONTRACEPTIVES
Birth control pills.

OSTEOARTHRITIS
A disease in which the lining of the joints is inflamed, causing pain, swelling and redness of the joints. It can sometimes be very debilitating.

OSTEOBLAST
A cell which plays a key role in forming new bone for bone growth, repair of damaged bone and replacement of old bone.

OSTEOCLAST
A cell which resorbs and removes old bone tissue.

OSTEOPENIA
Decrease in bone density level below normal range, yet not low enough to be termed osteoporotic. By World Health Organization (WHO) diagnostic criteria a T-Score between −1 and −2.5 Standard Deviations below normal. An individual with osteopenia is considered to be at risk for osteoporotic fracture.

OSTEOPOROSIS
By World Health Organization (WHO) definition a disease characterized by low bone density and deterioration of the structure of the bone tissue leading to enhanced bone fragility and an increased susceptibility to fractures. By WHO diagnostic criteria a T-Score of –2.5 or below.

OVARY
The female reproductive gland where female eggs are made and released. Estrogen, progesterone and some testosterone are produced in this gland.

PARATHYROID HORMONE (PTH)
Hormone secreted by the parathyroid gland. PTH regulates the level of calcium in the blood by adjusting the activity of cells in bone (osteoblasts and osteoclasts) and in the kidney. Through the action of PTH and vitamin D, the body maintains a constant and consistent level of calcium in the blood.

PEAK BONE MASS
The stage at which bones have reached maximum density and strength and after which the rate of bone removal exceeds the rate of bone renewal.

PITUITARY GLAND
A gland at the base of the brain which secretes various hormones, i.e., luteinizing hormone, growth hormone.

PLAQUE
Atheromatous blockage of arteries.

POSTMENOPAUSAL OSTEOPOROSIS
Bone loss accelerated by estrogen deficiency that occurs at menopause. This is now called Type I osteoporosis.

PRIMARY OSTEOPOROSIS
A category of osteoporosis that includes postmenopausal or Type I and age-related, also known as senile or Type II.

PROGESTERONE
A hormone produced in the ovaries after ovulation occurs.

PROGRESSION
Increasing frequency, intensity and duration of exercise over a time period to improve.

PUBERTY
The age at which the reproductive organs develop and become capable of reproduction.

RECEPTOR
A structure in a specific cell which, acted upon by a hormone or a local factor, produces a chemical reaction within the cell.

REPETITION
Also known as a REP. One complete movement of an exercise. From starting position ⇒ to performance of the exercise ⇒ back to starting position

RESORPTION
A physiological process involving the remodeling of bone during which old bone is dissolved and eliminated by osteoclasts.

RESPIRATION
Intake of oxygen and exhalation of carbon dioxide (the act of breathing).

RISK FACTOR
Factors that may put you at higher risk for a certain disease. For example risk factors for osteoporosis put you at high risk for the development of osteoporosis.

SECONDARY OSTEOPOROSIS
A category used to indicate that bone loss is the result of a disease rather than the primary natural causes of osteoporosis, menopausal estrogen deficiency and age.

SENILE OSTEOPOROSIS
Bone loss relating to aging. Called Type II osteoporosis.

SET
A number of repetitions (complete movements) performed without a rest. For example, one set of bicep curls might consists of eight reps.

SPECIFICITY
Choosing types of exercise to effect a particular type of fitness. For example, a marathon runner would choose cardiovascular exercises. A wrestler would choose muscular strength exercises.

STEROIDS
A class of chemical compounds that have the same basic chemical structure. The estrogens, testosterone, progesterone and cortisone are all steroids.

STRENGTH
Ability to exert force with a muscle.

STRENGTH TRAINING
Increasing the strength of a muscle through training.

SURGICAL MENOPAUSE
Refers to menopause by the surgical removal of the ovaries in a woman who is still having menstrual periods.

TESTOSTERONE
A predominantly male sex hormone. The most potent of the naturally occurring androgens. Made in the adrenal cortex, the male testes and the female ovaries. In females, has been found to have a relationship with the female sex drive.

THORACIC SPINE
The 12 vertebrae that make up the upper back from the base of the neck to just above the waist. Also called the dorsal spine.

TONE
Normal tension in healthy muscle firmness.

TRABECULAR BONE
Also known as spongy bone because it has a porous, sponge-like structure. Comprises the interior of vertebral bodies and smaller amounts in the ends of long bones. This portion of bone may be preferentially lost in postmenopausal osteoporosis. Makes up about 20 percent of all bone. It has a faster metabolic rate than cortical (compact or hard) bone, so it is remodeled at a much faster rate than cortical bone.

TRACE MINERALS
Minerals needed in very small amounts to stay healthy. Examples are manganese, boron, copper and strontium.

TRIGLYCERIDE
Fat made up of three fatty acids and glycerol.

UNIVERSAL MACHINE
A type of weight machine in which weights are on rails or tracks and lifted by pulleys and levers.

VALSALVA MANEUVER
Holding your breath with extreme effort causing increased pressure in the abdominal and thoracic cavities.

VERTEBRAE
Bones of the spine.

VITAMIN D
Enables calcium to be absorbed in the intestine and stimulates the kidneys to reabsorb calcium from the urine and keep it in the bloodstream. Some Vitamin D is stored in an inactivated form in our skin and some is stored in our liver.

VITAMIN K
Involved in the synthesis of osteocalcin. A deficiency is thought to contribute to the development of osteoporotic fractures.

WARM UP
Low-intensity movements to warm up the muscles, joints, heart, lungs for more intense exercise. Generally 5-10 minutes of low-intensity movements of the type of exercise to be done or low-intensity walking, stationary bike, etc.

WEIGHT BEARING EXERCISE

Working against gravity. Exercise that requires you support the weight of your body. Walking is a weight-bearing exercise . Swimming is not considered a weight- bearing exercise because of the water's buoyancy.

WEIGHT TRAINING

A regimen of dumbbells, barbells or machines to improve muscle strength and endurance.

ZINC

A trace mineral. Zinc deficiency is thought to contribute to the development of osteoporosis.

Exercise-Related Resources

Aerobics & Fitness Association
for Sports Medicine
15250 Ventura Blvd., Ste.200
Sherman Oaks, CA 91403
800-445-4950

All Pro Exercise Products
P.O. Box 8268
Longboat Key, FL 34228
941-387-9432
www.allproweights.com

American College of Sports Medicine
P.O. Box 1440
Indianapolis, IN 46206-1440
317-637-9200

American Council on Exercise
P.O. Box 910449
San Diego, CA 92191-0049
216-929-7227/ 800-537-5512

FDA Consumer
5600 Fisher's Lane
Room 15A19
Rockville, MD 20857
301-443-3220

Gym Source
40 E. 52nd Street
New York, NY 10022
212-688-4222

National Academy of Sports Medicine
699 Hampshire Road, Ste. 105
Westlake Village, CA 91361
805-449-1370

National Strength and Conditioning Association
P.O. Box 38909
Colorado Springs, CO 80937-8909
719-632-6722

President's Council on Physical
Fitness & Sports
Washington, DC
202-690-9000

Fitness Disributors
25 Washingtoon St
Natick, MA 01760
800-244-1882
Fax 508-650-0448

MC Sports
3070 Shaffer St. S.E.
Grand Rapids, MI 59512
800 626-1762
Fax 616 942-1973

Cybex
2100 Smithtown Ave.
Ronkonkoma, NY 11779
516-585-9000

DynaBandFitness Wholesale
895-A Hampshire Road
Stow, OH 44224

Parabody
14150 Sunfish Lake Blvd.
Ramsey, MN 55303-4803
612-323-4500
800-328-9714
Fax:612-323-4794

Paramount Fitness Corp.
6450 E. Bandini Blvd.
Los Angeles, CA 90040
213-721-2121
800-721-2121

Paragon Sporting Goods
867 Broadway
New York, NY 10003
212-255-8036
Fax 212-929-1831

Universal Gym Equipment
515 N. Flager Dr.
4th Floor Pavillion
W. Palm Beach, FL 33401
561-833-2320
800-843-3906
Fax: 561-802-5620

York Barbell
Box 1707
York, PA
717-767-6481
800-358-YORK

Country Technology, Inc.
P.O. Box 87
Gays Mills, WI 54631
608-735-4718
Fax 608-735-4859

Other Health-Related Resources

National Osteoporosis Foundation
1150 17th Street N.W., Ste. 500
Washington, DC 20036-4603
202-223-2226
800-223-9994

North American Menopause Society
C/o Cleveland Menopause Clinic
29001 Cedar Rd. #600
Cleveland, Ohio 44124

The Arthritis Foundation
National Office
1314 Spring St., N.W.
Atlanta, GA 30309
404-872-7100
800-283-7800

Administration on Aging
300 Independence Avenue, SW
Washington, DC 20201
202-619-0641

National Arthritis and Musculoskeletal and
Skin Diseases Information Clearing House
Box AMS
Bethesda, MD 20982
301-496-4000

Osteoporosis and Related Bone Diseases
National Resource Center
1150 17th St, NY, Suite 500
Washington, D.C. 20036-4603
800 624-BONE
Fax 202 223-2237

National Dairy Council
10255 W. Higgins Rd. Suite. 900
Rosemont, IL 60018
847-803-200

American College of Obstetricians and
Gynecologists
409 12th St. S.W.
Washington, DC 20024
202-638-5577

American Academy of Orthopedic Surgeons
6300 N. River Rd.
Rosemont, IL 60018
847-7186

Health and Medical Research Foundation
4900 Broadway
San Antonio, TX 78209
210-824-4200

American Association of Retired Persons
601 E. Street, NW
Washington, DC 20201
202-434-2277

National Center for Nutrition and Dietetics
American Dietetic Association
216 West Jackson Blvd.
Chicago, IL 60606-6995
800-366-1655

National Chronic Pain Outreach Association
7979 Old Georgetown Road
Bethesda, MD 20814
301-652-4948

Support Groups Services
National Osteoporosis Foundation Chicago Office
C/o AMA
515 North State Street
Chicago, IL 60610
312-464-5110
312-464-5863 (fax)

Office on Smoking and Health
National Center for Chronic Disease
Prevention US Department of Health and Human Services
1600 Clifton Road NE
Atlanta, GA 30333

Women's Sports Foundation
Eisenhower Park
East Meadow, NY 11554
516-542-4700
516-542-4716 FAX

American Heart Association
7272 Greenville Avenue
Dallas, TX 75231
214-373-6300

American Anorexia/Bulimia Association
165 West 46th Street 1108
New York, NY 10036

Aids for Arthritis
3 Little Knoll Court
Medford, New Jersey 08055
609-654-6918

Older Women's League
666 Eleventh Street NW, Sutie 700
Washington, DC 20001
202-783-6686 or 1-800-TAKE-OWL

Women's Health America
429 Gammon Place
PO 9690
Madison, WI 53715
608-833-9102

National Women's Health Resource Center
Suite 325, 2440 M St. N.W.
Washington, DC 20037
202-293-6045

National Women's Health Network
10th Street NW, Ste.402
Washington, DC 20004
202-347-1140

National Clearinghouse for Alcohol and Drug Information
P.O. Box 2345
Rockville, MD 20847-2345
301-468-2600 or 800 662-4357

National Women's Health Network
514 10th Street NW, Suite 400
Washington, DC 20004
202-347-1140

American Society for Bone and Mineral Research
1200 19th Street, NW, Ste. 300
Washington, DC 20036
202-857-1161
Fax: 202-223-4579

Foundation for Osteoporosis Research and Education
27th Street, Ste. 103
Oakland, CA 94612
888-266-3015
Fax: 510-208-7174

International Society for Clinical Densitometry
ISCD Headquarters
1200 19th Street, NW , Ste. 300
Washington, DC 20036-2422
202-828-6056
Fax: 202-857-1102

National Institute on Aging Information Center
PO Box 8057
Gaithersburg, MD 20898-8057
800-222-2225

Index

The Author

Dr. Raymond E. Cole

Certified Personal Fitness Trainer (C.P.T.) by the National Association of Sports Medicine (NASM)
Certified Family Physician (D.O.) by the American Osteopathic Association (AOA)
Certified Clinical Densitometrist (C.C.D.) in Osteoporosis by the International Society of Clinical Densitometry (ISCD)

Graduate of Chicago College of Osteopathic Medicine 1974 – Graduated third in class
Family physician for more than 26 years
Former Director of The Michigan Health & Wellness Institute
Medical Director of the Osteoporosis Testing Center of Michigan
Chairman (2001-2002) of the Department of Family Practice Doctor's Hospital, Jackson, Michigan.
Former weekly newspaper columnist (River Rouge & Ecorse Newspapers 1977-1985)
Host of Weekly TV Medical Talk Show "Focus On Health"
Frequent speaker for patient and physician audiences

Authored three books:
> Osteoporosis: Unmasking a Silent Thief. ISBN 0-917073-03-7
> Exercising Your Wellpower, ISBN 0-917073-00-2
> Choices for Health, ISBN 0-917073-02-9

National Award Winning Author (First Place National Marion Laboratory Writing Award in clinical writing 1975)

Published in medical journals
> A Comprehensive Program for Health Utilizing the Team Approach to the Education of the Patient With Chronic Obstructive Pulmonary Disease, Published in The Journal of The American Osteopathic Association June 1975. A paper concerning the optimal treatment of COPD utilizing the team approach. This paper won the National Marion Laboratory Writing Award for excellence in clinical writing in 1975.

> Education of the Subject in Clinical Research, Published in The Journal of The American Osteopathic Association 1975. A paper concerning the pitfalls to avoid and proper method of obtaining an informed consent in medical research.

> Learning To Live With Chronic Respiratory Disease, Published in The Osteopathic Health Magazine 1976. A paper for the general public about what they can do for themselves if they have chronic obstructive pulmonary disease.

Occasionally writes feature health articles for local newspapers on various topics.

Member of:
> National Osteoporosis Foundation (NOF)
> International Society For Clinical Densitometry (ISCD)
> International Bone and Mineral Society
> The American Society For Bone and Mineral Research (ASBMR)
> American Osteopathic Association (AOA)
> Michigan Osteopathic Association (MOA)

Assistant Clinical Professor, Michigan State University College of Osteopathic Medicine 1984-86

Notes From The Author's Life *Which Led Him To Write...*

Best Body Best Bones *Your Doctor's Exercise* **R$_x$** *Prescription*

A former "jock," team captain of undefeated football teams three out of four years in high school, award-winning scholar-athlete, after a brief stint playing football the first year of college, I became a "weekend warrior" for many years. From athletics to intellectual pursuits, then through medical school, I balanced the life of husband and primary supporter of a family. At mid-life age 45, I ballooned up to 235 pounds (6' tall) with typical middle age spread, bulging size 40 belt line, cholesterol 232, HDL 31, LDL 160, and triglycerides over 400.

Over the years I observed that patients in their late 90s who remained active seemed to be the healthiest and most energetic. I witnessed patients in their 80s with disuse atrophy and muscle wasting turn their lives around with a controlled regular exercise program. I noticed as these elderly individuals became stronger, more vigorous and active, they also developed more zest for life and optimism about their future. The most dramatic trurn-arounds seemed to occur the more inactive and debilitated the person was when they initially started. My research into effective osteoporosis treatments also led me to the realization that regular exercise is the best natural way to build stronger bone, increase muscle mass and flexibility, and improve balance and posture.

Introspectively, I observed when I was physically fit my energy level, sense of well being, and vitality tremendously increased. Taking charge of my personal life again with a firm personal commitment in my 50s, I incorporated medical knowledge with professional training as a fitness trainer and embarked on a lifelong journey into living a life of sound physical health and optimal well-being. With regular exercise and improved nutrition my weight decreased to 180 pounds, body fat decreased from 31 percent to 19 percent, and my vitality and energy increased. I feel and know I look younger, and my cholesterol is now 167, HDL 50, LDL 70, and triglycerides 77. I also feel much more in control and have a greater sense of self-mastery of my life.

Patient after patient noticed my transformation and wanted to know how I did it and if it could work for them. All individuals look for role models and, of course, patients look for their personal physician to be a role model. Each day inquisitive patients requested information on how they could do the same. Since I was explaining it hundreds of times, I finally wrote it down in a simple, easy-to-understand basic program.

From first-hand experience in my own life, as a Family Physician treating thousands of patients over a quarter of a century, as a motivator and speaker for many patient and physician audiences, and as a fitness trainer, I feel keenly in touch with what individuals want to know and the questions they want to have answered concerning fitness, health and the development of a strong body and strong bones.

The problem in saying a program is an absolute for everyone is that we all come in many shapes and sizes, and the circumstances and particulars of our lives are so vastly different. Because of these disparities the intensity, duration and even the type of fitness exercise will differ depending on one's particular physical abilities and personal desired goals. Exercising will also vary from person to person depending on one's age and particular life circumstances. The exercises of **THE BEST BODY BEST BONES FIT FOR LIFE PROGRAM** are a starting point only, not a fixed program in stone. As you customize your personal program, remember to design it as a lifelong investment in your health and not a short-term gain for the day! *Exercise Fit For a Lifetime!!!*

Best Body Best Bones

ISBN 0-917073-04-5

Book Order Form

Name_____

Address_____

City_____ State_____Zip_____

Phone_____

❏ Check   ❏ VISA   ❏ Mastercard   ❏ Discover

Card #_____Exp. Date_____

Signature_____

Make Checks payable to: WELLPOWER PUBLICATIONS

*BEST BODY BEST BONES*_____copies @ $24.95 ea.   = $_____
20% Discount for two or more books (above line X .20) Substract   = $-_____
                                                            Subtotal = $_____
Michigan Residents add 6% sales tax (adjusted subtotal X .06) add   = $+_____
Shipping & Handling ($5.00 for first book)   = $+_____
Shipping & Handling ($2.00 for each additional book)   = $+_____

TOTAL   Please pay this amount = $_____

To order by phone please call 1 517 592-WELL(9355) or 1 877 DOC-COLE
Or Fax order to   1 517 592-2540

Mail order to: WELLPOWER PUBLICATIONS
               107 Chicago St.
               Brooklyn, MI 49230

A portion of the sale of each book is donated to **KIWANIS** to help the local community clubs, national and international service programs and to assist in **KIWANIANS FOR A FIT AMERICA!**

Suggestions For Future Publications

Your Suggestions and Comments are Deeply Appreciated for Future Publications.

Please mail to:

> **Dr. Raymond Cole**
> **Wellpower Publications**
> **107 Chicago St.**
> **Brooklyn, Michigan 49230**

or E-mail to: recfcc@aol.com

_____

_____

_____

_____

_____

_____

_____

_____

_____

_____

_____

by Dr. Raymond Cole

PIN THIS UP

STEP-BY-STEP
FOLLOW-ALONG CHART OF THE
BEST BODY BEST BONES
FIT FOR LIFE PROGRAM

Putting it All Together to keep
Fit For A Lifetime

A good safe and simple beginning exercise program for most individuals is

30 minutes of WALKING

then

30 minutes of WEIGHTS

The weight exercises are muscle-strengthening, balance and posture exercises with 5- to 10-lb. dumbbells and 5- to 10-lb. ankle weights (The 4-1-4-4 Program) three times a week on alternating days (i.e. M-W-F). The fitness program always finishes with stretching.

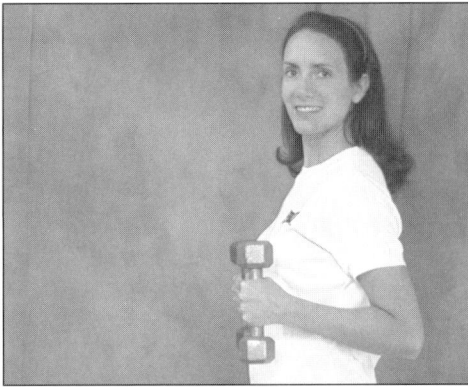 

Forward

Backward

Out

Up and Down

FOUR UPPER EXERCISES

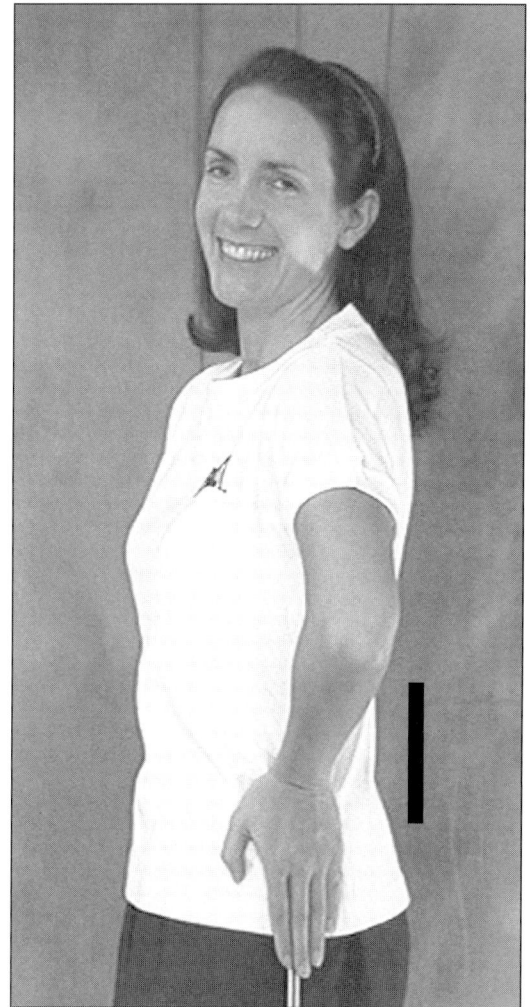

Contract Abdomen and Flatten Back

Forward

Backward

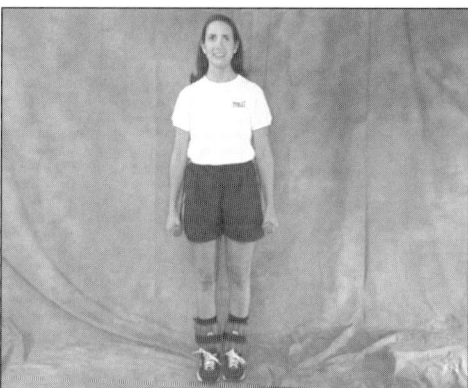 

Out

Up and Down

FOUR LOWER EXERCISES

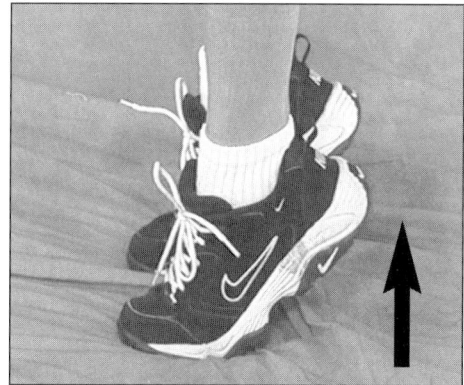

Forward Raise (Raise up on toes)

Backward (Go back on heels)

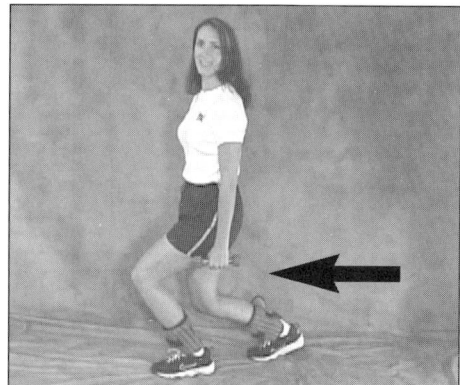

Out to Side (Stationary Lunge) Do Left & Right Sides

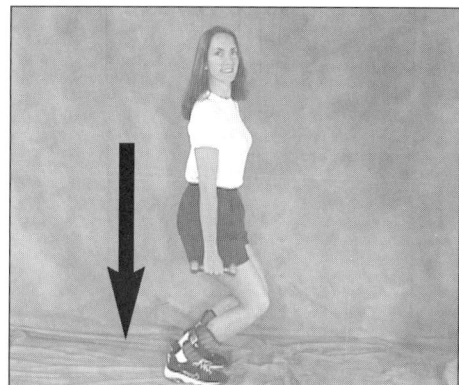

Up and Down (Squat)

FOUR BALANCE & POSTURE EXERCISES

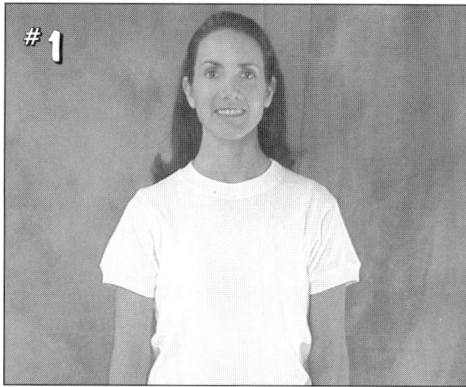

Begin Upper Extremity Stretches

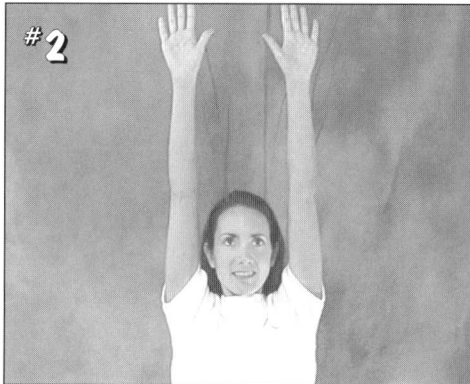

Overhead Stretch

Hand Stretch

Right Side Stretch

Arm on Hip

Arm Down Leg

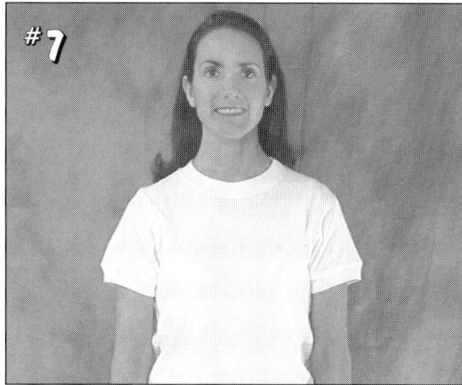

Neutral

Repeat Overhead Stretch

Repeat Hand Stretch

Left Side Stretch

Arm on Hip

Arm Down Leg

USE SCISSORS – CUT ALONG DOTTED LINE AND TAPE UP ON YOUR WALL

"You're under arrest"

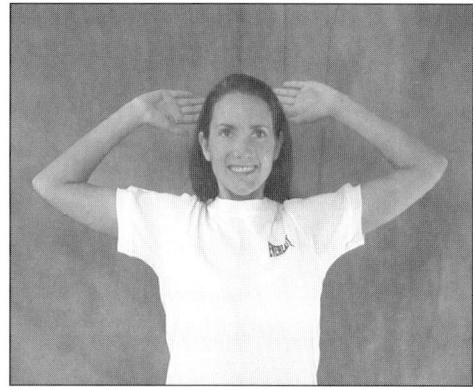

"Put your arms behind your head"

"But Officer, I didn't do anything"

"You're under arrest, I'm going to cuff ya"

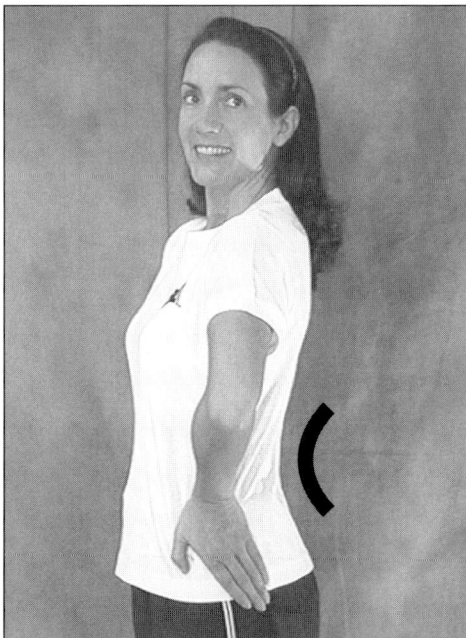

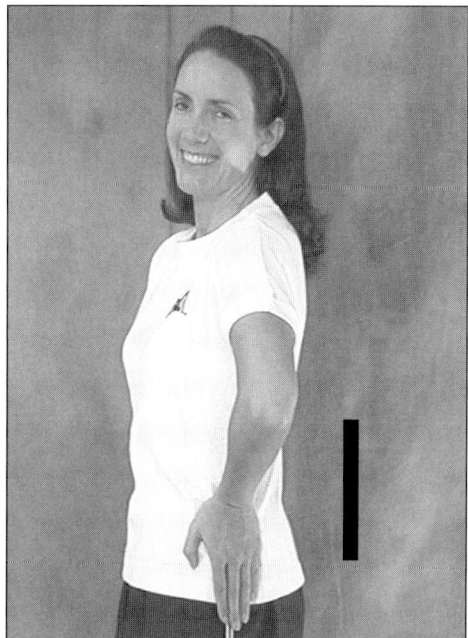

Abdominal Flattening/Low Back Flattening Stretch

Adductor Right Stretch

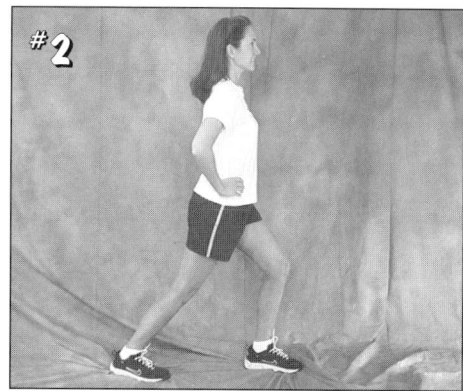

Achilles *(back heel on ground)*

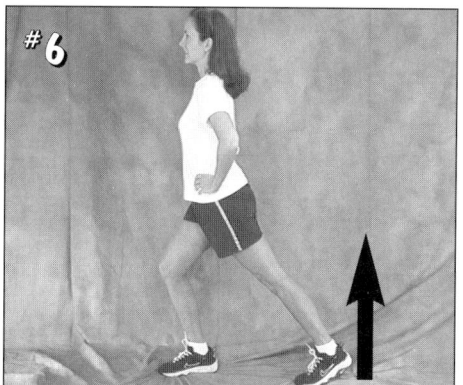

Hip Flexor *(back heel off ground)*

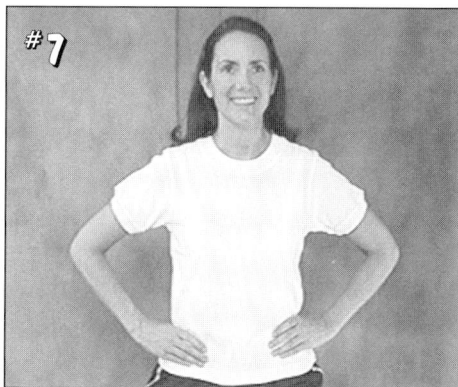

Adductor Left Stretch

Achilles *(heel on ground)*

Hip Flexor *(back heel off ground)*

Finish

LOWER EXTREMITY STRETCHES